Storm Blueprints: Patterns for Distributed Real-time Computation

Use Storm design patterns to perform distributed, real-time big data processing, and analytics for real-world use cases

P. Taylor Goetz

Brian O'Neill

[PACKT] **open source***

PUBLISHING   community experience distilled

BIRMINGHAM - MUMBAI

Storm Blueprints: Patterns for Distributed Real-time Computation

First published: March 2014

Production Reference: 1200314

Published by Packt Publishing Ltd.
Livery Place
35 Livery Street
Birmingham B3 2PB, UK.

ISBN 978-1-78216-829-4

www.packtpub.com

Cover Image by Prashant Timappa Shetty (sparkling.spectrum.123@gmail.com)

Credits

Authors

P. Taylor Goetz

Brian O'Neill

Reviewers

Vincent Gijsen

Sonal Raj

James Xu

Acquisition Editors

Usha Iyer

James Jones

Lead Technical Editor

Arun Nadar

Technical Editors

Kapil Hemnani

Monica John

Edwin Moses

Copy Editors

Roshni Banerjee

Sarang Chari

Brandt D'Mello

Mradula Hegde

Gladson Monteiro

Project Coordinator

Mary Alex

Proofreaders

Simran Bhogal

Maria Gould

Graphics

Ronak Dhruv

Valentina Dsilva

Disha Haria

Yuvraj Mannari

Abhinash Sahu

Indexer

Tejal Soni

Production Coordinator

Conidon Miranda

Cover Work

Conidon Miranda

About the Authors

P. Taylor Goetz is an Apache Storm committer and release manager and has been involved with the usage and development of Storm since it was first released as open source in October of 2011. As an active contributor to the Storm user community, Taylor leads a number of open source projects that enable enterprises to integrate Storm into heterogeneous infrastructure.

Presently, he works at Hortonworks where he leads the integration of Storm into **Hortonworks Data Platform (HDP)**. Prior to joining Hortonworks, he worked at Health Market Science where he led the integration of Storm into HMS' next generation Master Data Management platform with technologies including Cassandra, Kafka, Elastic Search, and the Titan graph database.

I would like to thank my amazing wife, children, family, and friends whose love, support, and sacrifices made this book possible. I owe you all a debt of gratitude.

Brian O'Neill is a husband, hacker, hiker, and kayaker. He is a fisherman and father as well as big data believer, innovator, and distributed computing dreamer.

He has been a technology leader for over 15 years and is recognized as an authority on big data. He has experience as an architect in a wide variety of settings, from start-ups to Fortune 500 companies. He believes in open source and contributes to numerous projects. He leads projects that extend Cassandra and integrate the database with indexing engines, distributed processing frameworks, and analytics engines. He won InfoWorld's Technology Leadership award in 2013. He authored the Dzone reference card on Cassandra and was selected as a Datastax Cassandra MVP in 2012 and 2013.

In the past, he has contributed to expert groups within the **Java Community Process** (**JCP**) and has patents in artificial intelligence and context-based discovery. He is proud to hold a B.S. in Computer Science from Brown University.

Presently, Brian is Chief Technology Officer for **Health Market Science (HMS)**, where he heads the development of their big data platform focused on data management and analysis for the healthcare space. The platform is powered by Storm and Cassandra and delivers real-time data management and analytics as a service.

For my family...To my wife Lisa, We put our faith in the wind. And our mast has carried us to the clouds. Rooted to the earth by our children, and fastened to the bedrock of those that have gone before us, our hands are ever entwined by the fabric of our family. Without all of you, this ink would never have met this page.

About the Reviewers

Vincent Gijsen is essentially a people's person, and he is passionate about any stuff related to technology. His background and area of interest broadly lies in Embedded Systems Engineering and Information Science. He started his career at a marketing -research company as an IT Manager. After that, he started his own company, and specialized in VOIP communications. Currently, he works at ScienceRockstars, a start-up, which is all about persuasive profiling and large data. In his spare time, he likes to get his hands dirty with lasers, quad-copters, eBay purchases, hacking stuff, and beers.

Sonal Raj is a geek, a "Pythonista", and a technology enthusiast. He is the founder and Executive Head at Enfoss. He holds a bachelor's degree in Computer Science and Engineering from National Institute of Technology, Jamshedpur. He was a Research Fellow at SERC, IISc Bangalore, and he pursued projects on distributed computing and real-time operations. He also worked as an intern at HCL Infosystems, Delhi.

He has given talks at PyCon India on Storm and Neo4J and has published articles and research papers in leading magazines and international journals.

James Xu is a committer of Apache Storm and a Java/Clojure programmer working in e-commerce. He is passionate about new technologies such as Storm and Clojure. He works in Alibaba Group, which is the leading e-ecommerce platform in China.

www.PacktPub.com

Support files, eBooks, discount offers and more

You might want to visit www.PacktPub.com for support files and downloads related to your book.

Did you know that Packt offers eBook versions of every book published, with PDF and ePub files available? You can upgrade to the eBook version at www.PacktPub.com and as a print book customer, you are entitled to a discount on the eBook copy. Get in touch with us at service@packtpub.com for more details.

At www.PacktPub.com, you can also read a collection of free technical articles, sign up for a range of free newsletters and receive exclusive discounts and offers on Packt books and eBooks.

http://PacktLib.PacktPub.com

Do you need instant solutions to your IT questions? PacktLib is Packt's online digital book library. Here, you can access, read and search across Packt's entire library of books.

Why Subscribe?

- Fully searchable across every book published by Packt
- Copy and paste, print and bookmark content
- On demand and accessible via web browser

Free Access for Packt account holders

If you have an account with Packt at www.PacktPub.com, you can use this to access PacktLib today and view nine entirely free books. Simply use your login credentials for immediate access.

Table of Contents

Preface

The demand for timely, actionable information is pushing software systems to process an increasing amount of data in a decreasing amount of time. Additionally, as the number of connected devices increases and as these devices are applied to a broadening spectrum of industries, that demand is becoming increasingly pervasive. Traditional enterprise operational systems are being forced to operate on scales of data that were originally associated only with Internet-scale companies. This monumental shift is forcing the collapse of more traditional architectures and approaches that separated online transactional systems and offline analysis. Instead, people are reimagining what it means to extract information from data. Frameworks and infrastructure are likewise evolving to accommodate this new vision.

Specifically, data generation is now viewed as a series of discrete events. Those event streams are associated with data flows, some operational and some analytical, but processed by a common framework and infrastructure.

Storm is the most popular framework for real-time stream processing. It provides the fundamental primitives and guarantees required for fault-tolerant distributed computing in high-volume, mission-critical applications. It is both an integration technology as well as a data flow and control mechanism. Many large companies are using Storm as the backbone of their big data platforms.

Using design patterns from this book, you will learn to develop, deploy, and operate data processing flows capable of processing billions of transactions per hour/day.

Storm Blueprints: Patterns for Distributed Real-time Computation covers a broad range of distributed computing topics, including not only design and integration patterns but also domains and applications to which the technology is immediately useful and commonly applied. This book introduces the reader to Storm using real-world examples, beginning with simple Storm topologies. The examples increase in complexity, introducing advanced Storm concepts as well as more sophisticated approaches to deployment and operational concerns.

What this book covers

Chapter 1, Distributed Word Count, introduces the core concepts of distributed stream processing with Storm. The distributed word count example demonstrates many of the structures, techniques, and patterns required for more complex computations. In this chapter, we will gain a basic understanding of the structure of Storm computations. We will set up a development environment and understand the techniques used to debug and develop Storm applications.

Chapter 2, Configuring Storm Clusters, provides a deeper look into the Storm technology stack and the process of setting up and deploying to a Storm cluster. In this chapter, we will automate the installation and configuration of a multi-node cluster using the Puppet provisioning tool.

Chapter 3, Trident Topologies and Sensor Data, covers Trident topologies. Trident provides a higher-level abstraction on top of Storm that abstracts away the details of transactional processing and state management. In this chapter, we will apply the Trident framework to process, aggregate, and filter sensor data to detect a disease outbreak.

Chapter 4, Real-time Trend Analysis, introduces trend analysis techniques using Storm and Trident. Real-time trend analysis involves identifying patterns in data streams. In this chapter, you will integrate with Apache Kafka and will implement a sliding window to compute moving averages.

Chapter 5, Real-time Graph Analysis, covers graph analysis using Storm to persist data to a graph database and query that data to discover relationships. Graph databases are databases that store data as graph structures with vertices, edges, and properties and focus primarily on relationships between entities. In this chapter, you will integrate Storm with Titan, a popular graph database, using Twitter as a data source.

Chapter 6, Artificial Intelligence, applies Storm to an artificial intelligence algorithm typically implemented using recursion. We expose some of the limitations of Storm, and examine patterns to accommodate those limitations. In this chapter, using **Distributed Remote Procedure Call (DRPC)**, you will implement a Storm topology capable of servicing synchronous queries to determine the next best move in tic-tac-toe.

Chapter 7, Integrating Druid for Financial Analytics, demonstrates the complexities of integrating Storm with non-transactional systems. To support such integrations, the chapter presents a pattern that leverages ZooKeeper to manage the distributed state. In this chapter, you will integrate Storm with Druid, which is an open source infrastructure for exploratory analytics, to deliver a configurable real-time system for analysis of financial events.

Chapter 8, Natural Language Processing, introduces the concept of Lambda architecture, pairing real time and batch processing to create a resilient system for analytics. Building on the *Chapter 7, Integrating Druid for Financial Analytics* you will incorporate the Hadoop infrastructure and examine a MapReduce job to backfill analytics in Druid in the event of a host failure.

Chapter 9, Deploying Storm on Hadoop for Advertising Analysis, demonstrates converting an existing batch process, written in Pig script running on Hadoop, into a real-time Storm topology. To do this, you will leverage Storm-YARN, which allows users to leverage YARN to deploy and run Storm clusters. Running Storm on Hadoop allows enterprises to consolidate operations and utilize the same infrastructure for both real time and batch processing.

Chapter 10, Storm in the Cloud, covers best practices for running and deploying Storm in a cloud-provider hosted environment. Specifically, you will leverage Apache Whirr, a set of libraries for cloud services, to deploy and configure Storm and its supporting technologies to infrastructure provisioned via **Amazon Web Services (AWS) Elastic Compute Cloud (EC2)**. Additionally, you will leverage Vagrant to create clustered environments for development and testing.

What you need for this book

The following is a list of software used in this book:

Chapter number	Software required
1	Storm (0.9.1)
2	Zookeeper (3.3.5)
	Java (1.7)
	Puppet (3.4.3)
	Hiera (1.3.1)
3	Trident (via Storm 0.9.1)
4	Kafka (0.7.2)
	OpenFire (3.9.1)
5	Twitter4J (3.0.3)
	Titan (0.3.2)
	Cassandra (1.2.9)
6	No new software
7	MySQL (5.6.15)
	Druid (0.5.58)

Chapter number	Software required
8	Hadoop (0.20.2)
9	Storm-YARN (1.0-alpha)
	Hadoop (2.1.0-beta)
10	Whirr (0.8.2)
	Vagrant (1.4.3)

Who this book is for

Storm Blueprints: Patterns for Distributed Real-time Computation benefits both beginner and advanced users, by describing broadly applicable distributed computing patterns grounded in real-world example applications. The book presents the core primitives in Storm and Trident alongside the crucial techniques required for successful deployment and operation.

Although the book focuses primarily on Java development with Storm, the patterns are applicable to other languages, and the tips, techniques, and approaches described in the book apply to architects, developers, systems, and business operations.

Hadoop enthusiasts will also find this book a good introduction to Storm. The book demonstrates how the two systems complement each other and provides potential migration paths from batch processing to the world of real-time analytics.

The book provides examples that apply Storm to a broad range of problems and industries, which should translate to other domains faced with problems associated with processing large datasets under tight time constraints. As such, solution architects and business analysts will benefit from the high-level system architectures and technologies introduced in these chapters.

Conventions

In this book, you will find a number of styles of text that distinguish between different kinds of information. Here are some examples of these styles, and an explanation of their meaning.

Code words in text, database table names, folder names, filenames, file extensions, pathnames, dummy URLs, user input, and Twitter handles are shown as follows: "All the Hadoop configuration files are located in `$HADOOP_CONF_DIR`. The three key configuration files for this example are: `core-site.xml`, `yarn-site.xml`, and `hdfs-site.xml`."

A block of code is set as follows:

```
<configuration>
    <property>
        <name>fs.default.name</name>
        <value>hdfs://master:8020</value>
    </property>
</configuration>
```

When we wish to draw your attention to a particular part of a code block, the relevant lines or items are set in bold:

```
13/10/09 21:40:10 INFO yarn.StormAMRMClient: Use NMClient to launch
supervisors in container.
13/10/09 21:40:10 INFO impl.ContainerManagementProtocolProxy: Opening
proxy : slave05:35847
13/10/09 21:40:12 INFO yarn.StormAMRMClient: Supervisor
log: http://slave05:8042/node/containerlogs/
container_1381197763696_0004_01_000002/boneill/supervisor.log
13/10/09 21:40:14 INFO yarn.MasterServer: HB: Received allocated
containers (1) 13/10/09 21:40:14 INFO yarn.MasterServer: HB:
Supervisors are to run, so queueing (1) containers...
13/10/09 21:40:14 INFO yarn.MasterServer: LAUNCHER: Taking container
with id (container_1381197763696_0004_01_000004) from the queue.
13/10/09 21:40:14 INFO yarn.MasterServer: LAUNCHER:
Supervisors are to run, so launching container id
(container_1381197763696_0004_01_000004)
13/10/09 21:40:16 INFO yarn.StormAMRMClient: Use NMClient to
launch supervisors in container.  13/10/09 21:40:16 INFO impl.
ContainerManagementProtocolProxy: Opening proxy : dlwolfpack02.
hmsonline.com:35125
13/10/09 21:40:16 INFO yarn.StormAMRMClient: Supervisor
log: http://slave02:8042/node/containerlogs/
container_1381197763696_0004_01_000004/boneill/supervisor.log
```

Any command-line input or output is written as follows:

```
hadoop fs -mkdir /user/bone/lib/
hadoop fs -copyFromLocal ./lib/storm-0.9.0-wip21.zip /user/bone/lib/
```

New terms and **important words** are shown in bold. Words that you see on the screen, in menus or dialog boxes for example, appear in the text like this: "From the **Filter** drop-down menu at the top of the page select **Public images**."

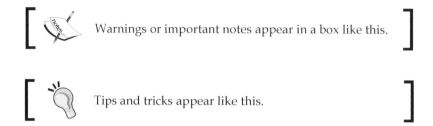

Warnings or important notes appear in a box like this.

Tips and tricks appear like this.

Reader feedback

Feedback from our readers is always welcome. Let us know what you think about this book—what you liked or may have disliked. Reader feedback is important for us to develop titles that you really get the most out of.

To send us general feedback, simply send an e-mail to feedback@packtpub.com, and mention the book title via the subject of your message.

If there is a topic that you have expertise in and you are interested in either writing or contributing to a book, see our author guide on www.packtpub.com/authors.

Customer support

Now that you are the proud owner of a Packt book, we have a number of things to help you to get the most from your purchase.

Downloading the example code

You can download the example code files for all Packt books you have purchased from your account at http://www.packtpub.com. If you purchased this book elsewhere, you can visit http://www.packtpub.com/support and register to have the files e-mailed directly to you.

Errata

Although we have taken every care to ensure the accuracy of our content, mistakes do happen. If you find a mistake in one of our books—maybe a mistake in the text or the code—we would be grateful if you would report this to us. By doing so, you can save other readers from frustration and help us improve subsequent versions of this book. If you find any errata, please report them by visiting `http://www.packtpub.com/submit-errata`, selecting your book, clicking on the **errata submission form** link, and entering the details of your errata. Once your errata are verified, your submission will be accepted and the errata will be uploaded on our website, or added to any list of existing errata, under the Errata section of that title. Any existing errata can be viewed by selecting your title from `http://www.packtpub.com/support`.

Piracy

Piracy of copyright material on the Internet is an ongoing problem across all media. At Packt, we take the protection of our copyright and licenses very seriously. If you come across any illegal copies of our works, in any form, on the Internet, please provide us with the location address or website name immediately so that we can pursue a remedy.

Please contact us at `copyright@packtpub.com` with a link to the suspected pirated material.

We appreciate your help in protecting our authors, and our ability to bring you valuable content.

Questions

You can contact us at `questions@packtpub.com` if you are having a problem with any aspect of the book, and we will do our best to address it.

1
Distributed Word Count

In this chapter, we will introduce you to the core concepts involved in creating distributed stream processing applications with Storm. We do this by building a simple application that calculates a running word count from a continuous stream of sentences. The word count example involves many of the structures, techniques, and patterns required for more complex computation, yet it is simple and easy to follow.

We will begin with an overview of Storm's data structures and move on to implementing the components that comprise a fully fledged Storm application. By the end of the chapter, you will have gained a basic understanding of the structure of Storm computations, setting up a development environment, and techniques for developing and debugging Storm applications.

This chapter covers the following topics:

- Storm's basic constructs – topologies, streams, spouts, and bolts
- Setting up a Storm development environment
- Implementing a basic word count application
- Parallelization and fault tolerance
- Scaling by parallelizing computation tasks

Introducing elements of a Storm topology – streams, spouts, and bolts

In Storm, the structure of a distributed computation is referred to as a **topology** and is made up of streams of data, spouts (stream producers), and bolts (operations). Storm topologies are roughly analogous to jobs in batch processing systems such as Hadoop. However, while batch jobs have clearly defined beginning and end points, Storm topologies run forever, until explicitly killed or undeployed.

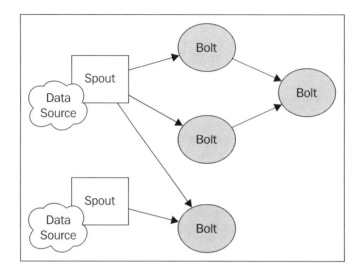

A Storm topology

Streams

The core data structure in Storm is the *tuple*. A tuple is simply a list of named values (key-value pairs), and a Stream is an unbounded sequence of tuples. If you are familiar with **complex event processing (CEP)**, you can think of Storm tuples as *events*.

Spouts

Spouts represent the main entry point of data into a Storm topology. Spouts act as adapters that connect to a source of data, transform the data into tuples, and emit the tuples as a stream.

As you will see, Storm provides a simple API for implementing spouts. Developing a spout is largely a matter of writing the code necessary to consume data from a raw source or API. Potential data sources include:

- Click streams from a web-based or mobile application
- Twitter or other social network feeds
- Sensor output
- Application log events

Since spouts typically don't implement any specific business logic, they can often be reused across multiple topologies.

Bolts

Bolts can be thought of as the *operators* or *functions* of your computation. They take as input any number of streams, process the data, and optionally emit one or more streams. Bolts may subscribe to streams emitted by spouts or other bolts, making it possible to create a complex network of stream transformations.

Bolts can perform any sort of processing imaginable and like the Spout API, the bolt interface is simple and straightforward. Typical functions performed by bolts include:

- Filtering tuples
- Joins and aggregations
- Calculations
- Database reads/writes

Introducing the word count topology data flow

Our word count topology (depicted in the following diagram) will consist of a single spout connected to three downstream bolts.

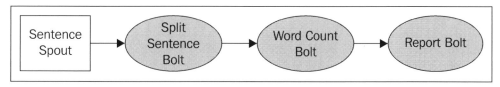

Word count topology

Sentence spout

The `SentenceSpout` class will simply emit a stream of single-value tuples with the key name `"sentence"` and a string value (a sentence), as shown in the following code:

```
{ "sentence":"my dog has fleas" }
```

To keep things simple, the source of our data will be a static list of sentences that we loop over, emitting a tuple for every sentence. In a real-world application, a spout would typically connect to a dynamic source, such as tweets retrieved from the Twitter API.

Introducing the split sentence bolt

The split sentence bolt will subscribe to the sentence spout's tuple stream. For each tuple received, it will look up the `"sentence"` object's value, split the value into words, and emit a tuple for each word:

```
{ "word" : "my" }
{ "word" : "dog" }
{ "word" : "has" }
{ "word" : "fleas" }
```

Introducing the word count bolt

The word count bolt subscribes to the output of the `SplitSentenceBolt` class, keeping a running count of how many times it has seen a particular word. Whenever it receives a tuple, it will increment the counter associated with a word and emit a tuple containing the word and the current count:

```
{ "word" : "dog", "count" : 5 }
```

Introducing the report bolt

The report bolt subscribes to the output of the `WordCountBolt` class and maintains a table of all words and their corresponding counts, just like `WordCountBolt`. When it receives a tuple, it updates the table and prints the contents to the console.

Implementing the word count topology

Now that we've introduced the basic Storm concepts, we're ready to start developing a simple application. For now, we'll be developing and running a Storm topology in local mode. Storm's local mode simulates a Storm cluster within a single JVM instance, making it easy to develop and debug Storm topologies in a local development environment or IDE. In later chapters, we'll show you how to take Storm topologies developed in local mode and deploy them to a fully clustered environment.

Setting up a development environment

Creating a new Storm project is just a matter of adding the Storm library and its dependencies to the Java classpath. However, as you'll learn in *Chapter 2, Configuring Storm Clusters*, deploying a Storm topology to a clustered environment requires special packaging of your compiled classes and dependencies. For this reason, it is highly recommended that you use a build management tool such as Apache Maven, Gradle, or Leinengen. For the distributed word count example, we will use Maven.

Let's begin by creating a new Maven project:

```
$ mvn archetype:create -DgroupId=storm.blueprints
-DartifactId=Chapter1 -DpackageName=storm.blueprints.chapter1.v1
```

Next, edit the `pom.xml` file and add the Storm dependency:

```
<dependency>
    <groupId>org.apache.storm</groupId>
    <artifactId>storm-core</artifactId>
    <version>0.9.1-incubating</version>
</dependency>
```

Then, test the Maven configuration by building the project with the following command:

```
$ mvn install
```

Downloading the example code

You can download the example code files for all Packt books you have purchased from your account at http://www.packtpub.com. If you purchased this book elsewhere, you can visit http://www.packtpub.com/ support and register to have the files e-mailed directly to you.

Maven will download the Storm library and all its dependencies. With the project set up, we're now ready to begin writing our Storm application.

Implementing the sentence spout

To keep things simple, our `SentenceSpout` implementation will simulate a data source by creating a static list of sentences that gets iterated. Each sentence is emitted as a single field tuple. The complete spout implementation is listed in *Example 1.1*.

Example 1.1: SentenceSpout.java

```java
public class SentenceSpout extends BaseRichSpout {

    private SpoutOutputCollector collector;
    private String[] sentences = {
        "my dog has fleas",
        "i like cold beverages",
        "the dog ate my homework",
        "don't have a cow man",
        "i don't think i like fleas"
    };
    private int index = 0;

    public void declareOutputFields(OutputFieldsDeclarer declarer) {
        declarer.declare(new Fields("sentence"));
    }

    public void open(Map config, TopologyContext context,
            SpoutOutputCollector collector) {
        this.collector = collector;
    }

    public void nextTuple() {
        this.collector.emit(new Values(sentences[index]));
        index++;
        if (index >= sentences.length) {
            index = 0;
        }
        Utils.waitForMillis(1);
    }
}
```

The `BaseRichSpout` class is a convenient implementation of the `ISpout` and `IComponent` interfaces and provides default implementations for methods we don't need in this example. Using this class allows us to focus only on the methods we need.

The `declareOutputFields()` method is defined in the `IComponent` interface that all Storm components (spouts and bolts) must implement and is used to tell Storm what streams a component will emit and the fields each stream's tuples will contain. In this case, we're declaring that our spout will emit a single (default) stream of tuples containing a single field (`"sentence"`).

The `open()` method is defined in the `ISpout` interface and is called whenever a spout component is initialized. The `open()` method takes three parameters: a map containing the Storm configuration, a `TopologyContext` object that provides information about a components placed in a topology, and a `SpoutOutputCollector` object that provides methods for emitting tuples. In this example, we don't need to perform much in terms of initialization, so the `open()` implementation simply stores a reference to the `SpoutOutputCollector` object in an instance variable.

The `nextTuple()` method represents the core of any spout implementation. Storm calls this method to request that the spout emit tuples to the output collector. Here, we just emit the sentence at the current index, and increment the index.

Implementing the split sentence bolt

The `SplitSentenceBolt` implementation is listed in *Example 1.2*.

Example 1.2 – SplitSentenceBolt.java

```java
public class SplitSentenceBolt extends BaseRichBolt{
    private OutputCollector collector;

    public void prepare(Map config, TopologyContext context,
  OutputCollector collector) {
        this.collector = collector;
    }

    public void execute(Tuple tuple) {
        String sentence = tuple.getStringByField("sentence");
        String[] words = sentence.split(" ");
        for(String word : words){
            this.collector.emit(new Values(word));
        }
    }

    public void declareOutputFields(OutputFieldsDeclarer declarer) {
        declarer.declare(new Fields("word"));
    }
}
```

The BaseRichBolt class is another convenience class that implements both the IComponent and IBolt interfaces. Extending this class frees us from having to implement methods we're not concerned with and lets us focus on the functionality we need.

The prepare() method defined by the IBolt interface is analogous to the open() method of ISpout. This is where you would prepare resources such as database connections during bolt initialization. Like the SentenceSpout class, the SplitSentenceBolt class does not require much in terms of initialization, so the prepare() method simply saves a reference to the OutputCollector object.

In the declareOutputFields() method, the SplitSentenceBolt class declares a single stream of tuples, each containing one field ("word").

The core functionality of the SplitSentenceBolt class is contained in the execute() method defined by IBolt. This method is called every time the bolt receives a tuple from a stream to which it subscribes. In this case, it looks up the value of the "sentence" field of the incoming tuple as a string, splits the value into individual words, and emits a new tuple for each word.

Implementing the word count bolt

The WordCountBolt class (Example 1.3) is the topology component that actually maintains the word count. In the bolt's prepare() method, we instantiate an instance of HashMap<String, Long> that will store all the words and their corresponding counts. It is common practice to instantiate most instance variables in the prepare() method. The reason behind this pattern lies in the fact that when a topology is deployed, its component spouts and bolts are serialized and sent across the network. If a spout or bolt has any non-serializable instance variables instantiated before serialization (created in the constructor, for example) a NotSerializableException will be thrown and the topology will fail to deploy. In this case, since HashMap<String, Long> is serializable, we could have safely instantiated it in the constructor. However, in general, it is best to limit constructor arguments to primitives and serializable objects and instantiate non-serializable objects in the prepare() method.

In the declareOutputFields() method, the WordCountBolt class declares a stream of tuples that will contain both the word received and the corresponding count. In the execute() method, we look up the count for the word received (initializing it to 0 if necessary), increment and store the count, and then emit a new tuple consisting of the word and current count. Emitting the count as a stream allows other bolts in the topology to subscribe to the stream and perform additional processing.

Example 1.3 – WordCountBolt.java

```java
public class WordCountBolt extends BaseRichBolt{
    private OutputCollector collector;
    private HashMap<String, Long> counts = null;

    public void prepare(Map config, TopologyContext context,
            OutputCollector collector) {
        this.collector = collector;
        this.counts = new HashMap<String, Long>();
    }

    public void execute(Tuple tuple) {
        String word = tuple.getStringByField("word");
        Long count = this.counts.get(word);
        if(count == null){
            count = 0L;
        }
        count++;
        this.counts.put(word, count);
        this.collector.emit(new Values(word, count));
    }

    public void declareOutputFields(OutputFieldsDeclarer declarer) {
        declarer.declare(new Fields("word", "count"));
    }
}
```

Implementing the report bolt

The purpose of the ReportBolt class is to produce a report of the counts for each word. Like the WordCountBolt class, it uses a HashMap<String, Long> object to record the counts, but in this case, it just stores the count received from the counter bolt.

One difference between the report bolt and the other bolts we've written so far is that it is a terminal bolt—it only receives tuples. Because it does not emit any streams, the declareOutputFields() method is left empty.

The report bolt also introduces the cleanup() method defined in the IBolt interface. Storm calls this method when a bolt is about to be shutdown. We exploit the cleanup() method here as a convenient way to output our final counts when the topology shuts down, but typically, the cleanup() method is used to release resources used by a bolt, such as open files or database connections.

One important thing to keep in mind about the `IBolt.cleanup()` method when writing bolts is that there is no guarantee that Storm will call it when a topology is running on a cluster. We'll discuss the reasons behind this when we talk about Storm's fault tolerance mechanisms in the next chapter. But for this example, we'll be running Storm in a development mode where the `cleanup()` method is guaranteed to be called.

The full source for the `ReportBolt` class is listed in Example 1.4.

Example 1.4 – ReportBolt.java

```
public class ReportBolt extends BaseRichBolt {

    private HashMap<String, Long> counts = null;

    public void prepare(Map config, TopologyContext context,
OutputCollector collector) {
        this.counts = new HashMap<String, Long>();
    }

    public void execute(Tuple tuple) {
        String word = tuple.getStringByField("word");
        Long count = tuple.getLongByField("count");
        this.counts.put(word, count);
    }

    public void declareOutputFields(OutputFieldsDeclarer declarer) {
        // this bolt does not emit anything
    }

    public void cleanup() {
        System.out.println("--- FINAL COUNTS ---");
        List<String> keys = new ArrayList<String>();
        keys.addAll(this.counts.keySet());
        Collections.sort(keys);
        for (String key : keys) {
            System.out.println(key + " : " + this.counts.get(key));
        }
        System.out.println("-------------");
    }
}
```

Implementing the word count topology

Now that we've defined the spout and bolts that will make up our computation, we're ready to wire them together into a runnable topology (refer to *Example 1.5*).

Example 1.5 – WordCountTopology.java

```java
public class WordCountTopology {

    private static final String SENTENCE_SPOUT_ID = "sentence-spout";
    private static final String SPLIT_BOLT_ID = "split-bolt";
    private static final String COUNT_BOLT_ID = "count-bolt";
    private static final String REPORT_BOLT_ID = "report-bolt";
    private static final String TOPOLOGY_NAME = "word-count-topology";

    public static void main(String[] args) throws Exception {

        SentenceSpout spout = new SentenceSpout();
        SplitSentenceBolt splitBolt = new SplitSentenceBolt();
        WordCountBolt countBolt = new WordCountBolt();
        ReportBolt reportBolt = new ReportBolt();


        TopologyBuilder builder = new TopologyBuilder();

        builder.setSpout(SENTENCE_SPOUT_ID, spout);
        // SentenceSpout --> SplitSentenceBolt
        builder.setBolt(SPLIT_BOLT_ID, splitBolt)
                .shuffleGrouping(SENTENCE_SPOUT_ID);
        // SplitSentenceBolt --> WordCountBolt
        builder.setBolt(COUNT_BOLT_ID, countBolt)
                .fieldsGrouping(SPLIT_BOLT_ID, new Fields("word"));
        // WordCountBolt --> ReportBolt
        builder.setBolt(REPORT_BOLT_ID, reportBolt)
                .globalGrouping(COUNT_BOLT_ID);

        Config config = new Config();

        LocalCluster cluster = new LocalCluster();

        cluster.submitTopology(TOPOLOGY_NAME, config, builder.
createTopology());
        waitForSeconds(10);
        cluster.killTopology(TOPOLOGY_NAME);
        cluster.shutdown();
    }
}
```

Storm topologies are typically defined and run (or submitted if the topology is being deployed to a cluster) in a Java `main()` method. In this example, we begin by defining string constants that will serve as unique identifiers for our Storm components. We begin the `main()` method by instantiating our spout and bolts and creating an instance of `TopologyBuilder`. The `TopologyBuilder` class provides a fluent-style API for defining the data flow between components in a topology. We start by registering the sentence spout and assigning it a unique ID:

```
builder.setSpout(SENTENCE_SPOUT_ID, spout);
```

The next step is to register `SplitSentenceBolt` and establish a subscription to the stream emitted by the `SentenceSpout` class:

```
builder.setBolt(SPLIT_BOLT_ID, splitBolt)
            .shuffleGrouping(SENTENCE_SPOUT_ID);
```

The `setBolt()` method registers a bolt with the `TopologyBuilder` class and returns an instance of `BoltDeclarer` that exposes methods for defining the input source(s) for a bolt. Here we pass in the unique ID we defined for the `SentenceSpout` object to the `shuffleGrouping()` method establishing the relationship. The `shuffleGrouping()` method tells Storm to shuffle tuples emitted by the `SentenceSpout` class and distribute them evenly among instances of the `SplitSentenceBolt` object. We will explain stream groupings in detail shortly in our discussion of parallelism in Storm.

The next line establishes the connection between the `SplitSentenceBolt` class and the `WordCountBolt` class:

```
builder.setBolt(COUNT_BOLT_ID, countBolt)
            .fieldsGrouping(SPLIT_BOLT_ID, new
                        Fields("word"));
```

As you'll learn, there are times when it's imperative that tuples containing certain data get routed to a specific instance of a bolt. Here, we use the `fieldsGrouping()` method of the `BoltDeclarer` class to ensure that all tuples containing the same `"word"` value get routed to the same `WordCountBolt` instance.

The last step in defining our data flow is to route the stream of tuples emitted by the `WordCountBolt` instance to the `ReportBolt` class. In this case, we want all tuples emitted by `WordCountBolt` routed to a single `ReportBolt` task. This behavior is provided by the `globalGrouping()` method, as follows:

```
builder.setBolt(REPORT_BOLT_ID, reportBolt)
            .globalGrouping(COUNT_BOLT_ID);
```

With our data flow defined, the final step in running our word count computation is to build the topology and submit it to a cluster:

```
Config config = new Config();

LocalCluster cluster = new LocalCluster();

        cluster.submitTopology(TOPOLOGY_NAME, config, builder.
createTopology());
        waitForSeconds(10);
        cluster.killTopology(TOPOLOGY_NAME);
        cluster.shutdown();
```

Here, we're running Storm in local mode using Storm's `LocalCluster` class to simulate a full-blown Storm cluster within our local development environment. Local mode is a convenient way to develop and test Storm applications without the overhead of deploying to a distributed cluster. Local mode also allows you to run Storm topologies within an IDE, setting breakpoints, halting execution, inspecting variables and profiling the application in ways that are much more time consuming or near impossible when deploying to a Storm cluster.

In this example, we create a `LocalCluster` instance and call the `submitTopology()` method with the topology name, an instance of `backtype.storm.Config`, and the `Topology` object returned by the `TopologyBuilder` class' `createTopology()` method. As you'll see in the next chapter, the `submitTopology()` method used to deploy a topology in local mode has the same signature as the method to deploy a topology in remote (distributed) mode.

Storm's `Config` class is simply an extension of `HashMap<String, Object>`, which defines a number of Storm-specific constants and convenience methods for configuring a topology's runtime behavior. When a topology is submitted, Storm will merge its predefined default configuration values with the contents of the `Config` instance passed to the `submitTopology()` method, and the result will be passed to the `open()` and `prepare()` methods of the topology spouts and bolts respectively. In this sense, the `Config` object represents a set of configuration parameters that are global to all components in a topology.

We're now ready to run the `WordCountTopology` class. The `main()` method will submit the topology, wait for ten seconds while it runs, kill (undeploy) the topology, and finally shut down the local cluster. When the program run is complete, you should see console output similar to the following:

```
--- FINAL COUNTS ---
a : 1426
ate : 1426
beverages : 1426
cold : 1426
cow : 1426
dog : 2852
don't : 2851
fleas : 2851
has : 1426
have : 1426
homework : 1426
i : 4276
like : 2851
man : 1426
my : 2852
the : 1426
think : 1425
-------------
```

Introducing parallelism in Storm

Recall from the introduction that Storm allows a computation to scale horizontally across multiple machines by dividing the computation into multiple, independent *tasks* that execute in parallel across a cluster. In Storm, a task is simply an instance of a spout or bolt running somewhere on the cluster.

To understand how parallelism works, we must first explain the four main components involved in executing a topology in a Storm cluster:

- **Nodes (machines)**: These are simply machines configured to participate in a Storm cluster and execute portions of a topology. A Storm cluster contains one or more nodes that perform work.

- **Workers (JVMs)**: These are independent JVM processes running on a node. Each node is configured to run one or more workers. A topology may request one or more workers be assigned to it.

- **Executors (threads)**: These are Java threads running within a worker JVM process. Multiple tasks can be assigned to a single executor. Unless explicitly overridden, Storm will assign one task for each executor.

- **Tasks (bolt/spout instances)**: Tasks are instances of spouts and bolts whose `nextTuple()` and `execute()` methods are called by executor threads.

WordCountTopology parallelism

So far in our word count example, we have not explicitly used any of Storm's parallelism APIs; instead, we allowed Storm to use its default settings. In most cases, unless overridden, Storm will default most parallelism settings to a factor of one.

Before changing the parallelism settings for our topology, let's consider how our topology will execute with the default settings. Assuming we have one machine (node), have assigned one worker to the topology, and allowed Storm to one task per executor, our topology execution would look like the following:

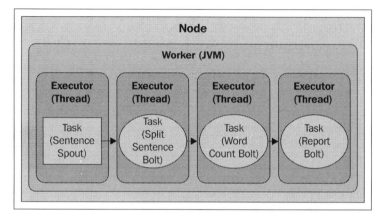

Topology execution

As you can see, the only parallelism we have is at the thread level. Each task runs on a separate thread within a single JVM. How can we increase the parallelism to more effectively utilize the hardware we have at our disposal? Let's start by increasing the number of workers and executors assigned to run our topology.

Adding workers to a topology

Assigning additional workers is an easy way to add computational power to a topology, and Storm provides the means to do so through its API as well as pure configuration. Whichever method we choose, our component spouts and bolts do not have to change, and can be reused as is.

In the previous version of the word count topology, we introduced the Config object that gets passed to the submitTopology() method at deployment time but left it largely unused. To increase the number of workers assigned to a topology, we simply call the setNumWorkers() method of the Config object:

```
Config config = new Config();
config.setNumWorkers(2);
```

This assigns two workers to our topology instead of the default of one. While this will add computation resources to our topology, in order to effectively utilize those resources, we will also want to adjust the number of executors in our topology as well as the number of tasks per executor.

Configuring executors and tasks

As we've seen, Storm creates a single task for each component defined in a topology, by default, and assigns a single executor for each task. Storm's parallelism API offers control over this behavior by allowing you to set the number of executors per task as well as the number of tasks per executor.

The number of executors assigned to a given component is configured by setting a parallelism hint when defining a stream grouping. To illustrate this feature, let's modify our topology definition to parallelize SentenceSpout such that it is assigned two tasks and each task is assigned its own executor thread:

```
builder.setSpout(SENTENCE_SPOUT_ID, spout, 2);
```

If we're using one worker, the execution of our topology now looks like the following:

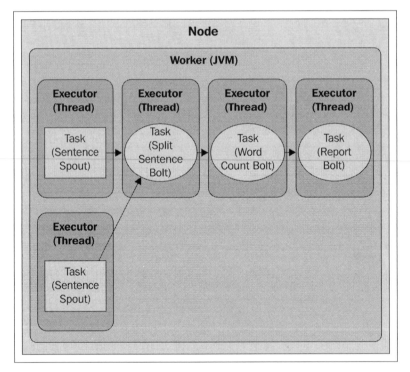

Two spout tasks

Next, we will set up the split sentence bolt to execute as four tasks with two executors. Each executor thread will be assigned two tasks to execute (4 / 2 = 2). We'll also configure the word count bolt to run as four tasks, each with its own executor thread:

```
builder.setBolt(SPLIT_BOLT_ID, splitBolt, 2)
           .setNumTasks(4)
              .shuffleGrouping(SENTENCE_SPOUT_ID);

builder.setBolt(COUNT_BOLT_ID, countBolt, 4)
              .fieldsGrouping(SPLIT_BOLT_ID, new
              Fields("word"));
```

With two workers, the execution of the topology will now look like the following diagram:

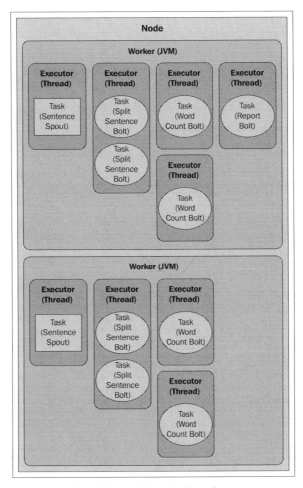

Parallelism with multiple workers

With the topology parallelism increased, running the updated `WordCountTopology` class should yield higher total counts for each word:

```
--- FINAL COUNTS ---
a : 2726
ate : 2722
beverages : 2723
cold : 2723
cow : 2726
dog : 5445
don't : 5444
fleas : 5451
has : 2723
have : 2722
homework : 2722
i : 8175
like : 5449
man : 2722
my : 5445
the : 2727
think : 2722
-------------
```

Since spout emits data indefinitely and only stops when the topology is killed, the actual counts will vary depending on the speed of your computer and what other processes are running on it, but you should see an overall increase in the number of words emitted and processed.

It's important to point out that increasing the number of workers has no effect when running a topology in local mode. A topology running in local mode always runs in a single JVM process, so only task and executor parallelism settings have any effect. Storm's local mode offers a decent approximation of cluster behavior and is very useful for development, but you should always test your application in a true clustered environment before moving to production.

Understanding stream groupings

Based on the previous example, you may wonder why we did not bother increasing the parallelism of `ReportBolt`. The answer is that it does not make any sense to do so. To understand why, you need to understand the concept of stream groupings in Storm.

A stream grouping defines how a stream's tuples are distributed among bolt tasks in a topology. For example, in the parallelized version of the word count topology, the `SplitSentenceBolt` class was assigned four tasks in the topology. The stream grouping determines which one of those tasks will receive a given tuple.

Storm defines seven built-in stream groupings:

- **Shuffle grouping**: This randomly distributes tuples across the target bolt's tasks such that each bolt receives an equal number of tuples.

- **Fields grouping**: This routes tuples to bolt tasks based on the values of the fields specified in the grouping. For example, if a stream is grouped on the `"word"` field, tuples with the same value for the `"word"` field will always be routed to the same bolt task.

- **All grouping**: This replicates the tuple stream across all bolt tasks such that each task will receive a copy of the tuple.

- **Global grouping**: This routes all tuples in a stream to a single task, choosing the task with the lowest task ID value. Note that setting a parallelism hint or number of tasks on a bolt when using the global grouping is meaningless since all tuples will be routed to the same bolt task. The global grouping should be used with caution since it will route all tuples to a single JVM instance, potentially creating a bottleneck or overwhelming a specific JVM/machine in a cluster.

- **None grouping**: The none grouping is functionally equivalent to the shuffle grouping. It has been reserved for future use.

- **Direct grouping**: With a direct grouping, the source stream decides which component will receive a given tuple by calling the `emitDirect()` method. It and can only be used on streams that have been declared direct streams.

- **Local or shuffle grouping**: The local or shuffle grouping is similar to the shuffle grouping but will shuffle tuples among bolt tasks running in the same worker process, if any. Otherwise, it will fall back to the shuffle grouping behavior. Depending on the parallelism of a topology, the local or shuffle grouping can increase topology performance by limiting network transfer.

In addition to the predefined groupings, you can define your own stream grouping by implementing the `CustomStreamGrouping` interface:

```
public interface CustomStreamGrouping extends Serializable {

void prepare(WorkerTopologyContext context,
GlobalStreamId stream, List<Integer> targetTasks);

List<Integer> chooseTasks(int taskId, List<Object> values);
}
```

The `prepare()` method is called at runtime to initiate the grouping with information the grouping implementation can use to make decisions on how to group tuples to receiving tasks. The `WorkerTopologyContext` object provides contextual information about the topology, and the `GlobalStreamId` object provides metadata about the stream being grouped on. The most useful parameter is `targetTasks`, which is a list of all the task identifiers the grouping needs to take into account. You will usually want to store the `targetTasks` parameter as an instance variable for reference in the implementation of the `chooseTasks()` method.

The `chooseTasks()` method returns a list of task identifiers to which a tuple should be sent. Its parameters are the task identifier of the component emitting the tuple and the values of the tuple.

To illustrate the importance of stream groupings, let's introduce a bug into our topology. Begin by modifying the `nextTuple()` method of `SentenceSpout` so it only emits each sentence once:

```
public void nextTuple() {
        if(index < sentences.length){
            this.collector.emit(new Values(sentences[index]));
            index++;
        }
        Utils.waitForMillis(1);
    }
```

Now run the topology to get the following output:

```
--- FINAL COUNTS ---
a : 2
ate : 2
beverages : 2
cold : 2
cow : 2
dog : 4
don't : 4
fleas : 4
has : 2
have : 2
homework : 2
i : 6
like : 4
man : 2
my : 4
the : 2
think : 2
-------------
```

Now change the field grouping on the CountBolt parameter to a shuffle grouping and rerun the topology:

```
builder.setBolt(COUNT_BOLT_ID, countBolt, 4)
                .shuffleGrouping(SPLIT_BOLT_ID);
```

The output should look like the following:

```
--- FINAL COUNTS ---
a : 1
ate : 2
beverages : 1
cold : 1
cow : 1
dog : 2
don't : 2
fleas : 1
has : 1
have : 1
homework : 1
i : 3
like : 1
man : 1
my : 1
the : 1
think : 1
--------------
```

Our counts are off because the CountBolt parameter is stateful: it maintains a count for each word it's seen. In this case, the accuracy of our computation depends on the ability to group based on a tuple's content when components have been parallelized. The bug we introduced will only be manifested if the parallelism of the CountBolt parameter is greater than one. This underscores the importance of testing topologies with various parallelism configurations.

 In general, you should avoid storing state information in a bolt since any time a worker fails and/or has its tasks reassigned, that information will be lost. One solution is to periodically take a snapshot of state information to a persistent store, such as a database, so it can be restored if a task is reassigned.

Guaranteed processing

Storm provides an API that allows you to guarantee that a tuple emitted by a spout is fully processed. So far in our example, we've not worried about failures. We've seen that a spout stream can be split and can generate any number of streams in a topology, depending on the behavior of downstream bolts. What happens in the event of a failure? As an example, consider a bolt that persists information to tuple data based on a database. How do we handle situations where the database update fails?

Reliability in spouts

In Storm, guaranteed message processing begins with the spout. A spout that supports guaranteed processing needs a way to keep track of tuples it has emitted and be prepared to re-emit a tuple if downstream processing of that tuple, or any child tuples, fails. A child tuple can be thought of as any tuple emitted as a result of a tuple originating from a spout. Another way to look at it is to consider the spout's stream(s) as the trunk of a tuple tree (shown in the following diagram):

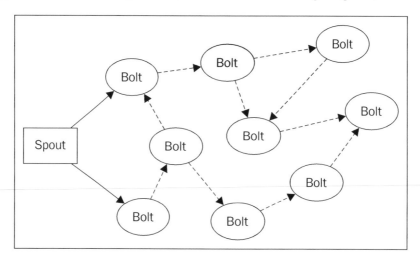

Tuple tree

In the preceding diagram, the solid lines represent the original trunk tuples emitted by a spout, and the dotted lines represent tuples derived from the original tuple. The resulting graph represents the tuple **tree**. With guaranteed processing, each bolt in the tree can either acknowledge (ack) or fail a tuple. If all bolts in the tree acknowledge tuples derived from the trunk tuple, the spout's ack method will be called to indicate that message processing is complete. If any of the bolts in the tree explicitly fail a tuple, or if processing of the tuple tree exceeds the time-out period, the spout's fail method will be called.

Storm's `ISpout` interface defines three methods involved in the reliability API: `nextTuple`, `ack`, and `fail`.

```
public interface ISpout extends Serializable {
    void open(Map conf, TopologyContext context, SpoutOutputCollector
collector);
    void close();
    void nextTuple();
    void ack(Object msgId);
    void fail(Object msgId);
}
```

As we've seen before, when Storm requests that a spout emit a tuple, it calls the `nextTuple()` method. The first step in implementing guaranteed processing is to assign the outbound tuple a unique ID and pass that value to the `emit()` method of `SpoutOutputCollector`:

```
collector.emit(new Values("value1", "value2") , msgId);
```

Assigning the tuple a message ID tells Storm that a spout would like to receive notifications either when the tuple tree is completed or if it fails at any point. If processing succeeds, the spout's `ack()` method will be called with the message ID assigned to the tuple. If processing fails or times out, the spout's `fail` method will be called.

Reliability in bolts

Implementing a bolt that participates in guaranteed processing involves two steps:

1. Anchoring to an incoming tuple when emitting a derived tuple.
2. Acknowledging or failing tuples that have been processed successfully or unsuccessfully, respectively.

Anchoring to a tuple means that we are creating a link between an incoming tuple and derived tuples such that any downstream bolts are expected to participate in the tuple tree by acknowledging the tuple, failing the tuple, or allowing it to time out.

You can anchor to a tuple (or a list of tuples) by calling one of the overloaded `emit` methods of `OutputCollector`:

```
collector.emit(tuple, new Values(word));
```

Here, we're anchoring to the incoming tuple and emitting a new tuple that downstream bolts should acknowledge or fail. An alternative form of the `emit` method will emit unanchored tuples:

```
collector.emit(new Values(word));));
```

Unanchored tuples do not participate in the reliability of a stream. If an unanchored tuple fails downstream, it will not cause a replay of the original root tuple.

After successfully processing a tuple and optionally emitting new or derived tuples, a bolt processing a reliable stream should acknowledge the inbound tuple:

```
this.collector.ack(tuple);
```

If tuple processing fails in such a way that the spout must replay (re-emit) the tuple, the bolt should explicitly fail the tuple:

```
this.collector.fail(tuple)
```

If tuple processing fails as a result of a time out or through an explicit call, the `OutputCollector.fail()` method, the spout that emitted the original tuple, will be notified, allowing it to re-emit the tuple, as you'll see shortly.

Reliable word count

To further illustrate reliability, let's begin by enhancing the `SentenceSpout` class to make it support guaranteed delivery. It will need to keep track of all tuples emitted and assign each one a unique ID. We'll use a `HashMap<UUID, Values>` object to store the tuples that are pending. For each tuple we emit, we'll assign a unique identifier and store it in our map of pending tuples. When we receive an acknowledgement, we'll remove the tuple from our pending list. On failure, we'll replay the tuple:

```
public class SentenceSpout extends BaseRichSpout {


    private ConcurrentHashMap<UUID, Values> pending;
    private SpoutOutputCollector collector;
    private String[] sentences = {
        "my dog has fleas",
        "i like cold beverages",
        "the dog ate my homework",
        "don't have a cow man",
        "i don't think i like fleas"
    };
```

```
    private int index = 0;

    public void declareOutputFields(OutputFieldsDeclarer declarer) {
        declarer.declare(new Fields("sentence"));
    }

    public void open(Map config, TopologyContext context,
            SpoutOutputCollector collector) {
        this.collector = collector;
        this.pending = new ConcurrentHashMap<UUID, Values>();
    }

    public void nextTuple() {
        Values values = new Values(sentences[index]);
        UUID msgId = UUID.randomUUID();
        this.pending.put(msgId, values);
        this.collector.emit(values, msgId);
        index++;
        if (index >= sentences.length) {
            index = 0;
        }
        Utils.waitForMillis(1);
    }

    public void ack(Object msgId) {
        this.pending.remove(msgId);
    }

    public void fail(Object msgId) {
        this.collector.emit(this.pending.get(msgId), msgId);
    }
}
```

Modifying the bolts to provide guaranteed processing simply involves anchoring outbound tuples to the incoming tuple and then acknowledging the inbound tuple:

```
public class SplitSentenceBolt extends BaseRichBolt{
    private OutputCollector collector;

    public void prepare(Map config, TopologyContext context,
OutputCollector collector) {
        this.collector = collector;
    }
```

```
public void execute(Tuple tuple) {
    String sentence = tuple.getStringByField("sentence");
    String[] words = sentence.split(" ");
    for(String word : words){
        this.collector.emit(tuple, new Values(word));
    }
    this.collector.ack(tuple);
}

public void declareOutputFields(OutputFieldsDeclarer declarer) {
    declarer.declare(new Fields("word"));
}
}
```

Summary

In this chapter, we've built a simple distributed computation application using Storm's core API and covered a large part of Storm's feature set, all without even installing Storm or setting up a cluster. Storm's local mode is powerful in terms of productivity and ease of development, but to see Storm's true power and horizontal scalability, you'll want to deploy applications to a real cluster.

In the next chapter, we'll walk through the process of installing and setting up a clustered Storm environment and deploying topologies in a distributed environment.

2
Configuring Storm Clusters

In this chapter, you'll take a deeper look at the Storm technology stack, its software dependencies, and the process of setting up and deploying it to a Storm cluster.

We will begin by installing Storm in the pseudo-distributed mode where all components are collocated on the same machine, rather than distributed across multiple machines. Once you have an understanding of the basic steps involved in installing and configuring Storm, we will move on to automating these processes using the Puppet provisioning tool, which will greatly reduce the time and effort required to set up a multi-node cluster.

Specifically, we will cover:

- The various components and services that compose a cluster
- The Storm technology stack
- Installing and configuring Storm on Linux
- Storm's configuration parameters
- Storm's command-line interface
- Using the Puppet provisioning tool to automate the installation

Introducing the anatomy of a Storm cluster

Storm clusters follow a master/slave architecture similar to distributed computing technologies such as Hadoop but with slightly different semantics. In a master/slave architecture, there is typically a master node that is either statically assigned through configuration or dynamically elected at runtime. Storm uses the former approach. While the master/slave architecture can be criticized as a setup that introduces a single point of failure, we'll show that Storm is semi-tolerant of a master node failure.

A Storm cluster consists of one master node (called **nimbus**) and one or more worker nodes (called **supervisors**). In addition to the nimbus and supervisor nodes, Storm also requires an instance of Apache ZooKeeper, which itself may consist of one or more nodes as shown in the following diagram:

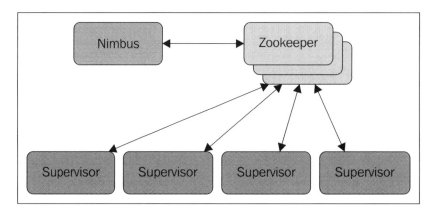

Both the nimbus and supervisor processes are daemon processes provided by Storm and do not need to be isolated from individual machines. In fact, it is possible to create a single-node pseudo-cluster with the nimbus, supervisor, and ZooKeeper processes all running on the same machine.

Understanding the nimbus daemon

The nimbus daemon's primary responsibility is to manage, coordinate, and monitor topologies running on a cluster, including topology deployment, task assignment, and task reassignment in the event of a failure.

Deploying a topology to a Storm cluster involves *submitting* the prepackaged topology JAR file to the nimbus server along with topology configuration information. Once nimbus has received the topology archive, it in turn distributes the JAR file to the necessary number of supervisor nodes. When the supervisor nodes receive the topology archive, nimbus then assigns tasks (spout and bolt instances) to each supervisor and signals them to spawn the necessary workers to perform the assigned tasks.

Nimbus tracks the status of all supervisor nodes and the tasks assigned to each. If nimbus detects that a specific supervisor node has failed to heartbeat or has become unavailable, it will reassign that supervisor's tasks to other supervisor nodes in the cluster.

As mentioned earlier, nimbus is not a single point of failure in the strictest sense. This quality is due to the fact that nimbus does not take part in topology data processing, rather it merely manages the initial deployment, task assignment, and monitoring of a topology. In fact, if a nimbus daemon dies while a topology is running, the topology will continue to process data as long as the supervisors and workers assigned with tasks remain healthy. The main caveat is that if a supervisor fails while nimbus is down, data processing will fail since there is no nimbus daemon to reassign the failed supervisor's tasks to another node.

Working with the supervisor daemon

The supervisor daemon waits for task assignments from nimbus and spawns and monitors workers (JVM processes) to execute tasks. Both the supervisor daemon and the workers it spawns are separate JVM processes. If a worker process spawned by a supervisor exits unexpectedly due to an error (or even if the process is being forcibly terminated with the UNIX `kill -9` or Windows `taskkill` command), the supervisor daemon will attempt to respawn the worker process.

At this point, you may be wondering how Storm's guaranteed delivery features fit into its fault tolerance model. If a worker or even an entire supervisor node fails, how does Storm guarantee the delivery of the tuples that were in process at the time of failure?

The answer lies in Storm's tuple anchoring and acknowledgement mechanism. When reliable delivery is enabled, tuples routed to the task on the failed node will not be acknowledged, and the original tuple will eventually be replayed by the spout after it is timed out. This process will repeat until the topology has recovered and normal processing has resumed.

Introducing Apache ZooKeeper

ZooKeeper provides a service for maintaining centralized information in a distributed environment using a small set of primitives and group services. It has a simple yet powerful distributed synchronization mechanism that allows client applications to watch or subscribe to individual data or sets of data and receive notifications when that data is created, updated, or modified. Using common ZooKeeper patterns or recipes, developers can implement a number of different constructs needed by distributed applications such as leader election, distributed locks and queues.

Storm uses ZooKeeper primarily to coordinate state information such as task assignments, worker status, and topology metrics between nimbus and supervisors in a cluster. Nimbus and supervisor node communication is largely handled through a combination of ZooKeeper's state modifications and watch notifications.

Storm's use of ZooKeeper is relatively lightweight by design and does not incur a heavy resource burden. For heavier-weight data transfer operations, such as a one-time (at deployment time) transfer of topology JAR files, Storm relies on Thrift for communication. And as we'll see, data transfer operations between components in a topology — where performance matters most — is handled at a low level and optimized for performance.

Working with Storm's DRPC server

A common pattern among Storm applications involves the desire to leverage Storm's parallelization and distributed computation capabilities within a request-response paradigm where a client process or application submits a request and waits for a response synchronously. While such a paradigm may seem to counter the highly asynchronous, long-lived nature of a typical Storm topology, Storm includes a transactional capability that enables such a use case.

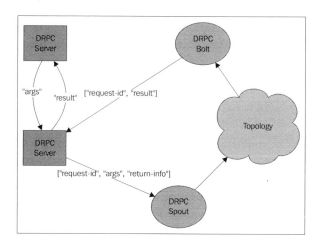

To enable this functionality, Storm uses the combination of an extra service (Storm DRPC) and a specialized spout and bolt that work together to provide a highly scalable Distributed RPC capability.

The use of Storm's DRPC capability is entirely optional. DRPC server nodes are only necessary when a Storm application leverages this functionality.

Introducing the Storm UI

Storm UI is an optional, but very useful, service that provides a web-based GUI to monitor Storm clusters and manage the running topologies to a certain degree. The Storm UI provides statistics for a given Storm cluster and its deployed topologies and is very useful when monitoring and tuning cluster and topology performance.

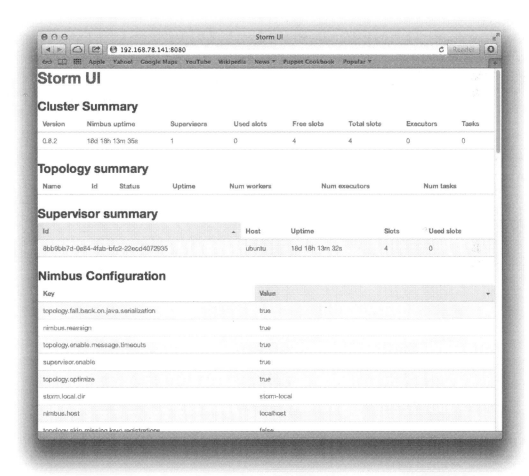

Storm UI only reports information gleaned from the nimbus thrift API and does not impart any other functionality to a Storm cluster. The Storm UI service can be started and stopped at any time without affecting any topology or cluster functionality and is in that respect completely stateless. It can also be configured to start, stop, pause, and rebalance topologies for easy management.

Introducing the Storm technology stack

Before we jump into installing Storm, let's take a look at the technologies with which Storm and topologies are built.

Java and Clojure

Storm runs on the Java Virtual Machine and is written with a roughly equal combination of Java and Clojure. Storm's primary interfaces are defined in Java, with the core logic being implemented mostly in Clojure. In addition to JVM languages, Storm uses Python to implement the Storm executable. Beyond those languages, Storm is a highly polyglot-friendly technology due in part to the fact that a number of its interfaces use Apache Thrift.

The components of Storm topologies (spouts and bolts) can be written in virtually any programming language supported by the operating system on which it's installed. JVM language implementations can run natively, and other implementations are possible through JNI and Storm's multilang protocol.

Python

All Storm daemons and management commands are run from a single executable file written in Python. This includes the nimbus and supervisor daemons, and as we'll see, all the commands to deploy and manage topologies. It is for this reason that a properly configured Python interpreter be installed on all machines participating in a Storm cluster as well as any workstation used for management purposes.

Installing Storm on Linux

Storm was originally designed to run on Unix-style operating systems, but as of Version 0.9.1, it supports deployment on Windows as well.

For our purposes, we will be using Ubuntu 12.04 LTS for its relative ease of use. We'll use the server version which by default does not include a graphical user interface since we won't need or use it. The Ubuntu 12.04 LTS server can be downloaded from http://releases.ubuntu.com/precise/ubuntu-12.04.2-server-i386.iso.

The instructions that follow the command work equally well on both the actual hardware as well as virtual machines. For the purpose of learning and development, you will likely find it much more convenient to work with virtual machines, especially if you don't have several networked computers readily available.

Virtualization software is readily available for OSX, Linux, and Windows. We recommend any one of the following software options:

- VMWare (OSX, Linux, and Windows)

  This software would need to be purchased. It is available at `http://www.vmware.com`.

- VirtualBox (OSX, Linux, and Windows)

  This software is available for free. It is available at `https://www.virtualbox.org`.

- Parallels Desktop (OSX)

  This software would need to be purchased. It is available at `http://www.parallels.com`.

Installing the base operating system

You can begin by booting from the Ubuntu installation disk (or disk image) and follow the onscreen instructions for a basic installation. When the **Package Selection** screen comes up, choose the option to install OpenSSH Server. This package will allow you to use `ssh` to remotely log into the server. In all other cases, you can simply accept the default options unless you choose to make modifications specific to your hardware.

By default, the primary user under Ubuntu will have administrative (sudo) privileges. If you are using a different user account or Linux distribution, make sure your account has administration privileges.

Installing Java

First, install a JVM. Storm is known to work with Java 1.6 and 1.7 JVMs from both the open source OpenJDK and Oracle. In this example, we'll update the apt repository information and install the OpenJDK distribution of Java 1.6:

```
sudo apt-get update
sudo apt-get --yes install openjdk-6-jdk
```

ZooKeeper installation

For our single-node pseudo-cluster, we'll install ZooKeeper alongside all other Storm components. Storm currently requires Version 3.3.x, so we'll install that version rather than the latest one using the following command:

```
sudo apt-get --yes install zookeeper=3.3.5* zookeeperd=3.3.5*
```

This command will install both the ZooKeeper binaries as well as the service scripts to start and stop ZooKeeper. It will also create a cron job that will periodically purge old ZooKeeper transaction logs and snapshot files, which will quickly consume large amounts of disk space if not purged on a regular basis as this is ZooKeeper's default behavior.

Storm installation

Storm's binary release distributions can be downloaded from the Storm website (http://storm.incubator.apache.org). The layout of the binary archives is geared more toward development activities than running a production system, so we'll make a few modifications to more closely follow UNIX conventions (such as logging to /var/log rather than Storm's home directory).

We begin by creating a Storm user and group. This will allow us to run the Storm daemons as a specific user rather than the default or root users:

```
sudo groupadd storm
sudo useradd --gid storm --home-dir /home/
storm --create-home --shell /bin/bash storm
```

Next, download and unzip the Storm distribution. We'll install Storm in /usr/share and symlink the version-specific directory to /usr/share/storm. This approach will allow us to easily install other versions and activate (or revert) the new version by changing a single symbolic link. We'll also link the Storm executable to /usr/bin/ storm:

```
sudo wget [storm download URL]
sudo unzip -o apache-storm-0.9.1-incubating.zip -d /usr/share/
sudo ln -s /usr/share/apache-storm-0.9.1-incubating /usr/share/storm
sudo ln -s /usr/share/storm/bin/storm /usr/bin/storm
```

By default, Storm will log information to `$STORM_HOME/logs` rather than the `/var/log` directory that most UNIX services use. To change this, execute the following commands to create the `storm` directory under `/var/log/` and configure Storm to write its log data there:

```
sudo mkdir /var/log/storm
sudo chown storm:storm /var/log/storm


sudo sed -i 's/${storm.home}\/logs/\/var\/log\/storm/
  g' /usr/share/storm/log4j/storm.log.properties
```

Finally, we'll move Storm's configuration file to `/etc/storm` and create a symbolic link so Storm can find it:

```
sudo mkdir /etc/storm
sudo chown storm:storm /etc/storm
sudo mv /usr/share/storm/conf/storm.yaml /etc/storm/
sudo ln -s /etc/storm/storm.yaml /usr/share/storm/conf/storm.yaml
```

With Storm installed, we're now ready to configure Storm and set up the Storm daemons so they start automatically.

Running the Storm daemons

All of the Storm daemons are fail-fast by design, meaning the process will halt whenever an unexpected error occurs. This allows individual components to safely fail and successfully recover without affecting the rest of the system.

This means that the Storm daemons need to be restarted immediately whenever they die unexpectedly. The technique for this is known as running a process under *supervision*, and fortunately there are a number of utilities available to perform this function. In fact, ZooKeeper is also a fail-fast system, and the upstart-based `init` scripts included in the ZooKeeper Debian distributions (Ubuntu is a Debian-based distribution) provide just that functionality—if the ZooKeeper process exits abnormally at any time, upstart will ensure it is restarted so the cluster can recover.

While the Debian upstart system is perfect for this situation, there are simpler options that are also available on other Linux distributions. To keep things simple, we'll use the supervisor package that's readily available on most distributions. Unfortunately, the supervisor name collides with the name of Storm's supervisor daemon. To clarify this distinction, we'll refer to the non-Storm process supervision daemon as *supervisord* (note the added *d* at the end) in the text, even though sample code and commands will use the proper name without the added *d*.

Under Debian-based Linux distributions, the `supervisord` package is named supervisor, while other distributions such as Red Hat use the name supervisord. To install it on Ubuntu, use the following command:

```
sudo apt-get --yes install supervisor
```

This will install and start the supervisord service. The main configuration file will be located at `/etc/supervisor/supervisord.conf`. Supervisord's configuration file will automatically include any files matching the pattern `*.conf` in the `/etc/supervisord/conf.d/` directory, and this is where we'll place our `config` files for to run the Storm daemons under supervision.

For each Storm daemon command we want to run under supervision, we'll create a configuration file that contains the following:

- A unique (within the supervisord configuration) name for the service under supervision.
- The command to run.
- The working directory in which to run the command.
- Whether or not the command/service should be automatically restarted if it exits. For fail-fast services, this should always be true.
- The user that will own the process. In this case, we will run all Storm daemons with the Storm user as the process owner.

Create the following three files to set up the Storm daemons to be automatically started (and restarted in the event of unexpected failure) by the supervisord service:

- `/etc/supervisord/conf.d/storm-nimbus.conf`

  Use the following code to create the file:

  ```
  [program:storm-nimbus]
  command=storm nimbus
  directory=/home/storm
  autorestart=true
  user=storm
  ```

- `/etc/supervisord/conf.d/storm-supervisor.conf`

  Use the following code to create the file:

  ```
  [program:storm-supervisor]
  command=storm supervisor
  directory=/home/storm
  autorestart=true
  user=storm
  ```

- `/etc/supervisord/conf.d/storm-ui.conf`

    Use the following code to create the file:

    ```
    [program:storm-ui]
    command=storm ui
    directory=/home/storm
    autorestart=true
    user=storm
    ```

Once those files have been created, stop and start the supervisord service with the following commands:

```
sudo /etc/init.d/supervisor stop
sudo /etc/init.d/supervisor start
```

The supervisord service will load the new configurations and start the Storm daemons. Wait a moment or two for the Storm services to start and then verify the Storm pseudo-cluster is up and running by visiting the following URL in a web browser (replace `localhost` with the host name or IP address of the actual machine):

```
http://localhost:8080
```

This will bring up the Storm UI graphical interface. It should indicate that the cluster is up with one supervisor node running with four available worker slots and no topologies are running (we'll deploy a topology to the cluster later).

If for some reason the Storm UI does not come up or fails to show an active supervisor in the cluster, check the following log files for errors:

- **Storm UI**: Check the `ui.log` file under `/var/log/storm` to check for errors
- **Nimbus**: Check the `nimbus.log` file under `/var/log/storm` to check for errors
- **Supervisor**: Check the `supervisor.log` file under `/var/log/storm` to check for errors

So far, we've relied on the default Storm configuration that defaults to using `localhost` for many cluster hostname parameters such as the ZooKeeper hosts as well as the location of the nimbus master. This is fine for a single-node pseudo-cluster where everything runs on the same machine, but setting up a real multi-node cluster requires overriding the default values. Next, we'll explore the various configuration options Storm provides and how they affect the behavior of a cluster and its topologies.

Configuring Storm

Storm's configuration consists of a series of YAML properties. When a Storm daemon starts, it loads the default values and then loads the `storm.yaml` (which we've symlinked to `/etc/storm/storm.yaml`) file under `$STORM_HOME/conf/`, substituting any values found there with the defaults.

The listing below provides a minimal `storm.yaml` file with entries that you must override:

```
# List of hosts in the zookeeper cluster
storm.zookeeper.servers:
    - "localhost"


# hostname of the nimbus node
nimbus.host: "localhost"


# supervisor worker ports
supervisor.slots.ports:
    - 6700
    - 6701
    - 6702
    - 6703


# where nimbus and supervisors should store state data
storm.local.dir: "/home/storm"


# List of hosts that are Storm DRPC servers (optional)
# drpc.servers:
#    - "localhost"
```

Mandatory settings

The following settings are mandatory for configuring working, multihost Storm clusters.

- `storm.zookeeper.servers`: This setting is a list of the hostnames in the ZooKeeper cluster. Since we're running a single node ZooKeeper on the same machine as the other Storm daemons, the default value of localhost is acceptable.

- `nimbus.host`: This is the hostname of the cluster's nimbus node. Workers need to know which node is the master in order to download topology JAR files and configurations.

- `supervisor.slots.ports`: This setting controls how many worker processes run on a supervisor node. It is defined as a list of port numbers that the workers will listen on, and the number of port numbers listed will control how many worker slots are available on the supervisor node. For example, if we have a cluster with three supervisor nodes, and each node is configured with three ports, the cluster will have a total of nine (3 * 3 = 9) worker slots. By default, Storm will use ports 6700-6703, a total of four slots per supervisor node.

- `storm.local.dir`: Both the nimbus and supervisor daemons store a small amount of transient state information as well as JAR and configuration files required by workers. This setting determines where the nimbus and supervisor processes will store that information. The directory specified here must exist with appropriate permissions so the process owner (in our case, the Storm user) can read and write to the directory. The contents of this directory must persist as long as the cluster is running, so it is best to avoid using `/tmp` where the contents might be deleted by the operating system.

Optional settings

In addition to the settings that are mandatory for an operational cluster, there are several other settings that you may find necessary to override. Storm configuration settings follow a dotted naming convention where the prefix identifies the category of the setting; this is shown in the following table:

Prefix	Category
`storm.*`	General configuration
`nimbus.*`	Nimbus configuration
`ui.*`	Storm UI configuration
`drpc.*`	DRPC server configuration
`supervisor.*`	Supervisor configuration
`worker.*`	Worker configuration
`zmq.*`	ZeroMQ configuration
`topology.*`	Topology configuration

For a complete list of the default configuration settings that are available, take a look at the `defaults.yaml` file in the Storm source code (`https://github.com/nathanmarz/storm/blob/master/conf/defaults.yaml`). Some of the more frequently overridden settings are outlined as follows:

- `nimbus.childopts` (default: "-Xmx1024m"): This setting is a list of JVM options that will be added to the Java command line when starting the nimbus daemon.

- `ui.port` (default: 8080): This specifies the listening port for the Storm UI web server.

- `ui.childopts` (default: "-Xmx1024m"): This specifies the JVM options that will be added to the Java command line when starting the Storm UI service.

- `supervisor.childopts` (default: "-Xmx1024m"): This specifies the JVM options that will be added to the Java command line when starting the supervisor daemon.

- `worker.childopts` (default: "-Xmx768m"): This specifies the JVM options that will be added to the Java command line when starting worker processes.

- `topology.message.timeout.secs` (default: 30): This configures the maximum amount of time (in seconds) for a tuple's tree to be acknowledged (fully processed) before it is considered failed (timed out). Setting this value too low may cause tuples to be replayed repeatedly. For this setting to take effect, a spout must be configured to emit anchored tuples.

- `topology.max.spout.pending` (default: null): With the default value of null, Storm will stream tuples from a spout as fast as the spout can produce them. Depending on the execute latency of downstream bolts, the default behavior can overwhelm the topology, leading to message timeouts. Setting this value to a non-null number greater than 0 will cause Storm to pause streaming tuples from spouts until the number of outstanding tuples falls below that number, essentially throttling the spout. This setting, along with `topology.message.timeout.secs`, are two of the most important parameters when tuning a topology for performance.

- `topology.enable.message.timeouts` (default: true): This sets the timeout behavior for anchored tuples. If false, anchored tuples will not time out. Use this setting with care. Consider altering `topology.message.timeout.secs` before setting this to false. For this setting to take effect, a spout must be configured to emit anchored tuples.

The Storm executable

The Storm executable is a multipurpose command used for everything from launching Storm daemons to performing topology management functions, such as deploying new topologies to a cluster, or simply running a topology in local mode during development and testing phases.

The basic syntax for the Storm command is as follows:

```
storm [command] [arguments...]
```

Setting up the Storm executable on a workstation

For running Storm commands that connect to a remote cluster, you will need to have the Storm distribution installed locally. Installing the distribution on a workstation is simple; just unzip the Storm distribution archive and add the Storm bin directory ($STORM_HOME/bin) to your PATH environment variable. Next, create the storm.yaml file under ~/.storm/ with a single line that tells Storm where to find the nimbus server for the cluster with which you want to interact:

Sample: ~/.storm/storm.yaml file.

nimbus.host: "nimbus01."

> In order for a Storm cluster to operate properly, it is imperative that the IP address name resolution be set up properly, either through the DNS system or entries in the hosts file under /etc.
>
> While it is possible to use IP addresses instead of hostnames throughout Storm's configuration, using the DNS system is preferred.

The daemon commands

Storm's daemon commands are used to launch Storm services, and should be run under supervision so they are relaunched in the event of unexpected failures. When starting, Storm daemons read configuration from $STORM_HOME/conf/storm.yaml. Any configuration parameters in this file will override Storm's built-in defaults.

Nimbus

Usage: `storm nimbus`

This launches the nimbus daemon.

Supervisor

Usage: `storm supervisor`

This launches the supervisor daemon.

UI

Usage: `storm ui`

This launches the Storm UI daemon that provides a web-based UI for monitoring Storm clusters.

DRPC

Usage: `storm drpc`

This launches the DRPC daemon.

The management commands

Storm's management commands are used to deploy and manage topologies running in a cluster. Management commands typically, but not necessarily, run from a workstation outside of the Storm cluster. They communicate to the nimbus Thrift API and thus need to know the hostname of the nimbus node. The management commands look for configuration from the `~/.storm/storm.yaml` file, and Storm's jars are appended to the classpath. The only required configuration parameter is the hostname of the nimbus node:

```
nimbus.host: "nimbus01"
```

Jar

Usage: `storm jar topology_jar topology_class [arguments...]`

The `jar` command is used to submit a topology to a cluster. It runs the `main()` method of `topology_class` with the specified arguments and uploads the `topology_jar` file to nimbus for distribution to the cluster. Once submitted, Storm will activate the topology and start processing.

The `main()` method in the topology class is responsible for calling the `StormSubmitter.submitTopology()` method and supplying a unique (within the cluster) name for the topology. If a topology with that name already exists on the cluster, the `jar` command will fail. It is common practice to specify the topology name in the command-line arguments so that the topology can be named at the time of submission.

Kill

Usage: `storm kill topology_name [-w wait_time]`

The `kill` command is used to undeploy. It kills the topology with the name `topology_name`. Storm will first deactivate the topology's spouts for the duration of the topology's configured `topology.message.timeout.secs` to allow all tuples actively being processed to complete. Storm will then halt the workers and attempt to clean up any saved states. Specifying a wait time with the `-w` switch will override `topology.message.timeout.secs` with the specified interval.

The functionality of the `kill` command is also available in the Storm UI.

Deactivate

Usage: `storm deactivate topology_name`

The `deactivate` command tells Storm to stop streaming tuples from the specified topology's spouts.

Topologies can also be deactivated from the Storm UI.

Activate

Usage: `storm activate topology_name`

The `activate` command tells Storm to resume streaming tuples from the specified topology's spouts.

Topologies can also be reactivated from the Storm UI.

Rebalance

Usage: `storm rebalance topology_name [-w wait_time] [-n worker_count] [-e component_name=executer_count]...`

The `rebalance` command instructs Storm to redistribute tasks among workers in a cluster without killing and resubmitting the topology. For example, this might be necessary when a new supervisor node has been added to a cluster—since it is a new node, none of the tasks of existing topologies would have been assigned to workers on that node.

The `rebalance` command also allows you to alter the number of workers assigned to a topology and change the number of executors assigned to a given task with the `-n` and `-e` switches respectively.

When the `rebalance` command is run, Storm will first deactivate the topology, wait for the configured time for outstanding tuples to finish processing, then redistribute workers evenly among supervisor nodes. After rebalancing, Storm will return the topology to its previous activation state (that is, if it was activated, Storm will reactivate it and vice versa).

The following example will rebalance the topology with the name `wordcount-topology` with a waiting time of 15 seconds, assign five workers to the topology, and set `sentence-spout` and `split-bolt` to use 4 and 8 executor threads respectively:

```
storm rebalance wordcount-topology -w 15 -n 5 -e
    sentence-spout=4 -e split-bolt=8
```

Remoteconfvalue

Usage: `storm remoteconfvalue conf-name`

The `remoteconfvalue` command is used to look up a configuration parameter on a remote cluster. Note that this applies to the global cluster configuration and does not take into account individual overrides made at the topology level.

Local debug/development commands

Storm's local commands are utilities for debugging and testing. Like the management commands, Storm's debug commands read `~/.storm/storm.yaml` and use those values to override Storm's built-in defaults.

REPL

Usage: `storm repl`

The `repl` command opens a Clojure REPL session configured with Storm's local classpath.

Classpath

Usage: `storm classpath`

The `classpath` command prints the classpath used by the Storm client.

Localconfvalue

Usage: `storm localconfvalue conf-name`

The `localconfvalue` command looks up a configuration key from the consolidated configuration, that is, from `~/.storm/storm.yaml` and Storm's built-in defaults.

Submitting topologies to a Storm cluster

Now that we have a running cluster, let's revisit our earlier word count example and modify it so we can deploy it to a cluster as well as run it in local mode. The previous example used Storm's `LocalCluster` class to run in local mode:

```
LocalCluster cluster = new LocalCluster();
          cluster.submitTopology(TOPOLOGY_NAME, config, builder.
createTopology());
```

Submitting a topology to a remote cluster is simply a matter of using Storm's `StormSubmitter` class, which exposes a method with the same name and signature:

```
StormSubmitter.submitTopology(TOPOLOGY_NAME, config,
   builder.createTopology());
```

When developing Storm topologies, you usually aren't going to want to change code and recompile them to switch between running in local mode and deploying to a cluster. The standard way to handle this is to add an if/else block that makes that determination based on a command-line argument. In our updated example, if there are no command line arguments, we run the topology in local mode; otherwise, we use the first argument as the topology name and submit it to the cluster, as shown in the following code:

```
public class WordCountTopology {

    private static final String SENTENCE_SPOUT_ID =
    "sentence-spout";
    private static final String SPLIT_BOLT_ID = "split-bolt";
    private static final String COUNT_BOLT_ID = "count-bolt";
    private static final String REPORT_BOLT_ID = "report-bolt";
```

```
    private static final String TOPOLOGY_NAME =
    "word-count-topology";

    public static void main(String[] args) throws Exception {

        SentenceSpout spout = new SentenceSpout();
        SplitSentenceBolt splitBolt = new SplitSentenceBolt();
        WordCountBolt countBolt = new WordCountBolt();
        ReportBolt reportBolt = new ReportBolt();


        TopologyBuilder builder = new TopologyBuilder();

        builder.setSpout(SENTENCE_SPOUT_ID, spout, 2);
        // SentenceSpout --> SplitSentenceBolt
        builder.setBolt(SPLIT_BOLT_ID, splitBolt, 2)
                .setNumTasks(4)
                .shuffleGrouping(SENTENCE_SPOUT_ID);
        // SplitSentenceBolt --> WordCountBolt
        builder.setBolt(COUNT_BOLT_ID, countBolt, 4)
                .fieldsGrouping(SPLIT_BOLT_ID,
                new Fields("word"));
        // WordCountBolt --> ReportBolt
        builder.setBolt(REPORT_BOLT_ID, reportBolt)
                .globalGrouping(COUNT_BOLT_ID);

        Config config = new Config();
        config.setNumWorkers(2);

        if(args.length == 0){
            LocalCluster cluster = new LocalCluster();
            cluster.submitTopology(TOPOLOGY_NAME, config,
            builder.createTopology());
            waitForSeconds(10);
            cluster.killTopology(TOPOLOGY_NAME);
            cluster.shutdown();
        } else{
            StormSubmitter.submitTopology(args[0],
            config, builder.createTopology());
        }
    }
}
```

To deploy the updated word count topology to a running cluster, first perform a Maven build in the `Chapter 2` source code directory:

```
mvn clean install
```

Next, run the `storm jar` command to deploy the topology:

```
storm jar ./target/Chapter1-1.0-SNAPSHOT.jar
  storm.blueprints.chapter1.WordCountTopology wordcount-topology
```

When the command completes, you should see the topology become active in the Storm UI and be able to click on the topology name to drill down and view the topology statistics.

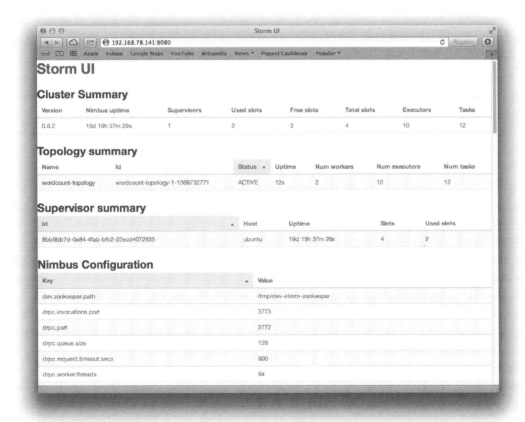

Automating the cluster configuration

So far, we've configured a single-node pseudo-cluster manually from the command line. While this approach certainly works with small clusters, it will quickly become untenable as the cluster size increases. Consider the situation where one needs to configure clusters consisting of tens, hundreds, or even thousands of nodes. The configuration tasks can be automated using shell scripts, but even a shell script-based automation solution is questionable in terms of scalability.

Fortunately, there are a number of technologies available to help address the issue of configuration and provisioning of large numbers of managed servers. Both Chef and Puppet offer a declarative approach to configuration that allows you to define **states** (that is, what packages are installed and how they are configured) as well as **classes** of machines (for example, an *Apache web server* class machine needs to have the Apache `httpd` daemon installed).

Automating the process of provisioning and configuring servers is a very broad topic that is far beyond the scope of this book. For our purposes, we will use Puppet and leverage a subset of its functionality in the hope that it will provide a basic introduction to the topic and encourage further exploration.

A rapid introduction to Puppet

Puppet (`https://puppetlabs.com`) is an IT automation framework that helps system administrators manage large network infrastructure resources using a flexible, declarative approach to IT automation.

At the heart of Puppet is the concept of a *manifest* that describes the desired *state* of an infrastructure resource. In Puppet terms, a state can include the following:

- Which software packages are installed
- Which services are running and which aren't
- Software configuration details

Puppet manifests

Puppet uses a declarative Ruby-based DSL to describe system configuration in collections of files known as manifests. An example Puppet manifest for ZooKeeper is listed as follows:

```
package { 'zookeeper':
    ensure => "3.3.5*",
}
```

```
package { 'zookeeperd':
    ensure => "3.3.5*",
    require => Package["zookeeper"],
}

service { 'zookeeperd':
    ensure => 'running',
    require => Package["zookeeperd"],
}
```

This simple manifest can be used to make sure ZooKeeper is installed as a service and that the service is running. The first package block tells Puppet to use the operating system's package manager (for example, apt-get for Ubuntu/Debian, yum for Red Hat, and so on) to ensure that the Version 3.3.5 of the zookeeper package is installed. The second package block ensures that the zookeeperd package is installed; it requires that the zookeeper package is already installed. Finally, the `service` block tells Puppet that it should ensure that the zookeeperd system service is running and that the service requires the zookeeperd package to be installed.

To illustrate how Puppet manifests translate to installed software and system's state, let's install Puppet and use the preceding example to install and start the zookeeperd service.

To get the latest version of Puppet, we need to configure apt-get to use the Puppet labs repository. Execute the following commands to do so and install the latest version of puppet:

```
wget http://apt.puppetlabs.com/puppetlabs-release-precise.deb
sudo dpkg -i puppetlabs-release-precise.deb
sudo apt-get update
```

Next, save the preceding example manifest to a file named init.pp and use Puppet to apply the manifest:

```
sudo puppet apply init.pp
```

When the command completes, check to see whether the zookeeper service is in fact running:

```
service zookeeper status
```

If we were to manually stop the zookeeper service and rerun the `puppet apply` command, Puppet would not install the packages again (since they are already there); however, it would restart the zookeeper service since the state defined in the manifest defines the service as *running*.

Puppet classes and modules

While standalone Puppet manifests make it easy to define the state of an individual resource, such an approach can quickly become unwieldy when the number of resources you're managing increases.

Fortunately, Puppet has the concept of classes and modules that can be leveraged to better organize and isolate specific configuration details.

Consider a situation with Storm where we have multiple classes of nodes. For example, a node in a Storm cluster may be a nimbus node, a supervisor node, or both. Puppet classes and modules provide a way to distinguish between multiple configuration roles that you can mix and match to easily define a network resource that performs multiple roles.

To illustrate this capability, let's revisit the manifest we used to install the zookeeper package and redefine it as a class that can be reused and included in multiple class types and manifests:

```
class zookeeper {

    include 'jdk'

    package { 'zookeeper':
        ensure => "3.3.5*",
    }
    package { 'zookeeperd':
        ensure => "3.3.5*",
        require => Package["zookeeper"],
    }

    service { 'zookeeperd':
        ensure => 'running',
        require => Package["zookeeperd"],
    }
}
```

In the preceding example, we've redefined the zookeeper manifest to be a `puppet` class that can be used in other classes and manifests. On the second line, the `zookeeper` class includes another class, `jdk`, which will include the class definition for a resource that will include the state necessary for a machine that requires a Java JDK.

Puppet templates

Puppet also leverages the Ruby ERB templating system that allows you to define templates for various files that will be populated when Puppet applies a manifest file. Placeholders in Puppet ERB templates are Ruby expressions and constructs that will be evaluated and replaced when Puppet runs. The Ruby code in ERB templates has full access to the Puppet variables defined in manifest files.

Consider the following Puppet file declaration that's used to generate the storm.yaml configuration file:

```
file { "storm-etc-config":
    path => "/etc/storm/storm.yaml",
    ensure => file,
    content => template("storm/storm.yaml.erb"),
    require => [File['storm-etc-config-dir'],
      File['storm-share-symlink']],
}
```

This declaration tells Puppet to create the file, storm.yaml, under /etc/storm/ from the storm.yaml.erb template:

```
storm.zookeeper.servers:
<% @zookeeper_hosts.each do |host| -%>
    - <%= host %>
<% end -%>

nimbus.host: <%= @nimbus_host %>

storm.local.dir: <%= @storm_local_dir %>

<% if @supervisor_ports != 'none' %>
supervisor.slots.ports:
<% @supervisor_ports.each do |port| -%>
    - <%= port %>
<% end -%>
<% end %>

<% if @drpc_servers != 'none' %>
<% @drpc_servers.each do |drpc| -%>
    - <%= drpc %>
<% end -%>
<% end %>
```

The conditional logic and variable expansion in the template allow us to define a single file that can be used for many environments. For example, if the environment we're configuring does not have any Storm DRPC servers, then the `drpc.servers` section of the generated `storm.yaml` file will be omitted.

Managing environments with Puppet Hiera

We've briefly introduced the concepts of Puppet manifests, classes, and templates. At this point, you're probably wondering how to define variables in a puppet class or manifest. Defining a variable within a `puppet` class or manifest is easy; simply define it at the beginning of the manifest or class definition as follows:

```
$java_version = "1.6.0"
```

Once defined, the `java_version` variable will be available throughout the class or manifest definition as well as any ERB templates; however, there is a drawback here in terms of reusability. If we hard-code information such as version numbers, we're effectively limiting the reuse of our class by pinning it to a hard-coded value. It would be better if we could externalize all potentially frequently changing variables to make configuration management more maintainable. This is where Hiera comes into play.

Introducing Hiera

Hiera is a key-value lookup tool that has been integrated into the latest version of the Puppet framework. Hiera allows you to define key-value hierarchies (hence the name) such that keys in a parent definition source can be overridden by child definition sources.

For example, consider a situation where we are defining configuration parameters for a number of machines that will participate in a Storm cluster. All machines will share a common set of key-values such as the version of Java we'd like to use. So, we'd define those values in a file called "`common.yaml`."

From there on, things start to diverge. We may have environments that are single-node pseudo-clusters, and we may have environments that are multi-node. For that, we'd like to store environment-specific configuration values in separate files such as "`single-node.yaml`" and "`cluster.yaml`."

Finally, we'd like to store true host-specific information in files that follow the naming convenion "**[hostname].yaml**."

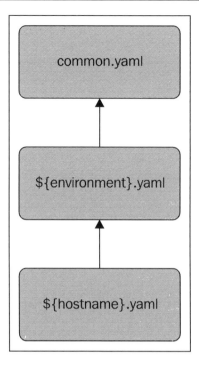

Puppet's Hiera integration allows you to do just that and use built-in Puppet variables to resolve filenames appropriately.

The examples in the Chapter 2 source code directory demonstrate how to implement this type of organization.

A typical common.yaml file might define global properties common to all hosts and looks like the following :

```
storm.version: apache-storm-0.9.1-incubating

# options are oracle-jdk, openjdk
jdk.vendor: openjdk
# options are 6, 7, 8
jdk.version: 7
```

At the environment level, we may want to distinguish between *standalone* and *cluster* configurations, in which case a `cluster.yaml` file might look like this:

```
# hosts entries for name resolution (template params for /etc/hosts)
hosts:
    nimbus01: 192.168.1.10
    zookeeper01: 192.168.1.11
    supervisor01: 192.168.1.12
    supervisor02: 192.168.1.13
    supervisor04: 192.168.1.14


storm.nimbus.host: nimbus01

storm.zookeeper.servers:
    - zookeeper01

storm.supervisor.slots.ports:
    - 6700
    - 6701
    - 6702
    - 6703
    - 6705
```

Finally, we may want to define host-specific parameters in files that use the naming convention [hostname].yaml, and define the Puppet classes that should be applied for that node.

For `nimbus01.yaml`, use the following code:

```
# this node only acts as a nimus node
classes:
    - nimbus
```

For `zookeeper01.yaml`, use the following code:

```
# this node is strictly a zookeeper node
classes:
    - zookeeper
```

We've only scratched the surface of what's possible with Puppet and Hiera. The `Chapter 2` source code directory contains additional examples and documentation on how to use Puppet to automate deployment and configuration tasks.

Summary

In this chapter, we've covered the steps necessary to install and configure Storm in both a single-node (pseudo-distributed) configuration as well as a fully distributed multi-node configuration. We've also introduced you to the Storm daemons and command line utilities used to deploy and manage running topologies.

Finally, we offered a brief introduction to the Puppet framework and showed how it can be used to manage multiple environment configurations.

We'd encourage you to explore the additional code and documentation included in the accompanied downloads.

In the next chapter, we will introduce Trident, which is a high-level abstraction layer on top of Storm for transactions and state management.

3
Trident Topologies and Sensor Data

In this chapter, we will explore Trident topologies. Trident provides a higher-level abstraction on top of Storm. Trident abstracts away the details of transactional processing and state management. Specifically, Trident provides batching of tuples into a discrete set of transactions. Additionally, Trident provides abstractions that allow topologies to perform operations on the data such as functions, filters, and aggregations.

We will use the sensor data as an example to gain a better understanding of Trident. Often, the sensor data forms streams that are read from many different locations. Some traditional examples include the weather or traffic information, but the pattern extends to a wide range of sources. For example, applications that run on cell phones generate a plethora of event information. Processing event streams from phones is another instance of sensor data processing.

The sensor data contains events emitted by many devices, often forming a never-ending stream. This is a perfect use case for Storm.

In this chapter, we will cover:

- Trident topologies
- Trident spouts
- Trident operations – filters and functions
- Trident aggregators – Combiners and Reducers
- The Trident state

Examining our use case

To better understand both the Trident topologies, as well as using Storm with sensor data, we will implement a Trident topology that collects medical reports to identify the outbreak of a disease.

The topology will process diagnosis events that contain the following pieces of information:

Latitude	Longitude	Timestamp	Diagnosis Code (ICD9-CM)
39.9522	-75.1642	03/13/2013 at 3:30 PM	320.0 (*Hemophilus meningitis*)
40.3588	-75.6269	03/13/2013 at 3:50 PM	324.0 (*Intracranial abscess*)

Each event will include the **Global Positioning System** (**GPS**) coordinates of the occurrence. The latitude and longitude are specified in the decimal format. The event also contains the ICD9-CM code, which indicates the diagnosis and a timestamp for the event. A complete list of ICD-9-CM codes are available at:

http://www.icd9data.com/.

To detect an outbreak, the system will count the occurrences of specific disease codes within a geographic location over a specified period of time. To simplify things for this example, we will map every diagnosis event to the closest city. In a real system, you would most likely perform more sophisticated geospatial clustering of the events.

Also, for the example, we will group the occurrences by hour since epoch. In a real-world system, you would most likely use a sliding window and calculate a trend against the moving average.

Finally, we will use a simple threshold to determine if there is an outbreak. If the count of occurrences for the hour is greater than some threshold, the system will send an alert and dispatch the National Guard.

To maintain a historical record, we will also persist the number of occurrences for each city, hour, and disease.

Introducing Trident topologies

To fulfill these requirements, we will need to count the occurrences in our topologies. This can be challenging while using standard Storm topologies because tuples can get replayed, which leads to double counting. As we will see in the next few sections, Trident provides primitives to solve this problem.

We will use the following topology:

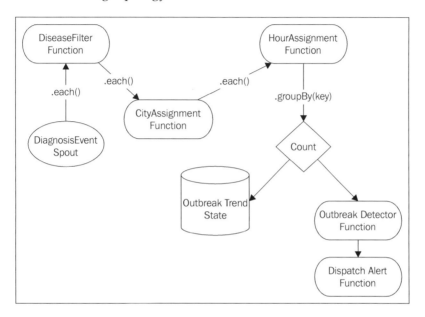

The code for the preceding topology is as follows:

```
public class OutbreakDetectionTopology {

    public static StormTopology buildTopology() {
    TridentTopology topology = new TridentTopology();
    DiagnosisEventSpout spout = new DiagnosisEventSpout();
    Stream inputStream = topology.newStream("event", spout);
    inputStream
    // Filter for critical events.
.each(new Fields("event"), new DiseaseFilter()))

            // Locate the closest city
        .each(new Fields("event"),
            new CityAssignment(), new Fields("city"))
```

```
            // Derive the hour segment
            .each(new Fields("event", "city"),
                  new HourAssignment(), new Fields("hour",
                  "cityDiseaseHour"))

            // Group occurrences in same city and hour
            .groupBy(new Fields("cityDiseaseHour"))

            // Count occurrences and persist the results.
            .persistentAggregate(new OutbreakTrendFactory(),
                                 new Count(),
                                 new Fields("count"))

            .newValuesStream()

            // Detect an outbreak
            .each(new Fields("cityDiseaseHour", "count"),
                  new OutbreakDetector(), new Fields("alert"))

            // Dispatch the alert
            .each(new Fields("alert"),
                  new DispatchAlert(), new Fields());

    }
}
```

The preceding code shows the wiring between the different Trident functions. First, the DiagnosisEventSpout function emits the events. The events are then filtered by the DiseaseFilter function, which filters out occurrences of diseases that we are not concerned with. After that, the event is associated with a city in the CityAssignment function. Then, the HourAssignment function assigns an hour to the event and adds a key to the tuple, which comprises the city, hour, and disease code. We then group by this key, which enables the counting and persisting of those counts in the persistAggregate function step in the topology. The counts are then passed along to the OutbreakDetector function, which thresholds the count, emitting an alert when the threshold is exceeded. Finally, the DispatchAlert function receives the alert, logs a message, and terminates the program. In the following section, we will take a deeper look into each of these steps.

Introducing Trident spouts

Let's first take a look at the spout in the topology. In contrast to Storm, Trident introduces the concept of **batches**. Unlike Storm spouts, Trident spouts must emit tuples in batches.

Each batch is given its own unique transaction identifier. A spout determines the composition of a batch based on the constraints of its contract. There are three types of contracts for spouts: **Non-transactional**, **Transactional**, and **Opaque**.

Non-transactional spouts provide no guarantee on the composition of the batches and might overlap. Two different batches might contain the same tuples. Transactional spouts guarantee that batches are non-overlapping and that the same batch always contains the same tuples. Opaque spouts guarantee that batches are non-overlapping, but the contents of a batch may change.

This is depicted in the following table:

Spout type	Batches may overlap	Batch contents may change
Non-transactional	X	X
Opaque		X
Transactional		

The interface for a spout looks like the following code snippet:

```
public interface ITridentSpout<T> extends Serializable {

    BatchCoordinator<T> getCoordinator(String txStateId,
                         Map conf, TopologyContext context);
    Emitter<T> getEmitter(String txStateId, Map conf,
                       TopologyContext context);

    Map getComponentConfiguration();

    Fields getOutputFields();
}
```

In Trident, the spout does not actually emit the tuples. Instead, the work is broken down between the BatchCoordinator and Emitter functions. The Emitter function is responsible for emitting the tuples, and the BatchCoordinator function is responsible for batch management and metadata such that the Emitter function can properly replay batches.

The `TridentSpout` function simply provides accessor methods to the `BatchCoordinator` and `Emitter` functions and declares the fields that the spout will emit. The following is the listing of the `DiagnosisEventSpout` function for our example:

```
public class DiagnosisEventSpout implements ITridentSpout<Long> {
  private static final long serialVersionUID = 1L;
  SpoutOutputCollector collector;
  BatchCoordinator<Long> coordinator = new DefaultCoordinator();
  Emitter<Long> emitter = new DiagnosisEventEmitter();

  @Override
  public BatchCoordinator<Long> getCoordinator(
          String txStateId, Map conf, TopologyContext context) {
      return coordinator;
  }

  @Override
  public Emitter<Long> getEmitter(String txStateId, Map conf,
                                  TopologyContext context) {
      return emitter;
  }

  @Override
  public Map getComponentConfiguration() {
      return null;
  }

  @Override
  public Fields getOutputFields() {
      return new Fields("event");
  }
}
```

As shown in the `getOutputFields()` method in the preceding code, in our example topology, the spout emits a single field called `event`, which contains the `DiagnosisEvent` class.

The `BatchCoordinator` class implements the following interface:

```
public interface BatchCoordinator<X> {
    X initializeTransaction(long txid, X prevMetadata);
    void success(long txid);
    boolean isReady(long txid);
    void close();
}
```

The `BatchCoordinator` class is a generic class. The generic class is the metadata that is required to replay a batch. In our example, the spout emits random events and thus the metadata is ignored. However, in real-world systems, the metadata might contain the identifiers of the messages or objects that comprise a batch. With that information, the opaque and transactional spouts can abide to their contracts and ensure that the contents of batches do not overlap, and in the case of the transactional spout, the batch contents do not change.

The `BatchCoordinator` class is implemented as a Storm Bolt operating in a single thread. Storm persists the metadata in Zookeeper. It notifies the coordinator when each transaction is complete.

For our example, if we do no coordination, the following is the coordination used in the `DiagnosisEventSpout` class:

```
public class DefaultCoordinator implements BatchCoordinator<Long>,
                                           Serializable {
    private static final long serialVersionUID = 1L;
private static final Logger LOG =
            LoggerFactory.getLogger(DefaultCoordinator.class);

@Override
public boolean isReady(long txid) {
    return true;
}

@Override
public void close() {
}
```

```
@Override
public Long initializeTransaction(long txid,
                                   Long prevMetadata) {
    LOG.info("Initializing Transaction [" + txid + "]");
    return null;
    }

@Override
public void success(long txid) {
    LOG.info("Successful Transaction [" + txid + "]");
}
}
```

The second component in a Trident spout is the Emitter function. The Emitter function performs the function of the Storm spout using a collector to emit tuples. The only distinction is that it uses a TridentCollector class, and the tuples must be included in a batch that was initialized by the BatchCoordinator class.

The interface for an Emitter function looks like the following code snippet:

```
public interface Emitter<X> {
void emitBatch(TransactionAttempt tx, X coordinatorMeta,
            TridentCollector collector);
void close();
}
```

As shown in the preceding code, the Emitter function has only one job—to emit the tuples for a given batch. To do this, the function is passed the metadata for the batch (which was constructed by the coordinator), information about the transaction, and the collector, which is what the Emitter function uses to emit the tuples. The listing for the DiagnosisEventEmitter class is as follows:

```
public class DiagnosisEventEmitter implements Emitter<Long>,
Serializable {

private static final long serialVersionUID = 1L;
AtomicInteger successfulTransactions = new AtomicInteger(0);

@Override
public void emitBatch(TransactionAttempt tx, Long
                coordinatorMeta, TridentCollector collector) {
    for (int i = 0; i < 10000; i++) {
        List<Object> events = new ArrayList<Object>();
        double lat =
```

```
                new Double(-30 + (int) (Math.random() * 75));
        double lng =
                new Double(-120 + (int) (Math.random() * 70));
        long time = System.currentTimeMillis();
        String diag = new Integer(320 +
                        (int) (Math.random() * 7)).toString();
        DiagnosisEvent event =
                    new DiagnosisEvent(lat, lng, time, diag);
        events.add(event);
        collector.emit(events);
    }
}

@Override
public void success(TransactionAttempt tx) {
    successfulTransactions.incrementAndGet();
}

@Override
public void close() {
}
}
```

The work is performed in the emitBatch() method. For this example, we will randomly assign a latitude and longitude, keeping it roughly within the United States, and we will use the System.currentTimeMillis() method for the timestamp on the diagnosis.

In real life, ICD-9-CM codes sparsely populate a range between 000 and 999. For this example, we will only use diagnosis codes between 320 and 327. These codes are listed as follows:

Code	Description
320	Bacterial meningitis
321	Meningitis due to other organisms
322	Meningitis of unspecified cause
323	Encephalitis myelitis and encephalomyelitis
324	Intracranial and intraspinal abscess
325	Phlebitis and thrombophlebitis of intracranial venous sinuses
326	Late effects of intracranial abscess or pyogenic infection
327	Organic sleep disorders

One of these diagnosis codes is randomly assigned to the event.

In this example, we will use an object to encapsulate the diagnosis event. Just as easily, we could have emitted each of the components as a separate field in the tuple. There is a balancing act between object encapsulation and use of fields in the tuple. Often, it is a good idea to keep the number of fields down to a manageable number, but it also makes sense to include data used for the control flow and/or grouping as fields in the tuple.

In our example, the `DiagnosisEvent` class is the key piece of data on which the topology is operating. That object looks like the following code snippet:

```
public class DiagnosisEvent implements Serializable {
    private static final long serialVersionUID = 1L;
    public double lat;
    public double lng;
    public long time;
    public String diagnosisCode;

    public DiagnosisEvent(double lat, double lng,
                        long time, String diagnosisCode) {
    super();
    this.time = time;
    this.lat = lat;
    this.lng = lng;
    this.diagnosisCode = diagnosisCode;
      }
   }
```

The object is a simple JavaBean. Time is stored as a long variable, which is the time since the epoch. The latitude and longitude are each stored as doubles. The `diagnosisCode` class is stored as a string, just in case the system needs to be able to process other types of codes that are not based on ICD-9, such as alphanumeric codes.

At this point, the topology is able to emit events. In a real implementation, we might integrate the topology into a medical claims processing engine or an electronic health records system at the point of practice.

Introducing Trident operations – filters and functions

Now that we have events being generated, the next step is to add the logic components that implement the business process. In Trident, these are known as **operations**. In our topology, we are using two different types of operations: filters and functions.

Operations are applied to streams via methods on the `Stream` object. In this example, we use the following methods on the `Stream` object:

```
public class Stream implements IAggregatableStream {
public Stream each(Fields inputFields, Filter filter) {
...
}

public IAggregatableStream each(Fields inputFields,
Function function,
Fields functionFields){
    ...
}

public GroupedStream groupBy(Fields fields) {
    ...
    }

public TridentState persistentAggregate(
StateFactory stateFactory,
CombinerAggregator agg,
Fields functionFields) {
        ...
}
}
```

Note that the methods in the preceding code return forms of the `Stream` objects or `TridentState` that can be used to create additional streams. With this, operations can be chained together using fluent-style Java.

Let's take another look at the critical lines in our example topology:

```
inputStream.each(new Fields("event"), new DiseaseFilter())
    .each(new Fields("event"), new CityAssignment(),
            new Fields("city"))

    .each(new Fields("event", "city"),
            new HourAssignment(),
          new Fields("hour", "cityDiseaseHour"))

    .groupBy(new Fields("cityDiseaseHour"))

    .persistentAggregate(new OutbreakTrendFactory(),
            new Count(), new Fields("count")).newValuesStream()

    .each(new Fields("cityDiseaseHour", "count"),
            new OutbreakDetector(), new Fields("alert"))

    .each(new Fields("alert"), new DispatchAlert(),
            new Fields());
```

Typically, operations are applied by declaring a set of input fields and a set of output fields also known as **function fields**. The second line of the topology in the preceding code declares that we want `CityAssignment` to execute on each tuple in the stream. From that tuple, `CityAssignment` will operate on the `event` field and emit a function field labelled `city`, which is appended to the tuple.

Each operation has slightly different fluent-style syntax, which depends on what information the operation requires. In the following sections, we will cover the details of the syntax and the semantics of the different operations.

Introducing Trident filters

The first piece of logic in our topology is a **filter**, which ignores disease events that are not of concern. In this example, the system will focus on meningitis. From the previous table, the only meningitis codes are 320, 321, and 322.

To filter events based on codes, we will leverage a Trident filter. Trident makes this easy by providing a `BaseFilter` class that we can subclass to filter tuples that the system does not care about. The `BaseFilter` class implements the `Filter` interface, which looks like the following code snippet:

```
public interface Filter extends EachOperation {
    boolean isKeep(TridentTuple tuple);
}
```

To filter tuples in a stream, the application simply implements this interface by extending the `BaseFilter` class. In the example, we will filter events using the following filter:

```
public class DiseaseFilter extends BaseFilter {
private static final long serialVersionUID = 1L;
private static final Logger LOG =
LoggerFactory.getLogger(DiseaseFilter.class);

@Override
public boolean isKeep(TridentTuple tuple) {
    DiagnosisEvent diagnosis = (DiagnosisEvent) tuple.getValue(0);
    Integer code = Integer.parseInt(diagnosis.diagnosisCode);
    if (code.intValue() <= 322) {
        LOG.debug("Emitting disease [" +
diagnosis.diagnosisCode + "]");
        return true;
    } else {
        LOG.debug("Filtering disease [" +
diagnosis.diagnosisCode + "]");
        return false;
    }
}
}
```

In the preceding code, we will extract the `DiagnosisEvent` class from the tuple and examine the disease code. Since all the meningitis codes are less than or equal to 322, and we are not emitting any other codes, we simply check to see if the code is less than 322 to determine if the event relates to meningitis.

Returning `True` from a `Filter` operation will result in the tuple flowing along to downstream operations. If the method returns `False`, the tuple will not flow to downstream operations.

In our topology, we apply the filter to each tuple in the stream using the `each(inputFields, filter)` method on the stream. The following line in our topology applies the filter to the stream:

```
inputStream.each(new Fields("event"), new DiseaseFilter())
```

Introducing Trident functions

In addition to filters, Storm provides an interface for generic functions. Functions are similar to Storm bolts in that they consume tuples and optionally emit new tuples. One distinction is that Trident functions are additive. The values emitted by functions are fields that are added to the tuple. They do not remove or mutate existing fields.

The interface for a function looks like the following code snippet:

```
public interface Function extends EachOperation {
void execute(TridentTuple tuple, TridentCollector collector);
}
```

Similar to a Storm bolt, the function implements a single method that contains the logic for that function. The function implementation can optionally use the `TridentCollector` to emit the tuple passed into the function. In this way, functions can also be used to filter tuples.

The first function in our topology is the `CityAssignment` function that looks like the following code snippet:

```
public class CityAssignment extends BaseFunction {
private static final long serialVersionUID = 1L;
private static final Logger LOG = LoggerFactory.
getLogger(CityAssignment.class);

private static Map<String, double[]> CITIES =
                      new HashMap<String, double[]>();

    { // Initialize the cities we care about.
        double[] phl = { 39.875365, -75.249524 };
        CITIES.put("PHL", phl);
        double[] nyc = { 40.71448, -74.00598 };
        CITIES.put("NYC", nyc);
        double[] sf = { -31.4250142, -62.0841809   };
        CITIES.put("SF", sf);
        double[] la = { -34.05374, -118.24307 };
        CITIES.put("LA", la);
    }

    @Override
    public void execute(TridentTuple tuple,
TridentCollector collector) {
        DiagnosisEvent diagnosis =
```

```
                          (DiagnosisEvent) tuple.getValue(0);
        double leastDistance = Double.MAX_VALUE;
        String closestCity = "NONE";

        // Find the closest city.
        for (Entry<String, double[]> city : CITIES.entrySet()) {
            double R = 6371; // km
            double x = (city.getValue()[0] - diagnosis.lng) *
                Math.cos((city.getValue()[0] + diagnosis.lng) / 2);
            double y = (city.getValue()[1] - diagnosis.lat);
            double d = Math.sqrt(x * x + y * y) * R;
            if (d < leastDistance) {
            leastDistance = d;
            closestCity = city.getKey();
            }
        }

        // Emit the value.
        List<Object> values = new ArrayList<Object>();
        Values.add(closestCity);
        LOG.debug("Closest city to lat=[" + diagnosis.lat +
                "], lng=[" + diagnosis.lng + "] == ["
                + closestCity + "], d=[" + leastDistance + "]");
        collector.emit(values);
    }
}
```

In this function, we use a static initializer to create a map of the cities we care about. For sample data, the function has a map that contains the coordinates for Philadelphia (PHL), New York City (NYC), San Francisco (SF), and Los Angeles (LA).

In the `execute()` method, the function loops through the cities and calculates the distance between the event and the city. In a real system, a geospatial index is likely more efficient.

Once the function determines the closest city, it emits the code for that city in the last few lines of the method. Remember that in Trident, instead of the function declaring what fields it will emit, the fields are declared when the operation is attached to the stream as the third parameter in the function call.

The number of function fields declared must align with the number of values emitted by the function. If they do not align, Storm will throw an `IndexOutOfBoundsException`.

The next function in our topology, `HourAssignment`, is used to convert the timestamp into an hour since epoch, which can then be used to group occurrences temporally. The code for `HourAssignment` looks as follows:

```
public class HourAssignment extends BaseFunction {
private static final long serialVersionUID = 1L;
private static final Logger LOG =
                LoggerFactory.getLogger(HourAssignment.class);

@Override
public void execute(TridentTuple tuple,
                    TridentCollector collector) {
    DiagnosisEvent diagnosis = (DiagnosisEvent) tuple.getValue(0);
    String city = (String) tuple.getValue(1);

    long timestamp = diagnosis.time;
    long hourSinceEpoch = timestamp / 1000 / 60 / 60;

    LOG.debug("Key =   [" + city + ":" + hourSinceEpoch + "]");
    String key = city + ":" + diagnosis.diagnosisCode + ":" +

                hourSinceEpoch;

    List<Object> values = new ArrayList<Object>();
    values.add(hourSinceEpoch);
    values.add(key);
    collector.emit(values);
}
}
```

We overload this function slightly by emitting both the *hours* as well as a composite key comprising the city, diagnosis code, and the hour. Effectively, this acts as a unique identifier for each aggregate count, which we will discuss more in detail.

The final two functions in our topology detect the outbreak and alert us about it. The code for the `OutbreakDetector` class is as follows:

```
public class OutbreakDetector extends BaseFunction {
    private static final long serialVersionUID = 1L;
    public static final int THRESHOLD = 10000;

    @Override
    public void execute(TridentTuple tuple,
```

```
                      TridentCollector collector) {
   String key = (String) tuple.getValue(0);
   Long count = (Long) tuple.getValue(1);

   if (count > THRESHOLD) {
       List<Object> values = new ArrayList<Object>();
       values.add("Outbreak detected for [" + key + "]!");
       collector.emit(values);
   }
 }
}
```

This function extracts the count for the specific city, disease, and hour and sees if it has exceeded the threshold. If it has, it emits a new field that contains an alert. In the preceding code, notice that this function effectively acts as a filter but was implemented as a function because we wanted to add an additional field to the tuple that contains the alert. Since filters do not mutate the tuple, we must use a function that allows us to not only filter but also add new fields.

The final function in our topology simply dispatches the alert (and terminates the program). The listing for this topology is as follows:

```
public class DispatchAlert extends BaseFunction {
    private static final long serialVersionUID = 1L;

    @Override
    public void execute(TridentTuple tuple,
                     TridentCollector collector) {
    String alert = (String) tuple.getValue(0);
    Log.error("ALERT RECEIVED [" + alert + "]");
    Log.error("Dispatch the national guard!");
    System.exit(0);
    }
}
```

This function is straightforward. It simply extracts the alert, logs the message, and terminates the program.

Introducing Trident aggregators – Combiners and Reducers

Akin to functions, **aggregators** allow topologies to combine tuples. Unlike functions, they replace tuple fields and values. There are three different types of aggregators: CombinerAggregator, ReducerAggregator, and Aggregator.

CombinerAggregator

A CombinerAggregator is used to combine a set of tuples into a single field. It has the following signature:

```
public interface CombinerAggregator {
    T init (TridentTuple tuple);
    T combine(T val1, T val2);
    T zero();
}
```

Storm calls the init() method with each tuple, and then repeatedly calls the combine() method until the partition is processed. The values passed into the combine() method are partial aggregations, the result of combining the values returned by calls to init(). Partitions are discussed more in the following sessions, but a partition is effectively a subset of a stream of tuples that resides on the same host. After combing the values from processing the tuples, Storm emits the result of combining those values as a single new field. If a partition is empty, then Storm emits the value returned by the zero() method.

ReducerAggregator

The ReducerAggregator has a slightly different signature:

```
public interface ReducerAggregator<T> extends Serializable {
    T init();
    T reduce(T curr, TridentTuple tuple);
}
```

Storm calls the init() method to retrieve the initial value. Then reduce() is called with each tuple until the partition is fully processed. The first parameter into the reduce() method is the cumulative partial aggregation. The implementation should return the result of incorporating the tuple into that partial aggregation.

Aggregator

The most general aggregation operation is the `Aggregator`. The signature for `Aggregator` is as follows:

```
public interface Aggregator<T> extends Operation {
    T init(Object batchId, TridentCollector collector);
    void aggregate(T val, TridentTuple tuple,
TridentCollector collector);
     void complete(T val, TridentCollector collector);
}
```

The `Aggregator` interface's `aggregate()` method is similar to the `execute()` method of a `Function` interface, but it also includes a parameter for the value. This allows the `Aggregator` to accumulate a value as it processes the tuples. Notice that with an `Aggregator`, since the collector is passed into both the `aggregate()` method as well as the `complete()` method, you can emit any arbitrary number of tuples.

In our example topology, we leveraged a built-in aggregator named `Count`. The implementation for `Count` looks like the following code snippet:

```
public class Count implements CombinerAggregator<Long> {
    @Override
    public Long init(TridentTuple tuple) {
        return 1L;
    }

    @Override
    public Long combine(Long val1, Long val2) {
        return val1 + val2;
    }

    @Override
    public Long zero() {
        return 0L;
    }
}
```

We apply both grouping and counting in our example topology to count the occurrences of a disease during a specific hour near a particular city. The specific lines that accomplish this are as follows:

```
.groupBy(new Fields("cityDiseaseHour"))
.persistentAggregate(new OutbreakTrendFactory(),
   new Count(), new Fields("count")).newValuesStream()
```

Recall that Storm partitions the stream across the available hosts. This is shown in the following diagram:

The `groupBy()` method forces a repartitioning of the data. It groups all the tuples that share the same value for the named field into the same partition. To do this, Storm must send the like tuples to the same host. The following diagram shows the repartitioning of the preceding data based on our `groupBy()` method:

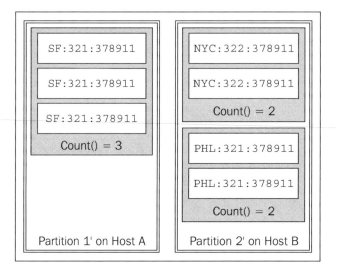

After repartitioning, the `aggregate` function is run on each group within each partition. In our example, we are grouping by city, hour, and disease code (using the key). Then, the `Count` aggregator is executed on each group, which in turn emits the occurrence count for downstream consumers.

Introducing the Trident state

Now that we have the counts for each aggregation, we want to persist with that information for further analysis. In Trident, persistence first starts with state management. Trident has a first-level primitive for state, but like the Storm API, it makes a few assumptions about what is being stored as state or how that state is persisted. At the highest level, Trident exposes a `State` interface as follows:

```
public interface State {
    void beginCommit(Long transactionId);
    void commit(Long transactionId);
}
```

As mentioned previously, Trident groups tuples into batches. Each batch has its own transaction identifier. In the preceding interface, Trident informs the `State` object when the state is being committed and when the commit should complete.

Like functions, there are methods on the `Stream` objects that introduce state-based operations into a topology. More specifically, there are two types of streams in Trident: `Stream` and `GroupedStream`. A `GroupedStream` is the result of performing a `groupBy` operation. In our topology, we group by the key generated by the `HourAssignment` function.

On the `Stream` object, the following methods allow the topology to read and write state information:

```
public class Stream implements IAggregatableStream {
    . . .
    public Stream stateQuery(TridentState state, Fields inputFields,
            QueryFunction function, Fields functionFields) {
    . . .
  }

public TridentState partitionPersist(StateFactory stateFactory,
Fields inputFields, StateUpdater updater,
Fields functionFields) {
    . . .
}

public TridentState partitionPersist(StateSpec stateSpec,
Fields inputFields, StateUpdater updater,
Fields functionFields) {
    . . .
}
```

```
public TridentState partitionPersist(StateFactory stateFactory,
Fields inputFields, StateUpdater updater) {
   ...
   }

public TridentState partitionPersist(StateSpec stateSpec,
Fields inputFields, StateUpdater updater) {
   ...
}
...
}
```

The stateQuery() method creates an input stream from state, and the various flavors of the partitionPersist() method allow a topology to update state information from tuples in a stream. The partitionPersist() method operates on each partition.

In addition to the methods on the Stream object, the GroupedStream object allows a topology to aggregate statistics from a set of tuples and simultaneously persist with the collected information to state. The following are the state-related methods on a GroupedStream class:

```
public class GroupedStream implements IAggregatableStream,
GlobalAggregationScheme<GroupedStream> {
...
    public TridentState persistentAggregate(
StateFactory stateFactory, CombinerAggregator agg,
Fields functionFields) {
...
}

public TridentState persistentAggregate(StateSpec spec,
CombinerAggregator agg, Fields functionFields) {
...
}

public TridentState persistentAggregate(
StateFactory stateFactory, Fields inputFields,
CombinerAggregator agg, Fields functionFields) {
...
}
```

```
public TridentState persistentAggregate(StateSpec spec,
Fields inputFields, CombinerAggregator agg,
Fields functionFields) {
...
}

public TridentState persistentAggregate(
StateFactory stateFactory, Fields inputFields,
ReducerAggregator agg, Fields functionFields) {
...
}

public TridentState persistentAggregate(StateSpec spec, Fields
inputFields, ReducerAggregator agg, Fields functionFields) {
...
}

public Stream stateQuery(TridentState state, Fields inputFields,
QueryFunction function, Fields functionFields) {
...
}

public TridentState persistentAggregate(
StateFactory stateFactory, ReducerAggregator agg,
Fields functionFields) {
...
}

public TridentState persistentAggregate(StateSpec spec,
ReducerAggregator agg, Fields functionFields) {
...
}

public Stream stateQuery(TridentState state,
    QueryFunction function, Fields functionFields) {
...
}
}
```

Like the base Stream object, the stateQuery() method creates an input stream from state. The various flavors of persistAggregate() allow a topology to update state information from tuples in a stream. Notice that the GroupedStream methods take an Aggregator, which it first applies before writing that information to the State object.

Now let's consider applying these functions to our example. In our system, we would like to persist with the occurrence counts by city, disease code, and hour. This would enable a report similar to the following table:

Disease	City	Date	Time	Occurrence Count
Bacterial meningitis	San Francisco	3/12/2013	3:00 PM	12
Bacterial meningitis	San Francisco	3/12/2013	4:00 PM	50
Bacterial meningitis	San Francisco	3/12/2013	5:00 PM	100
Smallpox	New York	3/13/2013	5:00 PM	6

To achieve this, we want to persist with the counts that we generate in the aggregation. We can use the `GroupedStream` interface (shown previously) returned by the `groupBy` function and call the `persistAggregate` method. Specifically, the following is the call we make in the example topology:

```
persistentAggregate(new OutbreakTrendFactory(),
    new Count(), new Fields("count")).newValuesStream()
```

To understand persistence, we will first focus on the first parameter to this method. Trident uses a factory pattern to generate instances of `State`. The `OutbreakTrendFactory` is the factory our topology provides to Storm. The listing for `OutbreakTrendFactory` is as follows:

```
public class OutbreakTrendFactory implements StateFactory {
private static final long serialVersionUID = 1L;

@Override
public State makeState(Map conf, IMetricsContext metrics,
int partitionIndex, int numPartitions) {
    return new OutbreakTrendState(new OutbreakTrendBackingMap());
}
}
```

The factory returns the `State` object that Storm uses to persist with information. In Storm, there are three types of state. Each type is described in the following table:

State type	Description
Non-Transactional	For persistence mechanisms that do not have rollback capabilities and where updates are permanent and commits are ignored.
Repeat Transactional	For persistence that is idempotent, provided the batch contains the same tuples.

State type	Description
Opaque Transactional	Updates are based on the previous value, which makes the persistence resilient to changes in batch composition.

To support counting and state updates in a distributed environment where batches can be replayed, Trident sequences state updates and uses different state update patterns to tolerate replays and faults. These are described in the following sections.

The Repeat Transactional state

For the Repeat Transactional state, the last committed batch identifier is stored with the data. The state is updated if and only if the batch identifier being applied is the next in sequence. If it is equal to or lower than the persisted identifier, then the update is ignored because it has already been applied.

To illustrate this approach, consider the following sequence of batches where the state update is an aggregate count of the occurrences of that key as it is in our example:

Batch #	State Update
1	{SF:320:378911 = 4}
2	{SF:320:378911 = 10}
3	{SF:320:378911 = 8}

The batches then complete processing in the following order:

1 à 2 à 3 à 3 (replayed)

This would result in the following state modifications, where the middle column is the persistence of the batch identifier indicating the most recent batch incorporated in the state:

Completed Batch #	State	
1	{ Batch = 1 }	{ SF:320:378911 = 4 }
2	{ Batch = 2 }	{ SF:320:378911 = 14 }
3	{ Batch = 3 }	{ SF:320:378911 = 22 }
3 (Replayed)	{ Batch = 3 }	{ SF:320:378911 = 22 }

Notice that when batch #3 completes the replay, it has no effect on the state because Trident has already incorporated its update in the state. For the Repeat Transactional state to function properly, batch contents cannot change between replays.

The Opaque state

The approach used in the Repeat Transactional state relies on the batch composition remaining constant, which may not be possible if a system encounters a fault. If the spout is emitting from a source that may have a partial failure, some of the tuples emitted in the initial batch might not be available for re-emission. The Opaque state allows the changing of batch composition by storing both current and previous states.

Assume that we have the same batches as in the previous example, but this time when Batch 3 is replayed, the aggregate count will be different since it contains a different set of tuples as shown in the following table:

Batch #	State update
1	{SF:320:378911 = 4}
2	{SF:320:378911 = 10}
3	{SF:320:378911 = 8}
3 (Replayed)	{SF:320:378911 = 6}

With Opaque state, the state would update as follows:

Completed batch #	Batch committed	Previous state	Current state
1	1	{}	{ SF:320:378911 = 4 }
2	2	{ SF:320:378911 = 4 }	{ SF:320:378911 = 14 }
3 (Applies)	3	{ SF:320:378911 = 14 }	{ SF:320:378911 = 22 }
3 (Replayed)	3	{ SF:320:378911 = 14 }	{ SF:320:378911 = 20 }

Notice that Opaque state stores the previous state information. Thus, when batch #3 is replayed, it can retransition the state using the new aggregate count.

You may wonder why we would reapply the batch if it had already been committed. The scenario we are concerned with is one whereby the state update succeeded, but the downstream processing failed. In our example topology, perhaps the alert failed to dispatch. Under such circumstances, Trident would retry the batch. Now, in the worst-case scenario, when the spout was asked to re-emit the batch, one or more sources of data may be unavailable.

In the case of a Transactional spout, it would need to wait until all the sources were again available. An Opaque Transactional spout would be able to emit the portion of the batch that was available, and processing could continue. Since Trident relies on sequential application of batches to state, it is imperative that no single batch be delayed, because that delays all processing in the system.

Given this approach, the choice of state should be based on the spout so as to guarantee idempotent behavior and not over-count or corrupt the state. The following table shows the possible pairings to guarantee idempotent behavior:

Type of Spout	Non-Transactional state	Opaque State	Repeat Transactional state
Non-Transactional spout			
Opaque spout		X	
Transactional spout		X	X

Fortunately, Storm provides map implementations that shield the persistence layer from the complexities of the state management. Specifically, Trident provides `State` implementations that maintain the additional information to adhere to the guarantees outlined previously. The objects are named appropriately: `NonTransactionalMap`, `TransactionalMap`, and `OpaqueMap`.

Returning to our example, since we have no transactional guarantees, we chose to use a `NonTransactionalMap` as our `State` object.

The `OutbreakTrendState` object looks like the following code snippet:

```
public class OutbreakTrendState extends NonTransactionalMap<Long> {
protected OutbreakTrendState(
OutbreakTrendBackingMap outbreakBackingMap) {
    super(outbreakBackingMap);
}
}
```

As shown in the preceding code, to leverage the MapState objects, we simply pass a backing map. In our example, this is the OutbreakTrendBackingMap. The code for that object is as follows:

```
public class OutbreakTrendBackingMap implements IBackingMap<Long> {
    private static final Logger LOG =
LoggerFactory.getLogger(OutbreakTrendBackingMap.class);
 Map<String, Long> storage =
new ConcurrentHashMap<String, Long>();

 @Override
 public List<Long> multiGet(List<List<Object>> keys) {
    List<Long> values = new ArrayList<Long>();
    for (List<Object> key : keys) {
        Long value = storage.get(key.get(0));
        if (value==null){
            values.add(new Long(0));
        } else {
            values.add(value);
        }
    }
    return values;
}

@Override
public void multiPut(List<List<Object>> keys, List<Long> vals) {
    for (int i=0; i < keys.size(); i++) {
        LOG.info("Persisting [" + keys.get(i).get(0) + "] ==> ["
+ vals.get(i) + "]");
        storage.put((String) keys.get(i).get(0), vals.get(i));
    }
}
}
```

In our example topology, we do not actually persist with the values. We simply put them in a ConcurrentHashMap. Obviously, that would not work across multiple hosts. The BackingMap is a clever abstraction, however. Simply changing the backing map instance that we pass into the constructor of the MapState object changes the persistence layer. We will see this in action in later chapters.

Executing the topology

The OutbreakDetectionTopology class has the following main method:

```
public static void main(String[] args) throws Exception {
    Config conf = new Config();
    LocalCluster cluster = new LocalCluster();
    cluster.submitTopology("cdc", conf, buildTopology());
    Thread.sleep(200000);
    cluster.shutdown();
}
```

Executing this method will submit the topology to a local cluster. The spout will immediately start emitting diagnosis events, which the Count aggregator will collect. The threshold in the OutbreakDetector class is set such that the count will quickly exceed the threshold, at which point the program terminates with the following set of commands:

```
INFO [Thread-18] DefaultCoordinator.success(31) | Successful Transaction
[8]

INFO [Thread-18] DefaultCoordinator.initializeTransaction(25) |
Initializing Transaction [9]

...

INFO [Thread-24] OutbreakTrendBackingMap.multiPut(34) | Persisting
[SF:320:378951] ==> [10306]

INFO [Thread-24] OutbreakTrendBackingMap.multiPut(34) | Persisting
[PHL:320:378951] ==> [893]

INFO [Thread-24] OutbreakTrendBackingMap.multiPut(34) | Persisting
[NYC:322:378951] ==> [1639]

INFO [Thread-24] OutbreakTrendBackingMap.multiPut(34) | Persisting
[SF:322:378951] ==> [10254]

INFO [Thread-24] OutbreakTrendBackingMap.multiPut(34) | Persisting
[SF:321:378951] ==> [10386]

...

00:04 ERROR: ALERT RECEIVED [Outbreak detected for [SF:320:378951]!]

00:04 ERROR: Dispatch the National Guard!
```

Notice that the coordinator is notified upon successful completion of the batches, and within a few batches, the threshold is exceeded, and the system instructs us with an error message, Dispatch the National Guard!.

Summary

In this chapter, we created a topology that processes diagnosis information to identify anomalies, which would indicate an outbreak. This same data flow could be applied to any type of data, including weather, seismic information, or traffic data. We exercised the fundamental primitives in Trident to construct a system that is capable of counting events even if batches are replayed. Later on in this book, we will leverage these same constructs and patterns to perform similar functions.

4
Real-time Trend Analysis

In this chapter, we will introduce you to trend analysis techniques using Storm and Trident. Real-time trend analysis involves identifying patterns in data streams, such as recognizing when the occurrence rate or count of certain events reaches a certain threshold. Common examples include trending topics in social media, such as when a specific hashtag becomes popular on Twitter or identifying trending search terms in a search engine. Storm originated as a project to perform real-time analytics on Twitter data, and it provides many of the core primitives required for analytical computation.

In the previous chapters, the spout implementations used were primarily simulations that used static sample data or randomly generated data. In this chapter, we will introduce an open source spout that emits data from a queue (Apache Kafka) and supports all three types of the Trident spout transaction (Non-transaction, Repeat Transaction, and Opaque Transactional). We will also implement a simple, generic method to populate the Kafka queue using a popular logging framework that will enable you to quickly begin real-time analysis of the existing applications and data with little or no source code modifications.

In this chapter, we will cover the following topics:

- Logging data to Apache Kafka and streaming it to Storm
- Streaming an existing application's log data to Storm for analysis
- Implementing an exponentially weighted moving average Trident function
- Using the XMPP protocol with Storm to send alerts and notifications

Use case

In our use case, we have an application or set of applications (websites, enterprise applications, and so on) that use the popular logback framework (http://logback. qos.ch) for logging structured messages to disk (access logs, errors, and so on). Currently, the only way to perform analytics on that data is to process the files in batches using something like Hadoop. The latency introduced by that process dramatically slows down our reaction time; patterns gleaned from the log data only emerge hours, sometimes days, after a particular event occurred and the opportunity to take responsive action has passed. It is much more desirable to be actively notified of patterns as they emerge, rather than after the fact.

This use case represents a common theme and has a broad range of applications across many business scenarios, including the following applications:

- Application Monitoring: For example, to notify system administrators when certain network errors reach a certain frequency
- Intrusion Detection: For example, to detect suspicious activity such as an increase in failed login attempts
- Supply Chain Management: For example, to identify spikes in sales of specific products and adjusting just-in-time delivery accordingly
- Online Advertising: For example, to recognize popular trends and dynamically changing ad delivery

Architecture

The architecture of our application is depicted in the following diagram, and it will include the following components:

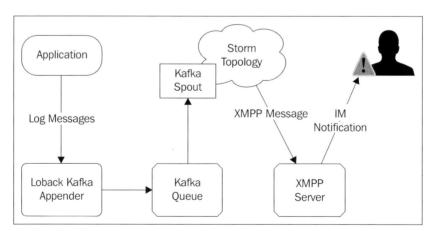

The source application

The source application component is any application that uses the logback framework for logging arbitrary log messages. For our purposes, we will create a simple application that logs structured messages at certain intervals. However, as you'll see, any existing application that uses either the logback or slf4j frameworks can be substituted with a simple configuration change.

The logback Kafka appender

The logback framework has an extension mechanism that allows you to add additional appenders to its configuration. A logback appender is simply a Java class that receives logging events and does something with them. The most commonly used appenders are one of several `FileAppender` subclasses that simply format and write log messages to a file on disk. Other appender implementations write log data to network sockets, relational databases, and to SMTP for e-mail notifications. For our purposes, we will implement an appender that writes log messages to an Apache Kafka queue.

Apache Kafka

Apache Kafka (`http://kafka.apache.org`) is an open source distributed publish-subscribe messaging system. Kafka is specifically designed and optimized for high-throughput, persistent real-time streams. Like Storm, Kafka is designed to scale horizontally on commodity software to support hundreds of thousands of messages per second.

Kafka spout

The Kafka spout reads data from a Kafka queue and emits it to a Storm or Trident topology. The Kafka spout was originally authored by Nathan Marz, and it is still a part of the storm-contrib project on GitHub (`https://github.com/nathanmarz/storm-contrib`). Prebuilt binaries of the Kafka spout are available from the `clojars.org` Maven repository (`https://clojars.org/storm/storm-kafka`). We will use the Kafka spout to read messages from the Kafka queue and stream them into our topology.

Our topology will consist of a collection of both built-in and custom Trident components (functions, filters, state, and so on) that detect patterns in the source data stream. When a pattern is detected, the topology will emit a tuple to a function that will send an XMPP message to an XMPP server to notify end users via an **instant message (IM)**.

The XMPP server

Extensible Messaging and Presence Protocol (**XMPP**) (http://xmpp.org) is an XML-based standard for instant messaging, presence information, and contact list maintenance. Many IM clients such as Adium (for OSX) (http://adium.im) and Pidgin (for OSX, Linus, and Windows) (http://www.pidgin.im) support the XMPP protocol, and if you have ever used Google Talk for instant messaging, you have used XMPP.

We will use the open source OpenFire XMPP server (http://www.igniterealtime.org/projects/openfire/) for its ease of setup and compatibility with OSX, Linux, and Windows.

Installing the required software

We'll begin by installing the necessary software: Apache Kafka and OpenFire. Although Kafka is a distributed messaging system, it will work just fine installed as a single node, or even locally as part of a development environment. In a production environment, you will need to set up a cluster of one or more machines depending on your scaling requirements. The OpenFire server is not a clustered system and can be installed on a single node or locally.

Installing Kafka

Kafka depends on ZooKeeper for storing certain state information, much like Storm. Since Storm imposes a relatively light load on ZooKeeper, in many cases it is acceptable to share the same ZooKeeper cluster between both Kafka and Storm. Since we've already covered ZooKeeper installation in *Chapter 2, Configuring Storm Clusters*, here we'll just cover the running of the local ZooKeeper server that ships with Kafka and is suitable for a development environment.

Begin by downloading the 0.7.x release of Apache Kafka from the following website:

http://kafka.apache.org/downloads.html

Next, unpack the source distribution and change the existing directory to the following directory:

```
tar -zxf kafka-0.7.2-incubating-src.tgz
cd kafka-0.7.2-incubating-src
```

Kafka is written in the Scala JVM language (`http://www.scala-lang.org`) and uses sbt (**Scala Build Tool**) (`http://www.scala-sbt.org`) for compiling and packaging. Fortunately, the Kafka source distribution includes `sbt` and can be built with the following command:

```
./sbt update package
```

Before starting Kafka, unless you already have a ZooKeeper service running, you will need to start the ZooKeeper service bundled with Kafka using the following command:

```
./bin/zookeeper-server-start.sh ./config/zookeeper.properties
```

Finally, in a separate terminal window, start the Kafka service with the following command:

```
./bin/kafka-server-start.sh ./config/server.properties
```

The Kafka service is now ready to use.

Installing OpenFire

OpenFire is available as an installer for OSX and Windows as well as a package for various Linux distributions, and it can be downloaded from the following website:

`http://www.ignitereialtime.org/downloads/index.jsp`

To install OpenFire, download the installer for your operating system and follow the appropriate installation instructions that can be found at the following website:

`http://www.ignitereialtime.org/builds/openfire/docs/latest/documentation/index.html`

Introducing the sample application

The application component is a simple Java class that uses the **Simple Logging Facade for Java** (**SLF4J**) (`http://www.slf4j.org`) to log messages. We will simulate an application that begins by generating warning messages at a relatively slow rate, then switches to a state where it generates warning messages at a much faster rate, and finally returns to the slow state as follows:

- Log a warning message every 5 seconds for 30 seconds (slow state)
- Log a warning message every second for 15 seconds (rapid state)
- Log a warning message every 5 seconds for 30 seconds (slow state)

The goal of the application is to generate a simple pattern that our storm topology can recognize and react to by sending notifications when certain patterns emerge and state changes occur as shown in the following code snippet:

```java
public class RogueApplication {
    private static final Logger LOG = LoggerFactory.
getLogger(RogueApplication.class);

    public static void main(String[] args) throws Exception {
        int slowCount = 6;
        int fastCount = 15;
        // slow state
        for(int i = 0; i < slowCount; i++){
            LOG.warn("This is a warning (slow state).");
            Thread.sleep(5000);
        }
        // enter rapid state
        for(int i = 0; i < fastCount; i++){
            LOG.warn("This is a warning (rapid state).");
            Thread.sleep(1000);
        }
        // return to slow state
        for(int i = 0; i < slowCount; i++){
            LOG.warn("This is a warning (slow state).");
            Thread.sleep(5000);
        }
    }
}
```

Sending log messages to Kafka

The logback framework provides a simple extension mechanism that allows you to plug in additional appenders. In our case, we want to implement an appender that can write log message data to Kafka.

Logback includes the `ch.qos.logback.core.AppenderBase` abstract class that makes it easy to implement the `Appender` interface. The `AppenderBase` class defines a single abstract method as follows:

```java
abstract protected void append(E eventObject);
```

The `eventObject` parameter represents a logging event and includes properties such as the date of the event, the log level (`DEBUG`, `INFO`, `WARN`, and so on), as well as the log message itself. We will override the `append()` method to write the `eventObject` data to Kafka.

In addition to the `append()` method, the `AppenderBase` class defines two additional lifecycle methods that we will need to override:

```
public void start();
public void stop();
```

The `start()` method is called during the initialization of the logback framework, and the `stop()` method is called upon deinitialization. We will override these methods to set up and tear down our connection to the Kafka service.

The source code for the `KafkaAppender` class is listed as follows:

```java
public class KafkaAppender extends AppenderBase<ILoggingEvent> {

    private String topic;
    private String zookeeperHost;
    private Producer<String, String> producer;
    private Formatter formatter;

    // java bean definitions used to inject
    // configuration values from logback.xml
    public String getTopic() {
        return topic;
    }

    public void setTopic(String topic) {
        this.topic = topic;
    }

    public String getZookeeperHost() {
        return zookeeperHost;
    }

    public void setZookeeperHost(String zookeeperHost) {
        this.zookeeperHost = zookeeperHost;
    }

    public Formatter getFormatter() {
        return formatter;
    }

    public void setFormatter(Formatter formatter) {
        this.formatter = formatter;
    }
```

```java
    // overrides
    @Override
    public void start() {
        if (this.formatter == null) {
            this.formatter = new MessageFormatter();
        }
        super.start();
        Properties props = new Properties();
        props.put("zk.connect", this.zookeeperHost);
        props.put("serializer.class", "kafka.serializer.
StringEncoder");
        ProducerConfig config = new ProducerConfig(props);
        this.producer = new Producer<String, String>(config);
    }

    @Override
    public void stop() {
        super.stop();
        this.producer.close();
    }

    @Override
    protected void append(ILoggingEvent event) {
        String payload = this.formatter.format(event);
        ProducerData<String, String> data = new ProducerData<String,
String>(this.topic, payload);
        this.producer.send(data);
    }

}
```

As you will see, the JavaBean-style accessors in this class allow us to configure the associated values via dependency injection at runtime when the logback framework initializes. The setters and getters for the `zookeeperHosts` property are used to initialize the `KafkaProducer` client, configuring it to discover Kafka hosts that have registered with ZooKeeper. An alternative method would be to supply a static list of Kafka hosts, but for simplicity's sake it is easier to use an auto-discovery mechanism. The `topic` property is used to tell the `KafkaConsumer` client from which Kafka topic it should read.

The `Formatter` property is somewhat special. It is an interface we've defined that provides an extension point for handling structured (that is, parseable) log messages as shown in the following code snippet:

```
public interface Formatter {
    String format(ILoggingEvent event);
}
```

A `Formatter` implementation's job is to take an `ILoggingEvent` object and turn it into a machine-readable string that can be processed by a consumer. A simple implementation listed in the following code snippet simply returns the log message, discarding any additional metadata:

```
public class MessageFormatter implements Formatter {

    public String format(ILoggingEvent event) {
        return event.getFormattedMessage();
    }
}
```

The following logback configuration file illustrates the usage of the appender. This example does not define a custom `Formatter` implementation, so the `KafkaAppender` class will default to using the `MessageFormatter` class and just write the log message data to Kafka and discard any additional information contained in the logging event, as shown in the following code snippet:

```
<?xml version="1.0" encoding="UTF-8" ?>
<configuration>
    <appender name="KAFKA"
        class="com.github.ptgoetz.logback.kafka.KafkaAppender">
        <topic>mytopic</topic>
        <zookeeperHost>localhost:2181</zookeeperHost>
    </appender>
    <root level="debug">
        <appender-ref ref="KAFKA" />
    </root>
</configuration>
```

The Storm application we're building is time sensitive: if we're tracking the rate at which each event occurs, we need to know exactly when an event occurs. A naïve approach would be to simply assign the event a time using the `System.currentTimeMillis()` method when the data enters our topology. However, Trident's batching mechanism doesn't guarantee that tuples will be delivered to a topology at the same rate with which they were received.

In order to account for this situation, we need to capture the time of the event when it occurs and include it in the data when we write to the Kafka queue. Fortunately, the ILoggingEvent class includes a timestamp, in milliseconds since the epoch, that the event occurred.

To include the metadata included in ILoggingEvent, we'll create a custom Formatter implementation that encodes the log event data in JSON format as follows:

```
public class JsonFormatter implements Formatter {
    private static final String QUOTE = "\"";
    private static final String COLON = ":";
    private static final String COMMA = ",";

    private boolean expectJson = false;

    public String format(ILoggingEvent event) {
        StringBuilder sb = new StringBuilder();
        sb.append("{");
        fieldName("level", sb);
        quote(event.getLevel().levelStr, sb);
        sb.append(COMMA);
        fieldName("logger", sb);
        quote(event.getLoggerName(), sb);
        sb.append(COMMA);
        fieldName("timestamp", sb);
        sb.append(event.getTimeStamp());
        sb.append(COMMA);
        fieldName("message", sb);
        if (this.expectJson) {
            sb.append(event.getFormattedMessage());
        } else {
            quote(event.getFormattedMessage(), sb);
        }

        sb.append("}");
        return sb.toString();
    }

    private static void fieldName(String name, StringBuilder sb) {
        quote(name, sb);
        sb.append(COLON);
    }
```

```
    private static void quote(String value, StringBuilder sb) {
        sb.append(QUOTE);
        sb.append(value);
        sb.append(QUOTE);
    }

    public boolean isExpectJson() {
        return expectJson;
    }

    public void setExpectJson(boolean expectJson) {
        this.expectJson = expectJson;
    }
}
```

The bulk of the `JsonMessageFormatter` class code uses a `java.lang.StringBuilder` class to create JSON from the `ILoggingEvent` object. While we could have used a JSON library to do the work, the JSON data we're generating is simple and adding an additional dependency just to generate JSON would be overkill.

The one JavaBean property exposed by `JsonMessageFormatter` is the `expectJson` Boolean used to specify whether the log message passed to the `Formatter` implementation should be treated as JSON. If set to `False`, the log message will be treated as a string and wrapped in double quotes, otherwise the message will be treated as a JSON object (`{...}`) or array (`[...]`).

The following is a sample logback configuration file that illustrates the usage of the `KafkaAppender` and `JsonFormatter` classes:

```
<?xml version="1.0" encoding="UTF-8" ?>
<configuration>
    <appender name="KAFKA"
        class="com.github.ptgoetz.logback.kafka.KafkaAppender">
        <topic>foo</topic>
        <zookeeperHost>localhost:2181</zookeeperHost>
        <!-- specify a custom formatter -->
        <formatter class="com.github.ptgoetz.logback.kafka.formatter.
JsonFormatter">
            <!--
            Whether we expect the log message to be JSON encoded or
not.
            If set to "false", the log message will be treated as
a string, and wrapped in quotes. Otherwise it will be treated as a
parseable JSON object.
            -->
```

```
        <expectJson>false</expectJson>
    </formatter>
  </appender>
  <root level="debug">
        <appender-ref ref="KAFKA" />
  </root>
</configuration>
```

Since the analytics topology we are building is more concerned with event timing than message content, the log messages we generate will be strings, so we set the `expectJson` property to `False`.

Introducing the log analysis topology

With the means to write our log data to Kafka, we're ready to turn our attention to the implementation of a Trident topology to perform the analytical computation. The topology will perform the following operations:

1. Receive and parse the raw JSON log event data.
2. Extract and emit necessary fields.
3. Update an exponentially-weighted moving average function.
4. Determine if the moving average has crossed a specified threshold.
5. Filter out events that do not represent a state change (for example, rate moved above/below threshold).
6. Send an instant message (XMPP) notification.

The topology is depicted in the following diagram with the Trident stream operations at the top and stream processing components at the bottom:

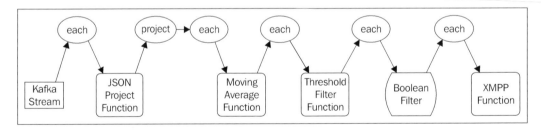

Kafka spout

The first step in creating the log analysis topology is to configure the Kafka spout to stream data received from Kafka into our topology as follows:

```
TridentTopology topology = new TridentTopology();

StaticHosts kafkaHosts = KafkaConfig.StaticHosts.
fromHostString(Arrays.asList(new String[] { "localhost" }), 1);
    TridentKafkaConfig spoutConf = new
TridentKafkaConfig(kafkaHosts, "log-analysis");
    spoutConf.scheme = new StringScheme();
    spoutConf.forceStartOffsetTime(-1);
    OpaqueTridentKafkaSpout spout = new OpaqueTridentKafkaSpout(s
poutConf);

Stream spoutStream = topology.newStream("kafka-stream",
spout);
```

This code first creates a new `TridentTopology` instance, and then uses the Kafka Java API to create a list of Kafka hosts with which to connect (since we're running a single, unclustered Kafka service locally, we specify a single host: `localhost`). Next, we create the `TridentKafkaConfig` object, passing it the host list and a unique identifier.

The data our application writes to Kafka is a simple Java string, so we use Storm-Kafka built-in `StringScheme` class. The `StringScheme` class will read data from Kafka as a string and output it in a tuple field named `str`.

By default, upon deployment the Kafka spout will attempt to read from the Kafka queue where it last left off by querying ZooKeeper for state information. This behavior can be overridden by calling the `forceOffsetTime(long time)` method of the `TridentKafkaConfig` class. The time parameter can be one of the following three values:

- **-2 (earliest offset)**: The spout will *rewind* and start reading from the beginning of the queue
- **-1 (latest offset)**: The spout will *fast forward* and read from the end of the queue
- **Time in milliseconds**: Given a specific date in milliseconds (for example, `java.util.Date.getTime()`), the spout will attempt to begin reading from that point in time

After setting up the spout configuration, we create an instance of the *Opaque Transactional* Kafka spout and set up a corresponding Trident stream.

The JSON project function

The data stream coming from the Kafka spout will contain a single field (str) containing the JSON data from the log event. We'll create a Trident function to parse the incoming data and output, or project requested fields as tuple values as shown in the following code snippet:

```
public class JsonProjectFunction extends BaseFunction {

    private Fields fields;

    public JsonProjectFunction(Fields fields) {
        this.fields = fields;
    }

    public void execute(TridentTuple tuple, TridentCollector
collector) {
        String json = tuple.getString(0);
        Map<String, Object> map = (Map<String, Object>)
            JSONValue.parse(json);
        Values values = new Values();
        for (int i = 0; i < this.fields.size(); i++) {
            values.add(map.get(this.fields.get(i)));
        }
        collector.emit(values);
    }

}
```

The JsonProjectFunction constructor takes a Fields object parameter that will determine what values to emit as a list of key names to look up from the JSON. When the function receives a tuple, it will parse the JSON in the tuple's str field, iterate the Fields object's values, and emit the corresponding value from the input JSON.

The following code creates a Fields object with a list of field names to extract from the JSON. It then creates a new Stream object from the spout stream, selects the str tuple field as the input to the JsonProjectFunction constructor, constructs the JsonProjectFunction constructor, and specifies that the fields selected from the JSON will also be output from the function:

```
        Fields jsonFields = new Fields("level", "timestamp",
"message", "logger");
        Stream parsedStream = spoutStream.each(new Fields("str"), new
JsonProjectFunction(jsonFields), jsonFields);
```

Consider that the following JSON message is received from the Kafka spout:

```
{
  "message" : "foo",
  "timestamp" : 1370918376296,
  "level" : "INFO",
  "logger" : "test"
}
```

This would mean that the function would output the following tuple values:

```
[INFO, 1370918376296, test, foo]
```

Calculating a moving average

In order to calculate the rate at which log events occur, without the need to store an inordinate amount of state, we will implement a function that performs what is known in statistics as an **exponentially weighted moving average**.

A moving average calculation is often used to smooth out short-term fluctuations and expose long-term trends in time series data. One of the most common examples of a moving average is its use in graphing the fluctuation of prices in the stock market, as shown in the following screenshot:

The smoothing effect of a moving average is achieved by taking into account historical values in the calculation. A moving average calculation can be performed with a very minimal amount of state. For a time series, we need only keep the time of the last event and the last calculated average.

In pseudo code, the calculation would look something like the following code snippet:

```
diff = currentTime - lastEventTime
currentAverage = (1.0 - alpha) * diff + alpha * lastAverage
```

The `alpha` value in the preceding calculation is a constant value between `0` and `1`. The `alpha` value determines the amount of smoothing that occurs over time. The closer the `alpha` value is to `1`, the more the historical values affect the current average. In other words, an `alpha` value closer to `0` will result in less smoothing and the moving average will be closer to the current value. An `alpha` value closer to `1` will have the opposite effect. The current average will be less affected by wild fluctuations and the historical values will have more weight in determining the current average.

Adding a sliding window

In some cases, we may want to discount historical values to reduce their effects on the moving average, for example, to reset the smoothing effect if a large amount of time has passed between receiving events. In case of a low alpha value, this may not be necessary since the smoothing effect is minimal. In the event of a high alpha, however, it may be desirable to counteract the smoothing effect.

Consider the following example.

We have an event (such as a network error and so on) that occurs infrequently. Occasionally, small spikes in frequency occur, but that's usually okay. So, we want to smooth out the small spikes. What we want to be notified of is if a *sustained* spike occurs.

If the event occurs once a week on average (well below our notification threshold), but one day spikes to many occurrences within an hour (above our notification threshold), the smoothing effect of the high alpha may negate the spike such that a notification is never triggered.

To counteract this effect, we can introduce the concept of a **sliding window** into our moving average calculation. Since we're already keeping track of both the time of the last event, and the current average, implementing a sliding window is simple as illustrated in the following pseudo code:

```
if (currentTime - lastEventTime) > slidingWindowInterval
    currentAverage = 0
end if
```

An implementation of an exponentially weighted moving average is listed as follows:

```java
public class EWMA implements Serializable {

    public static enum Time {
        MILLISECONDS(1), SECONDS(1000), MINUTES(SECONDS.getTime() *
60), HOURS(MINUTES.getTime() * 60), DAYS(HOURS
                .getTime() * 24), WEEKS(DAYS.getTime() * 7);

        private long millis;

        private Time(long millis) {
            this.millis = millis;
        }

        public long getTime() {
            return this.millis;
        }
    }

    // Unix load average-style alpha constants
    public static final double ONE_MINUTE_ALPHA = 1 - Math.exp(-5d /
60d / 1d);
    public static final double FIVE_MINUTE_ALPHA = 1 - Math.exp(-5d /
60d / 5d);
    public static final double FIFTEEN_MINUTE_ALPHA = 1 - Math.exp(-5d
/ 60d / 15d);

    private long window;
    private long alphaWindow;
    private long last;
    private double average;
    private double alpha = -1D;
    private boolean sliding = false;

    public EWMA() {
    }

    public EWMA sliding(double count, Time time) {
        return this.sliding((long) (time.getTime() * count));
    }
```

```
    public EWMA sliding(long window) {
        this.sliding = true;
        this.window = window;
        return this;
    }

    public EWMA withAlpha(double alpha) {
        if (!(alpha > 0.0D && alpha <= 1.0D)) {
            throw new IllegalArgumentException("Alpha must be between
0.0 and 1.0");
        }
        this.alpha = alpha;
        return this;
    }

    public EWMA withAlphaWindow(long alphaWindow) {
        this.alpha = -1;
        this.alphaWindow = alphaWindow;
        return this;
    }

    public EWMA withAlphaWindow(double count, Time time) {
        return this.withAlphaWindow((long) (time.getTime() * count));
    }

    public void mark() {
        mark(System.currentTimeMillis());
    }

    public synchronized void mark(long time) {
        if (this.sliding) {
            if (time - this.last > this.window) {
                // reset the sliding window
                this.last = 0;
            }
        }
        if (this.last == 0) {
            this.average = 0;
            this.last = time;
        }
        long diff = time - this.last;
        double alpha = this.alpha != -1.0 ? this.alpha : Math.exp(-1.0
* ((double) diff / this.alphaWindow));
```

```
            this.average = (1.0 - alpha) * diff + alpha * this.average;
            this.last = time;
    }

    public double getAverage() {
        return this.average;
    }

    public double getAverageIn(Time time) {
        return this.average == 0.0 ? this.average : this.average /
time.getTime();
    }

    public double getAverageRatePer(Time time) {
        return this.average == 0.0 ? this.average : time.getTime() /
this.average;
    }

}
```

The EWMA implementation defines three useful constant alpha values: ONE_MINUTE_
ALPHA, FIVE_MINUTE_ALPHA, and FIFTEEN_MINUTE_ALPHA. These correspond to the
standard alpha values used to calculate load averages in UNIX. The alpha value
can also be specified manually, or as a function of an *alpha* window.

The implementation uses a fluent-style *builder* API. For example, you can create an
EWMA instance with a sliding window of one minute and an alpha value equivalent
to the UNIX one-minute interval, as shown in use the following code snippet:

```
EWMA ewma = new EWMA().sliding(1.0, Time.MINUTES).withAlpha(EWMA.ONE_
MINUTE_ALPHA);
```

The mark() methods are used to update the moving average. Without arguments,
the mark() method will use the current time to calculate the average. Because we
want to use the original timestamp from the log event, we overload the mark()
method to allow the specification of a specific time.

The getAverage() method returns the average time between calls to mark() in
milliseconds. We also added the convenient getAverageIn() method, which will
return the average in the specified time unit of measure (seconds, minutes, hours,
and so on). The getAverageRatePer() method returns the rate of calls to mark()
in a specific time measurement.

As you'll probably notice, using an exponentially weighted moving average can be somewhat tricky. Finding the right set of values for an alpha as well as the optional sliding window varies quite a bit depending on the specific use case, and finding the right value is largely a matter of trial and error.

Implementing the moving average function

To use our EWMA class in a Trident topology, we'll create a subclass of Trident's BaseFunction abstract class named MovingAverageFunction that wraps an instance of EWMA, as shown in the following code snippet:

```
public class MovingAverageFunction extends BaseFunction {
    private static final Logger LOG = LoggerFactory.
getLogger(BaseFunction.class);

    private EWMA ewma;
    private Time emitRatePer;

    public MovingAverageFunction(EWMA ewma, Time emitRatePer){
        this.ewma = ewma;
        this.emitRatePer = emitRatePer;
    }

    public void execute(TridentTuple tuple, TridentCollector
collector) {
        this.ewma.mark(tuple.getLong(0));
        LOG.debug("Rate: {}", this.ewma.getAverageRatePer(this.
emitRatePer));
        collector.emit(new Values(this.ewma.getAverageRatePer(this.
emitRatePer)));
    }
}
```

The MovingAverage.execute() method gets the Long value of the incoming tuple's first field, uses the value to call the mark() method to update the current average, and emits the current average rate. Functions in Trident are additive, meaning they add values to the tuples in a stream. So, for example, consider that the tuple coming into our function looks like the following code snippet:

```
[INFO, 1370918376296, test, foo]
```

This means that after processing, the tuple might look like the following code snippet:

```
[INFO, 1370918376296, test, foo, 3.72234]
```

Here, the new value represents the new average rate.

To use the function, we create an instance of the EWMA class and pass it to the MovingAverageFunction constructor. We apply the function to the stream with the each() method, selecting the timestamp field as the input, as shown in the following code snippet:

```
        EWMA ewma = new EWMA().sliding(1.0, Time.MINUTES).
withAlpha(EWMA.ONE_MINUTE_ALPHA);
        Stream averageStream = parsedStream.each(new
Fields("timestamp"),
                new MovingAverageFunction(ewma, Time.MINUTES), new
Fields("average"));
```

Filtering on thresholds

For our use case, we want to be able to define a rate threshold that triggers a notification when exceeded. We also want notifications when the average rate falls back below that threshold (that is, returns to normal). We can accomplish this functionality using a combination of an additional function and a simple Trident filter.

The job of the function will be to determine whether the new value of the average rate field crosses a threshold, and if that represents a change from the previous value (that is, whether it has changed from *below threshold* to *above threshold* or vice versa). If the new average represents a state change, the function will emit the Boolean value True, otherwise it will emit False. We will leverage that value to filter out events that do not represent a state change. We'll implement the threshold tracking function in the ThresholdFilterFunction class as shown in the following code snippet:

```
public class ThresholdFilterFunction extends BaseFunction {
    private static final Logger LOG = LoggerFactory.getLogger(Threshol
dFilterFunction.class);

    private static enum State {
        BELOW, ABOVE;
    }

    private State last = State.BELOW;
    private double threshold;

    public ThresholdFilterFunction(double threshold){
        this.threshold = threshold;
    }
```

```
    public void execute(TridentTuple tuple, TridentCollector
collector) {
        double val = tuple.getDouble(0);
        State newState = val < this.threshold ? State.BELOW : State.
    ABOVE;

        boolean stateChange = this.last != newState;
        collector.emit(new Values(stateChange, threshold));
        this.last = newState;
        LOG.debug("State change? --> {}", stateChange);
    }
}
```

The `ThresholdFilterFunction` class defines an inner enumeration to represent the state (above threshold or below). The constructor takes a double argument that establishes the threshold we compare against. In the `execute()` method, we get the current rate value and determine whether it is below or above the threshold. We then compare it to the last state to see if it has changed and emit that value as a Boolean. Finally, we update the internal above/below state to the newly calculated value.

After passing through the `ThresholdFilterFunction` class, tuples in the input stream will contain a new Boolean value that we can use to easily filter out events that don't trigger a state change. To filter out non-state-change events, we'll use a simple `BooleanFilter` class as shown in the following code snippet:

```
public class BooleanFilter extends BaseFilter {

    public boolean isKeep(TridentTuple tuple) {
        return tuple.getBoolean(0);
    }
}
```

The `BooleanFilter.isKeep()` method simply reads a field from a tuple as a Boolean value and returns that value. Any tuples containing `False` for the input value will be filtered out of the resulting stream.

The following code fragment illustrates the usage of the `ThresholdFilterFuncation` class and the `BooleanFilter` class:

```
        ThresholdFilterFunction tff = new
    ThresholdFilterFunction(50D);
        Stream thresholdStream = averageStream.each(new
    Fields("average"), tff, new Fields("change", "threshold"));
```

```
Stream filteredStream = thresholdStream.each(new
Fields("change"), new BooleanFilter());
```

The first line creates a `ThresholdFilterFunction` instance with a threshold of `50.0`. We then create a new stream using the `averageStream` as input to the threshold function, and select the `average` tuple field as input. We also assign names (`change` and `threshold`) to the fields added by the function. Finally, we apply the `BooleanFilter` class to create a new stream that will only contain tuples that represent a change in threshold comparison.

At this point, we have everything necessary to implement notifications. The `filteredStream` we've created will only contain tuples that represent a threshold state change.

Sending notifications with XMPP

The XMPP protocol provides all the typical features you would expect in an instant messaging standard:

- Rosters (contact lists)
- Presence (knowing when others are online and their availability status)
- User-to-user instant messaging
- Group chats

The XMPP protocol uses an XML format for its communication protocol, but there are numerous high-level client libraries that handle most of the low-level details with a simple API. We will use the Smack API (`http://www.igniterealtime.org/projects/smack/`) as it is one of the most straightforward XMPP client implementations.

The following code snippet demonstrates the usage of the Smack API to send a simple instant message to another user:

```
// connect to XMPP server and login
ConnectionConfiguration config = new
    ConnectionConfiguration("jabber.org");
XMPPConnection client = new XMPPConnection(config);
client.connect();
client.login("username", "password");
```

```
// send a message to another user
Message message =
    new Message("myfriend@jabber.org", Type.normal);
message.setBody("How are you today?");
client.sendPacket(message);
```

The code connects to the XMPP server at `jabber.org` and logs in with a username and password. Behind the scenes, the Smack library handles the low-level communications with the server. When the client connects and authenticates, it also sends a presence message to the server. This allows a user's contacts (other users listed in their XMPP roster) to receive a notification that the person is now connected. Finally, we create and send a simple message addressed to `"myfriend@jabber.org"`.

Based on this simple example, we will create a class named `XMPPFunction` that sends XMPP notifications when it receives a Trident tuple. The class will establish a long-lived connection to an XMPP server in the `prepare()` method. Also, in the `execute()` method it will create an XMPP message based on the tuple received.

To make the `XMPPFunction` class more reusable, we'll introduce the `MessageMapper` interface that defines a method to format the data from a Trident tuple to a string suitable for an instant message notification, as shown in the following code snippet:

```
public interface MessageMapper extends Serializable {
    public String toMessageBody(TridentTuple tuple);
}
```

We'll delegate message formatting to an instance of `MessageMapper` in the `XMPPFunction` class as shown in the following code snippet:

```
public class XMPPFunction extends BaseFunction {
    private static final Logger LOG = LoggerFactory.
getLogger(XMPPFunction.class);

    public static final String XMPP_TO = "storm.xmpp.to";
    public static final String XMPP_USER = "storm.xmpp.user";
    public static final String XMPP_PASSWORD = "storm.xmpp.password";
    public static final String XMPP_SERVER = "storm.xmpp.server";

    private XMPPConnection xmppConnection;
    private String to;
    private MessageMapper mapper;
```

```
    public XMPPFunction(MessageMapper mapper) {
        this.mapper = mapper;
    }


    @Override
    public void prepare(Map conf, TridentOperationContext context) {
        LOG.debug("Prepare: {}", conf);
        super.prepare(conf, context);
        this.to = (String) conf.get(XMPP_TO);
        ConnectionConfiguration config = new ConnectionConfiguration((
    String) conf.get(XMPP_SERVER));
        this.xmppConnection = new XMPPConnection(config);
        try {
            this.xmppConnection.connect();
            this.xmppConnection.login((String) conf.get(XMPP_USER),
    (String) conf.get(XMPP_PASSWORD));
        } catch (XMPPException e) {
            LOG.warn("Error initializing XMPP Channel", e);
        }
    }


    public void execute(TridentTuple tuple, TridentCollector
    collector) {
        Message msg = new Message(this.to, Type.normal);
        msg.setBody(this.mapper.toMessageBody(tuple));
        this.xmppConnection.sendPacket(msg);

    }

}
```

The XMPPFunction class begins by defining several string constants that are used to look up values from the Storm configuration passed to the prepare() method, and it follows with the declaration of the instance variables that we'll populate when the function becomes active. The class' constructor takes a MessageMapper instance as a parameter that will be used in the execute() method to format the body of the notification message.

In the prepare() method, we look up the configuration parameters (server, username, to address, and so on) for the XMPPConnection class and open the connection. When a topology that uses this function is deployed, the XMPP client will send a presence packet and other users who have the configured user in their roster (buddy list) will receive a notification indicating that the user is now online.

The final necessary piece of our notification mechanism is to implement a
`MessageMapper` instance to format the contents of a tuple into a human-readable
message body as shown in the following code snippet:

```
public class NotifyMessageMapper implements MessageMapper {

    public String toMessageBody(TridentTuple tuple) {
        StringBuilder sb = new StringBuilder();
        sb.append("On " + new Date(tuple.getLongByField("timestamp"))
+ " ");
        sb.append("the application \"" + tuple.
getStringByField("logger") + "\" ");
        sb.append("changed alert state based on a threshold of " +
tuple.getDoubleByField("threshold") + ".\n");
        sb.append("The last value was " + tuple.
getDoubleByField("average") + "\n");
        sb.append("The last message was \"" + tuple.
getStringByField("message") + "\"");
        return sb.toString();
    }
}
```

The final topology

We now have all the components necessary to build our log analysis topology
as follows:

```
public class LogAnalysisTopology {

    public static StormTopology buildTopology() {
        TridentTopology topology = new TridentTopology();

        StaticHosts kafkaHosts = KafkaConfig.StaticHosts.
fromHostString(Arrays.asList(new String[] { "localhost" }), 1);
        TridentKafkaConfig spoutConf = new
TridentKafkaConfig(kafkaHosts, "log-analysis");
        spoutConf.scheme = new StringScheme();
        spoutConf.forceStartOffsetTime(-1);
        OpaqueTridentKafkaSpout spout = new OpaqueTridentKafkaSpout(s
poutConf);

        Stream spoutStream = topology.newStream("kafka-stream",
spout);
```

```
            Fields jsonFields = new Fields("level", "timestamp",
"message", "logger");
            Stream parsedStream = spoutStream.each(new Fields("str"), new
JsonProjectFunction(jsonFields), jsonFields);

            // drop the unparsed JSON to reduce tuple size
            parsedStream = parsedStream.project(jsonFields);

            EWMA ewma = new EWMA().sliding(1.0, Time.MINUTES).
withAlpha(EWMA.ONE_MINUTE_ALPHA);
            Stream averageStream = parsedStream.each(new
Fields("timestamp"),
                    new MovingAverageFunction(ewma, Time.MINUTES), new
Fields("average"));

            ThresholdFilterFunction tff = new
ThresholdFilterFunction(50D);
            Stream thresholdStream = averageStream.each(new
Fields("average"), tff, new Fields("change", "threshold"));

            Stream filteredStream = thresholdStream.each(new
Fields("change"), new BooleanFilter());

            filteredStream.each(filteredStream.getOutputFields(), new
XMPPFunction(new NotifyMessageMapper()), new Fields());

            return topology.build();
    }

    public static void main(String[] args) throws Exception {
        Config conf = new Config();
        conf.put(XMPPFunction.XMPP_USER, "storm@budreau.local");
        conf.put(XMPPFunction.XMPP_PASSWORD, "storm");
        conf.put(XMPPFunction.XMPP_SERVER, "budreau.local");
        conf.put(XMPPFunction.XMPP_TO, "tgoetz@budreau.local");

        conf.setMaxSpoutPending(5);
        if (args.length == 0) {
            LocalCluster cluster = new LocalCluster();
            cluster.submitTopology("log-analysis", conf,
buildTopology());
```

```
        } else {
            conf.setNumWorkers(3);
            StormSubmitter.submitTopology(args[0], conf,
    buildTopology());
        }
    }
}
```

Then, the `buildTopology()` method creates all the stream connections between the Kafka spout and our Trident functions and filters. The `main()` method then submits the topology to a cluster: a local cluster if the topology is being run in the local mode or a remote cluster when run in the distributed mode.

We begin by configuring the Kafka spout to read from the same topic that our application is configured to write log events. Because Kafka persists all the messages it receives, and because our application may have been running for some time (and thus logging many events), we tell the spout to fast-forward to the end of the Kafka queue by calling the `forceStartOffsetTime()` method with a value of `-1`. This will avoid the replay of all the old messages that we may not be interested in. Using a value of `-2` will force the spout to rewind to the beginning of the queue, and using a specific date in milliseconds will force it to rewind to a specific point in time. If the `forceFromStartTime()` method is not called, the spout will attempt to resume where it last left off by looking up an offset in ZooKeeper.

Next, we set up the `JsonProjectFunction` class to parse the raw JSON received from Kafka and emit the values that we're interested in. Recall that the Trident functions are additive. This means that our tuple stream, in addition to all the values extracted from the JSON, will also contain the original unparsed JSON string. Since we no longer need that data, we call the `Stream.project()` method with a list of fields we want to keep. The `project()` method is useful for paring down tuple streams to just the essential fields, and it is especially important while repartitioning streams that have large amounts of data.

The resulting stream now contains just the data we need. We set up an `EWMA` instance with a sliding window of one minute and configure the `MovingAverageFunction` class to emit the current rate in minutes. We create the `ThresholdFunction` class with a value of `50.0`, so we'll receive a notification any time the average rate goes above or falls below 50 events per minute.

Finally, we apply the `BooleanFilter` class and connect the resulting stream to the `XMPPFunction` class.

The `main()` method of the topology simply populates a `Config` object with the properties needed by the `XMPPFunction` class and submits the topology.

Running the log analysis topology

To run the analysis topology, first make sure that ZooKeeper, Kafka, and OpenFire are all up and running by using the procedures outlined earlier in the chapter. Then, run the `main()` method of the topology.

When the topology activates, the *storm* XMPP user will connect to the XMPP server and trigger a presence event. If you are logged into the same server with an XMPP client and have the *storm* user in your buddy list, you will see it become available. This is shown in the following screenshot:

Next, run the `RogueApplication` class and wait for a minute. You should receive an instant message notification indicating that the threshold has been exceeded, which will be followed by one indicating a return to normal (below threshold), as shown in the following screenshot:

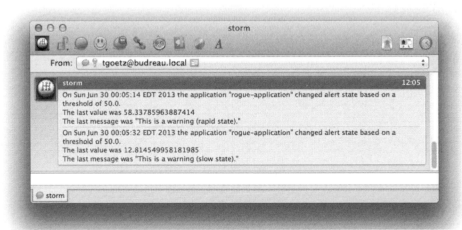

Summary

In this chapter, we've introduced you to real-time analytics by creating a simple yet powerful topology that can be adapted to a wide range of applications. The components we've built are generic and can easily be reused and extended in other projects. Finally, we introduced a real-world spout implementation that can be used for a multitude of purposes.

While the topic of real-time analytics is very broad, and admittedly we've only been able to scratch the surface in this chapter, we encourage you to explore the techniques presented in other chapters of this book and consider how they may be incorporated into your analytics toolbox.

In the next chapter, we'll introduce you to Trident's distributed state mechanism by building an application that continuously writes Storm-processed data to a graph database.

5
Real-time Graph Analysis

In this chapter, we will introduce you to graph analysis using Storm to persist data to a graph database and query that data to discover relationships. Graph databases are databases that store data as graph structures with vertices, edges, and properties, and focus primarily on relationships between the entities.

With the advent of social media sites such as Twitter, Facebook, and LinkedIn, social graphs have become ubiquitous. Analyzing relationships between people, the products they buy, the recommendations they make, and even the words they use can be analyzed to reveal patterns that would be difficult with traditional data models. For example, when LinkedIn shows that you are four steps away from another person based on your network, when Twitter offers suggestions of people to follow, or when Amazon suggests products you may be interested in, they are leveraging what they know about your relationship graph. Graph databases are designed for this type of relationship analysis.

In this chapter, we will build an application that ingests a subset of the Twitter firehose (the real-time feed of all tweets made by Twitter users) and based on the content of each message, creates nodes (vertices) and relationships (edges) in a graph database that we can then analyze. The most obvious graph structure within Twitter is based on the follows / followed by relationship between users, but we can infer additional relationships by looking beyond these explicit relationships. By looking at the content of messages, we can use message metadata (hashtags, user mentions, and so on) to identify, for example, users who mention the same subjects or tweet related hashtags. In this chapter, we will cover the following topics:

- Basic graph database concepts
- The TinkerPop graph APIs
- Graph data modeling
- Interacting with the Titan-distributed graph database
- Writing a Trident state implementation backed by a graph database

Use case

Today's social media websites capture a wealth of information. Many social media services such as Twitter, Facebook, and LinkedIn are based largely on relationships: who you follow, are friends with, or have a business connection to. Beyond the obvious and explicit relationships, social media interactions also create a persistent set of implicit connections that can be easily taken for granted. With Twitter, for example, the obvious relationships consist of those one follows and who one is followed by. The less obvious relationships are the connections created, perhaps unknowingly, just by using the service. Have you directly messaged someone on Twitter? If yes, then you've formed a connection. Tweeted a URL? If yes, again a connection. Liked a product, service, or comment on Facebook? Connection. Even the act of using a specific word or phrase in a tweet or post can be thought of as creating a connection. By using that word, you are forming a connection with it, and by using it repeatedly, you are strengthening that connection.

If we look at data as "everything is a connection," then we can build a structured dataset and analyze it to expose broader patterns. If Bob does not know Alice, but both Bob and Alice have tweeted the same URL, we can infer a connection from this fact. As our dataset grows, its value will also grow as the number of connections in the network increases (similar to Metcalfe's law: `http://en.wikipedia.org/wiki/Metcalfe's_law`).

When we begin querying our dataset, the value for storing data in a graph database will quickly become evident as we glean patterns from the growing network of connections. The graph analysis we perform is applicable to a number of real-world use cases that include the following:

- Targeted advertising
- Recommendation engines
- Sentiment analysis

Architecture

The architecture for our application is relatively simple. We will create a Twitter client application that reads a subset of the Twitter firehose and writes each message to a Kafka queue as a JSON data structure. We'll then use the Kafka spout to feed that data into our storm topology. Finally, our storm topology will analyze the incoming messages and populate the graph database.

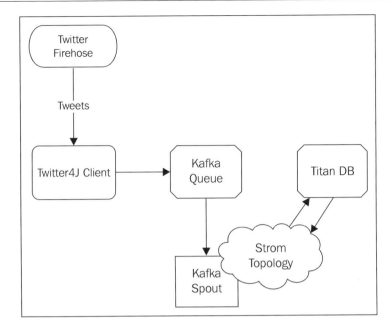

The Twitter client

Twitter provides a comprehensive RESTful API that in addition to a typical request-response interface also provides a streaming API that supports long-lived connections. The Twitter4J Java library (`http://twitter4j.org/`) offers full compatibility with the latest version of the Twitter API and takes care of all the low-level details (connection management, OAuth authentication, and JSON parsing) with a clean Java API. We will use Twitter4J to connect to the Twitter-streaming API.

Kafka spout

In the previous chapter, we developed a Logback Appender extension that allowed us to easily publish data to a Kafka queue, and we used Nathan Marz's Kafka spout (`https://github.com/nathanmarz/storm-contrib`) to consume the data in a Storm topology. While it would be easy enough to write a Storm spout using Twitter4J and the Twitter streaming API, using Kafka and the Kafka Spout gives us transactional, exactly-once semantics, and built-in fault tolerance that we would otherwise have to implement ourselves. For more information on installing and running Kafka refer to *Chapter 4*, *Real-time Trend Analysis*.

A titan-distributed graph database

Titan is a distributed graph database optimized for storing and querying graph structures. Like Storm and Kafka, Titan databases can run as a cluster and can scale horizontally to accommodate increasing data volume and user load. Titan stores its data in one of the three configurable storage backends: Apache Cassandra, Apache HBase, and Oracle Berkely Database. The choice of storage backend depends on which two properties of the CAP theorem are desired. In respect to a database, the CAP theorem stipulates that a distributed system cannot simultaneously make all of the following guarantees:

- **Consistency**: All clients see the current data regardless of modifications

- **Availability**: The system continues to operate as expected despite node failures

- **Partition Tolerance**: The system continues to operate as expected despite network or message failure

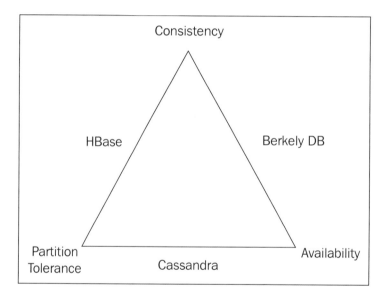

For our use case, consistency is not critical to our application. We are far more concerned with scalability and fault tolerance. If we look at the CAP theorem triangle, shown in the preceding diagram, it becomes clear that Cassandra is the storage backend of choice.

A brief introduction to graph databases

A graph is a network of objects (vertices) with directed connections (edges) between them. The following diagram illustrates a simple social graph similar to what one might find on Twitter:

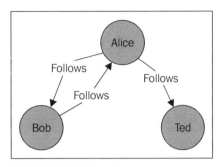

In this example, users are represented by vertices (nodes), and relationships are expressed as edges (connection). Note that the edges in the graph are directed, allowing an additional degree of expressiveness. This allows, for example, to express the fact that Bob and Alice follow one another, and Alice follows Ted but Ted does not follow Alice. This relationship would be more cumbersome to model without directed edges.

Many graph databases follow a property graph model. A property graph extends the basic graph model by allowing a set of properties (key-value pairs) to be assigned to vertices and edges as shown in the following diagram:

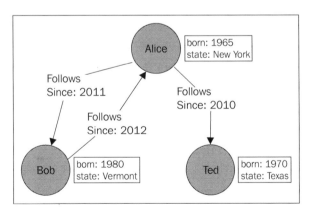

The ability to associate property metadata to objects and relationships in a graph model provides powerful support metadata for graph algorithms and queries. For example, adding the **since** property to the **Follows** edge would enable us to efficiently query for all the users who started following a particular user in a given year.

In contrast to relational databases, relationships in a graph database are explicit as opposed to implicit. Relationships in a graph database are full-blown data structures rather than implied connections (that is, foreign keys). Under the hood, graph databases' underlying data structures are heavily optimized for graph traversal. While it is entirely possible to model a graph in a relational database, it is often less efficient than a graph-centric model. In a relational data model, traversing a graph structure can be computationally expensive as it involves joining many tables. In a graph database, it is a more natural process of traversing links between nodes.

Accessing the graph – the TinkerPop stack

TinkerPop is a group of open source projects focused on graph technologies such as database access, data flow, and graph traversal. Blueprints, the foundation of the TinkerPop stack, is a generic Java API for interacting with property graphs in much the same way JDBC provides a generic interface to relational databases. Other projects in the stack add additional functionalities on top of that foundation so that they can be used with any graph database that implements the Blueprints API.

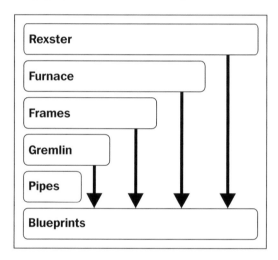

The components of the TinkerPop stack include the following:

- **Blueprints**: Graph API Blueprints is a collection of interfaces that provide access to a property graph data model. Implementations are available for graph databases including Titan, Neo4J, MongoDB, and many others.

- **Pipes**: Dataflow Processing Pipes is a dataflow framework for defining and connecting various data operations as a process graph. Manipulating data with Pipes' primitives closely resembles data processing in Storm. Pipes dataflow are **directed acyclic graphs (DAG)**, much like a Storm topology.

- **Gremlin**: Gremlin is a graph traversal language. It is a Java-based **domain specific language (DSL)** for graph traversal, query, analysis, and manipulation. The Gremlin distribution comes with a Groovy-based shell that allows the use of interactive analysis and modification of a Blueprints graph.

- **Frames**: Frames is an object-to-graph mapping framework analogous to an ORM but tailored for graphs.

- **Furnace**: The Furnace project aims to provide implementations of many common graph algorithms for Blueprints property graphs.

- **Rexster**: Rexster is a graph server that exposes Blueprints graphs through a REST API, as well as a binary protocol.

For our purposes, we will be focusing on the Blueprints API for populating a graph from a Storm topology and Gremlin for graph queries and analysis.

Manipulating the graph with the Blueprints API

The Blueprints API is very straightforward. The following code listing uses the Blueprints API to create the graph depicted in the previous diagram:

```
Graph graph = new TinkerGraph();

Vertex bob = graph.addVertex(null);
bob.setProperty("name", "Bob");
bob.setProperty("born", 1980);
bob.setProperty("state", "Vermont");

Vertex alice = graph.addVertex(null);
alice.setProperty("name", "Alice");
alice.setProperty("born", 1965);
alice.setProperty("state", "New York");

Vertex ted = graph.addVertex(null);
ted.setProperty("name", "Ted");
ted.setProperty("born", 1970);
ted.setProperty("state", "Texas");
```

```
Edge bobToAlice = graph.addEdge(null, bob, alice, "Follows");
bobToAlice.setProperty("since", 2012);

Edge aliceToBob = graph.addEdge(null, alice, bob, "Follows");
aliceToBob.setProperty("since", 2011);

Edge aliceToTed = graph.addEdge(null, alice, ted, "Follows");
aliceToTed.setProperty("since", 2010);

graph.shutdown();
```

The first line of code instantiates an implementation of the `com.tinkerpop.blueprints.Graph` interface. In this case, we're creating an in-memory, toy graph (`com.tinkerpop.blueprints.impls.tg.TinkerGraph`) for exploration. Later, we will demonstrate how to connect to a distributed graph database.

> You may be wondering why we are passing `null` as a parameter to the `addVertex()` and `addEdge()` methods at the first argument. This argument is essentially a suggestion to the underlying Blueprints implementation for a unique ID for the object. Passing in `null` as the ID simply has the effect of letting the underlying implementation assign an ID to the new object.

Manipulating the graph with the Gremlin shell

Gremlin is a high-level Java API built on the top of the Pipes and Blueprints APIs. In addition to the Java API, Gremlin also includes a Groovy-based API and ships with an interactive shell (or REPL) that allows you to directly interact with a Blueprints graph. The Gremlin shell allows you to create and/or connect to the shell and query virtually any Blueprints graph. The following code listing illustrates the process of executing the Gremlin shell:

```
./bin/gremlin.sh

        \,,,/
        (o o)
-----oOOo-(_)-oOOo-----
gremlin>
gremlin> g.V('name', 'Alice').outE('Follows').count()
==>2
```

In addition to querying a graph, it is also easy to create and manipulate graphs using Gremlin. The following code listing consists of Gremlin Groovy code that will create the same graph illustrated in the previous diagram and is the Groovy equivalent of the Java code:

```
g = new TinkerGraph()
bob = g.addVertex()
bob.name = "Bob"
bob.born = 1980
bob.state = "Vermont"
alice = g.addVertex()
alice.name = "Alice"
alice.born=1965
alice.state = "New York"
ted = g.addVertex()
ted.name = "Ted"
ted.born = 1970
ted.state = "Texas"
bobToAlice = g.addEdge(bob, alice, "Follows")
bobToAlice.since = 2012
aliceToBob = g.addEdge(alice, bob, "Follows")
aliceToBob.since = 2011
aliceToTed = g.addEdge(alice, ted, "Follows")
aliceToTed.since = 2010
```

You will learn more about using the Gremlin API and DSL later in the chapter once we've built a topology to populate a graph and are ready to analyze the graph data.

Software installation

The application we're building will utilize Apache Kafka and its dependencies (Apache ZooKeeper). If you haven't done so already, set up ZooKeeper and Kafka according to the instructions in the *ZooKeeper installation* section in Chapter 2, *Configuring Storm Clusters*, and the *Installing Kafka* section in Chapter 4, *Real-time Trend Analysis*.

Titan installation

To install Titan, download the Titan 0.3.x complete package from Titan's downloads page (`https://github.com/thinkaurelius/titan/wiki/Downloads`), and extract it to a convenient location by using the following command:

```
wget http://s3.thinkaurelius.com/downloads/titan/titan-all-0.3.2.zip
unzip titan-all-0.3.2.zip
```

Titan's complete distribution package includes everything that is necessary for running Titan with any of the supported storage backends: Cassandra, HBase, and BerkelyDB. There are also backend-specific distributions if you are only interested in using a specific storage backend.

> Both Storm and Titan use the Kryo (https://code.google. com/p/kryo/) library for Java object serialization. At the time of writing, Storm and Titan use different versions of the Kryo library, which will cause problems when the two are used in conjunction.

To patch Titan in order to properly enable serialization between Storm and Titan, replace the kryo.jar file in the Titan distribution with the kryo.jar file that comes with Storm:

```
cd titan-all-0.3.2/lib
rm kryo*.jar
cp $STORM_HOME/lib/kryo*.jar ./
```

At this point, you can test the installation by running the Gremlin shell:

```
$ cd titan
$ ./bin/gremlin.sh
         \,,,/
         (o o)
-----o0Oo-(_)-oO0o-----
gremlin> g = GraphOfTheGodsFactory.create('/tmp/storm-blueprints')
==>titangraph[local:/tmp/storm-blueprints]
gremlin> g.V.map
==>{name=saturn, age=10000, type=titan}
==>{name=sky, type=location}
==>{name=sea, type=location}
==>{name=jupiter, age=5000, type=god}
==>{name=neptune, age=4500, type=god}
==>{name=hercules, age=30, type=demigod}
==>{name=alcmene, age=45, type=human}
==>{name=pluto, age=4000, type=god}
==>{name=nemean, type=monster}
==>{name=hydra, type=monster}
==>{name=cerberus, type=monster}
==>{name=tartarus, type=location}
gremlin>
```

`GraphOfTheGodsFactory` is a class included with Titan that will create and populate a Titan database with a sample graph that represents the relationships between the characters and places in the Roman pantheon. Passing a directory path to the `create()` method will return a Blueprints graph implementation, specifically a `com.thinkaurelius.titan.graphdb.database.StandardTitanGraph` instance that uses a combination of BerkelyDB and Elasticsearch for a storage backend. Since the Gremlin shell is a Groovy REPL, we can easily verify this by looking at the class of the `g` variable:

```
gremlin> g.class.name
==>com.thinkaurelius.titan.graphdb.database.StandardTitanGraph
```

Setting up Titan to use the Cassandra storage backend

We've seen that Titan supports different storage backends. Exploring all three options is beyond the scope of this chapter (you can learn more about Titan and its configuration options at `http://thinkaurelius.github.io/titan/`), so we will focus on using the Cassandra (`http://cassandra.apache.org`) storage backend.

Installing Cassandra

In order to download and run Cassandra, we need to execute the following commands:

```
wget http://www.apache.org/dyn/closer.cgi?path=/cassandra/1.2.9/apache-cassandra-1.2.9-bin.tar.gz

tar -zxf ./cassandra-1.2.9.bin.tar.gz

cd cassandra-1.2.9

./bin/cassandra -f
```

The default file that comes with the Cassandra distribution will create a single-node Cassandra database running locally. If there is an error during the startup, you may need to configure Cassandra by editing the `${CASSANDRA_HOME}/conf/cassandra.yaml` and/or `${CASSANDRA_HOME}/conf/log4j-server.properties` files. The most common problems are usually related to the lack of file-write permissions on `/var/lib/cassandra` (where, by default, Cassandra stores its data) and `/var/log/cassandra` (the default Cassandra log location).

Starting Titan with the Cassandra backend

To run Titan with Cassandra, we need to configure it to connect to our Cassandra server. Create a new file called `storm-blueprints-cassandra.yaml` with the following contents:

```
storage.backend=cassandra
```

```
storage.hostname=localhost
```

As you can probably surmise, this configures Titan to connect to the Cassandra instance running locally.

> For this project, we may not need to actually run the Titan server. Since we're using Cassandra, Storm and Gremlin should be able to share the backend without any issues.

With the Titan backend configured, we are ready to create our data model.

Graph data model

The primary entity in our data model is a Twitter user. A Twitter user can perform the following relationship-forming actions when posting a tweet:

- Use a word
- Mention a hashtag
- Mention another user
- Mention a URL
- Retweet another user

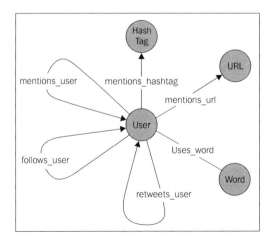

This concept maps very naturally into a graph model. In the model, we will have four different entity types (vertices):

- **User**: This represents a Twitter user account
- **Word**: This represents any word contained in a tweet
- **URL**: This represents any URL contained in a tweet
- **Hashtag**: This represents any hashtag contained in a tweet

Relationships (edges) will consist of the following actions:

- **mentions_user**: Using this action, a user mentions another user
- **retweets_user**: Using this action, a user retweets another user's post
- **follows_user**: Using this action, a user follows another user
- **mentions_hashtag**: Using this action, a user mentions a hashtag
- **uses_word**: Using this action, the user uses a specific word in a tweet
- **mentions_url**: Using this action, a user tweets a specific URL

The user vertex models a user's Twitter account information, which is shown in the following table:

User [vertex]		
type	String	`"user"`
user	String	Twitter screen name
name	String	Twitter name
location	String	Twitter location

The URL vertex provides a reference point for unique URLs:

URL [vertex]		
type	String	`"url"`
value	String	URL

The hashtag vertex allows us to store unique hashtags:

Hashtag [vertex]		
type	String	`"hashtag"`
value	String	

We store individual words in the word vertex:

Word [vertex]		
type	String	"word"
value	String	

The mentions_user edge is used for relationships between user objects:

mentions_user [edge]		
user	String	The ID of the user mentioned

The mentions_url edge represents a relationship between the User and URL objects:

mentions_url [edge]		
user	String	The ID of the user mentioned

Connecting to the Twitter stream

In order to connect to the Twitter API, we must first generate a set of OAuth tokens that will enable our application to authenticate with Twitter. This is done by creating a Twitter application that is associated with your account and then authorizing that application to access your account. If you do not already have a Twitter account, create one now and log in to it. Once you are logged in to Twitter, generate the OAuth tokens by following these steps:

1. Go to https://dev.twitter.com/apps/new and log in if necessary.

2. Enter a name and description for your application.

3. Enter a URL for your application. In our case, the URL is unimportant since we're not creating an app that will be distributed like a mobile app. Entering a placeholder URL here is fine.

4. Submit the form. The next page will display the details of the OAuth settings for your application. Note the **Consumer key** and **Consumer secret** values since we will need those for our application.

5. At the bottom of the page, click on the **Create my access token** button. This will generate an OAuth Access token and a secret key that will allow an application to access your account on your behalf. We will also need these values for our application. Do not share these values as they would allow someone else to authenticate as you.

Setting up the Twitter4J client

The Twitter4J client is broken down into a number of different modules that can be pieced together depending on our needs. For our purposes, we need the `core` module that provides essential functionalities such as HTTP transport, OAuth, and access to the basic Twitter API. We will also use the `stream` module for accessing the streaming API. These modules can be included in the project by adding the following Maven dependencies:

```
<dependency>
  <groupId>org.twitter4j</groupId>
  <artifactId>twitter4j-core</artifactId>
  <version>3.0.3</version>
</dependency>
<dependency>
  <groupId>org.twitter4j</groupId>
  <artifactId>twitter4j-stream</artifactId>
  <version>3.0.3</version>
</dependency>
```

The OAuth configuration

By default, Twitter4J will search the classpath for a `twitter4j.properties` file and load OAuth tokens from that file. The easiest way to do this is to create the file in the `resources` folder of your Maven project. Add the tokens you generated earlier to this file:

```
oauth.consumerKey=[your consumer key]
oauth.consumerSecret=[your consumer secret]
oauth.accessToken=[your access token]
oauth.accessTokenSecret=[your access token secret]
```

We're now ready to use the Twitter4J client to connect to Twitter's streaming API to consume tweets in real time.

The TwitterStreamConsumer class

The purpose of our Twitter client is straightforward; it will perform the following functions:

- Connect to the Twitter streaming API
- Request a stream of tweets filtered by a set of keywords
- Create a JSON data structure based on the status message
- Write the JSON data to Kafka for consumption by the Kafka spout

The main() method of the TwitterStreamConsumer class creates a TwitterStream object and registers an instance of StatusListener as a listener. The StatusListener interface is used as an asynchronous event handler that is notified whenever a stream-related event occurs:

```
    public static void main(String[] args) throws TwitterException,
IOException {

        StatusListener listener = new TwitterStatusListener();
        TwitterStream twitterStream = new TwitterStreamFactory().
getInstance();
        twitterStream.addListener(listener);

        FilterQuery query = new FilterQuery().track(args);
        twitterStream.filter(query);


    }
```

After registering the listener, we create a FilterQuery object to filter the stream based on a set of keywords. For convenience, we use the program arguments as the list of keywords so the filter criteria can be easily changed from the command line.

The TwitterStatusListener class

The TwitterStatusListener class performs most of the heavy lifting in our application. The StatusListener class defines several callback methods for events that can occur during the lifetime of a stream. The onStatus() method is our primary interest, since it is the method that gets calls whenever a new Tweet arrives. The following is the code for the TwitterStatusListener class:

```
    public static class TwitterStatusListener implements
StatusListener {
        public void onStatus(Status status) {

            JSONObject tweet = new JSONObject();
            tweet.put("user", status.getUser().getScreenName());
            tweet.put("name", status.getUser().getName());
            tweet.put("location", status.getUser().getLocation());
            tweet.put("text", status.getText());

            HashtagEntity[] hashTags = status.getHashtagEntities();
            System.out.println("# HASH TAGS #");
            JSONArray jsonHashTags = new JSONArray();
            for (HashtagEntity hashTag : hashTags) {
```

```
                System.out.println(hashTag.getText());
                jsonHashTags.add(hashTag.getText());
            }
            tweet.put("hashtags", jsonHashTags);

            System.out.println("@ USER MENTIONS @");
            UserMentionEntity[] mentions = status.
getUserMentionEntities();
            JSONArray jsonMentions = new JSONArray();
            for (UserMentionEntity mention : mentions) {
                System.out.println(mention.getScreenName());
                jsonMentions.add(mention.getScreenName());
            }
            tweet.put("mentions", jsonMentions);

            URLEntity[] urls = status.getURLEntities();
            System.out.println("$ URLS $");
            JSONArray jsonUrls = new JSONArray();
            for (URLEntity url : urls) {
                System.out.println(url.getExpandedURL());
                jsonUrls.add(url.getExpandedURL());
            }
            tweet.put("urls", jsonUrls);

            if (status.isRetweet()) {
                JSONObject retweetUser = new JSONObject();
                retweetUser.put("user", status.getUser().
getScreenName());
                retweetUser.put("name", status.getUser().getName());
                retweetUser.put("location", status.getUser().
getLocation());
                tweet.put("retweetuser", retweetUser);
            }
            KAFKA_LOG.info(tweet.toJSONString());
        }

        public void onDeletionNotice(StatusDeletionNotice
statusDeletionNotice) {
        }

        public void onTrackLimitationNotice(int
numberOfLimitedStatuses) {
```

```
            System.out.println("Track Limitation Notice: " +
    numberOfLimitedStatuses);
        }

        public void onException(Exception ex) {
            ex.printStackTrace();
        }

        public void onScrubGeo(long arg0, long arg1) {
        }

        public void onStallWarning(StallWarning arg0) {

        }
    }
```

In addition to the raw text of the status message, the `Status` object includes convenient methods for accessing all the associated metadata, such as user information, the hashtags, URLs, and user mentions contained in the tweet. The bulk of our `onStatus()` method builds up the JSON structure before finally logging it to the Kafka queue via the Logback Kafka Appender.

Twitter graph topology

The Twitter graph topology will read raw tweet data from the Kafka queue, parse out the relevant information, and then create nodes and relationships in the Titan graph database. Instead of writing to the graph database individually for each tuple received, we will implement a trident state implementation for performing persistence operations in bulk using Trident's transaction mechanism.

This approach offers several benefits. First, for graph databases, such as Titan that supports transactions, we can leverage this capability to provide additional exactly-once processing guarantees. Second, it allows us to perform a bulk-write followed by a bulk-commit (when supported) for an entire batch of tuples rather than a write-commit operation for each individual tuple. Finally, by using the generic Blueprints API, our Trident state implementation will be largely agnostic to the underlying graph database implementation, allowing any Blueprints graph database backend to be easily swapped in and out.

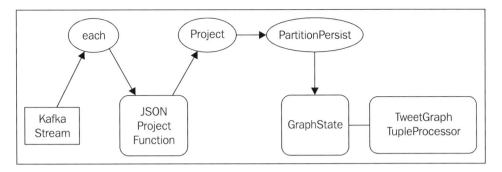

The first component of the topology consists of JSONProjectFunction, which we developed in *Chapter 7, Integrating Druid for Financial Analytics*, which simply parses the raw JSON data to extract only the information we are interested in. In this case, we are mainly interested in the timestamp of the message and the JSON representation of the Twitter status message.

The JSONProjectFunction class

The following is a code snippet explaining the JSONProjectFunction class:

```
public class JsonProjectFunction extends BaseFunction {

    private Fields fields;

    public JsonProjectFunction(Fields fields) {
        this.fields = fields;
    }

    public void execute(TridentTuple tuple, TridentCollector
collector) {
        String json = tuple.getString(0);
        Map<String, Object> map = (Map<String, Object>) JSONValue.
parse(json);
        Values values = new Values();
        for (int i = 0; i < this.fields.size(); i++) {
            values.add(map.get(this.fields.get(i)));
        }
        collector.emit(values);
    }

}
```

Implementing GraphState

The heart of the topology will be a Trident state implementation responsible for translating Trident tuples into graph structures and persisting them. Recall that a Trident state implementation consists of three components:

- `StateFactory`: The `StateFactory` interface defines the method Trident uses to create the persistent `State` objects.

- `State`: The Trident `State` interface defines the `beginCommit()` and `commit()` methods that are called before and after a Trident batch partition is written to the backing store. If the write succeeds (that is, all tuples are processed without error), Trident will call the `commit()` method.

- `StateUpdater`: The `StateUpdater` interface defines the `updateState()` method that is called to update the state, given that there is a batch of tuples. Trident passes three arguments to this method: the `State` object to be updated, a list of `TridentTuple` objects that represents a batch partition, and a `TridentCollector` instance that can be used to optionally emit additional tuples as a result of the state update.

In addition to these abstractions provided by Trident, we will introduce two additional interfaces that will support the use of any Blueprints graph database (`GraphFactory`) and isolate any use-case-specific business logic (`GraphTupleProcessor`). Before diving in to the Trident state implementation, let's quickly look at these interfaces.

GraphFactory

The `GraphFactory` interface contract is simple: given a `Map` object that represents the Storm and topology configuration, return a `com.tinkerpop.blueprints.Graph` implementation.

```
GraphFactory.java
public interface GraphFactory {
    public Graph makeGraph(Map conf);
}
```

This interface allows us to plug in any Blueprints-compatible graph implementation simply by providing an implementation of the `makeGraph()` method. Later, we will implement this interface to return a connection to a Titan graph database.

GraphTupleProcessor

The `GraphTupleProcessor` interface provides an abstraction between the Trident state implementation and any use-case-specific business logic.

```
public interface GraphTupleProcessor {

    public void process(Graph g, TridentTuple tuple, TridentCollector
collector);

}
```

Given a graph object, `TridentTuple`, and `TridentCollector`, manipulating the graph and optionally emitting additional tuples is the job of a `GraphTupleProcessor`. Later in the chapter, we will implement this interface to populate a graph based on the content of a Twitter status message.

GraphStateFactory

Trident's `StateFactory` interface represents the entry point for a state implementation. When a Trident topology using state components (via the `Stream.partitionPersist()` and `Stream.persistentAggregate()` methods) initializes, Storm calls the `StateFactory.makeState()` method to create a State instance for each batch partition. The number of batch partitions is determined by the parallelism of the stream. Storm passes this information to the `makeState()` method via the `numPartitions` and `partitionIndex` parameters, allowing state implementations to perform partition-specific logic if necessary.

In our use case, we're not concerned with partitions, so the `makeState()` method just uses a `GraphFactory` instance to instantiate a `Graph` instance used to construct a `GraphState` instance.

```
GraphStateFactory.java
public class GraphStateFactory implements StateFactory {

    private GraphFactory factory;

    public GraphStateFactory(GraphFactory factory){
        this.factory = factory;
    }
```

```
        public State makeState(Map conf, IMetricsContext metrics, int
partitionIndex, int numPartitions) {
            Graph graph = this.factory.makeGraph(conf);
            State state = new GraphState(graph);
            return state;
        }


    }
```

GraphState

Our `GraphState` class provides implementations for `State.beginCommit()` and `State.commit()` methods that will be called when a batch partition is about to take place and when it has successfully completed, respectively. In our case, we override the `commit()` method to check if the internal `Graph` object supports transactions, and if so, call the `TransactionalGraph.commit()` method to complete the transaction.

 The `State.beginCommit()` method may be called multiple times if there are failures within a Trident batch and the batch is replayed, while the `State.commit()` method will only get called once when all partition state updates have completed successfully.

The code snippet of the `GraphState` class is as follows:

```
GraphState.java
public class GraphState implements State {

    private Graph graph;

    public GraphState(Graph graph){
        this.graph = graph;
    }

    @Override
    public void beginCommit(Long txid) {}

    @Override
    public void commit(Long txid) {
        if(this.graph instanceof TransactionalGraph){
            ((TransactionalGraph)this.graph).commit();
        }
    }
```

```
    public void update(List<TridentTuple> tuples, TridentCollector
collector, GraphTupleProcessor processor){
        for(TridentTuple tuple : tuples){
            processor.process(this.graph, tuple, collector);
        }
    }

}
```

The `GraphState.update()` method does the core processing of the transaction between the calls to the `State.beginCommit()` and `State.commit()` methods. If the `update()` method succeeds for all batch partitions, the Trident transaction will complete and the `State.commit()` method will be called.

Notice that the `update()` method that actually updates the graph state is simply a public method of the `GraphState` class and not overridden. As you will see, we will have the opportunity to call this method directly in our `StateUpdater` implementation.

GraphUpdater

The `GraphUpdater` class implements the `updateState()` method that Storm will call (potentially repeatedly in the case of batch failures/replays) just after the call to `State.beginCommit()`. The first argument to the `StateUpdater.updateState()` method is a Java generics-typed instance of our state implementation that we use to call our `GraphState.update()` method.

```
GraphUpdater.java
public class GraphUpdater extends BaseStateUpdater<GraphState> {

    private GraphTupleProcessor processor;

    public GraphUpdater(GraphTupleProcessor processor){
        this.processor = processor;
    }

    public void updateState(GraphState state, List<TridentTuple>
tuples, TridentCollector collector) {
        state.update(tuples, collector, this.processor);
    }

}
```

Implementing GraphFactory

The `GraphFactory` interface we defined earlier creates a TinkerPop Graph
implementation, where a `Map` object represents a Storm configuration.
The following code illustrates how to create `TitanGraph` backed by Cassandra:

```
TitanGraphFactory.java
public class TitanGraphFactory implements GraphFactory {

    public static final String STORAGE_BACKEND = "titan.storage.
backend";
    public static final String STORAGE_HOSTNAME = "titan.storage.
hostname";

    public Graph makeGraph(Map conf) {
        Configuration graphConf = new BaseConfiguration();
        graphConf.setProperty("storage.backend", conf.get(STORAGE_
BACKEND));
        graphConf.setProperty("storage.hostname", conf.get(STORAGE_
HOSTNAME));

        return TitanFactory.open(graphConf);
    }
}
```

Implementing GraphTupleProcessor

In order to populate the graph database with relationships gleaned from Twitter
status messages, we need to implement the `GraphTupleProcessor` interface. The
following code illustrates parsing the Twitter status message's JSON object and
creating `"user"` and `"hashtag"` vertices with `"mentions"` relationships.

```
TweetGraphTupleProcessor.java
public class TweetGraphTupleProcessor implements GraphTupleProcessor {
    @Override
    public void process(Graph g, TridentTuple tuple, TridentCollector
collector) {
        Long timestamp = tuple.getLong(0);
        JSONObject json = (JSONObject)tuple.get(1);

        Vertex user = findOrCreateUser(g, (String)json.get("user"),
(String)json.get("name"));
```

```
        JSONArray hashtags = (JSONArray)json.get("hashtags");
        for(int i = 0; i < hashtags.size(); i++){
            Vertex v = findOrCreateVertex(g, "hashtag", ((String)
hashtags.get(i)).toLowerCase());
            createEdgeAtTime(g, user, v, "mentions", timestamp);
        }

    }
}
```

Putting it all together – the TwitterGraphTopology class

Creating our final topology consists of the following steps:

* Consume raw JSON from the Kafka spout
* Extract and project only the data we are interested in
* Build and connect the Trident GraphState implementation to our stream

The TwitterGraphTopology class

Let's look at the TwitterGraphTopology class in detail.

```
public class TwitterGraphTopology {
    public static StormTopology buildTopology() {
        TridentTopology topology = new TridentTopology();

        StaticHosts kafkaHosts = StaticHosts.fromHostString(Arrays.
asList(new String[] { "localhost" }), 1);
        TridentKafkaConfig spoutConf = new
TridentKafkaConfig(kafkaHosts, "twitter-feed");
        spoutConf.scheme = new StringScheme();
        spoutConf.forceStartOffsetTime(-2);
        OpaqueTridentKafkaSpout spout = new OpaqueTridentKafkaSpout(s
poutConf);

        Stream spoutStream = topology.newStream("kafka-stream",
spout);

        Fields jsonFields = new Fields("timestamp", "message");
        Stream parsedStream = spoutStream.each(spoutStream.
getOutputFields(), new JsonProjectFunction(jsonFields), jsonFields);
        parsedStream = parsedStream.project(jsonFields);
```

```
        // Trident State
        GraphFactory graphFactory = new TitanGraphFactory();
        GraphUpdater graphUpdater = new GraphUpdater(new
TweetGraphTupleProcessor());

        StateFactory stateFactory = new GraphStateFactory(graphFacto
ry);
        parsedStream.partitionPersist(stateFactory, parsedStream.
getOutputFields(), graphUpdater, new Fields());

        return topology.build();
    }


    public static void main(String[] args) throws Exception {
        Config conf = new Config();
        conf.put(TitanGraphFactory.STORAGE_BACKEND, "cassandra");
        conf.put(TitanGraphFactory.STORAGE_HOSTNAME, "localhost");

        conf.setMaxSpoutPending(5);
        if (args.length == 0) {
            LocalCluster cluster = new LocalCluster();
            cluster.submitTopology("twitter-analysis", conf,
buildTopology());

        } else {
            conf.setNumWorkers(3);
            StormSubmitter.submitTopology(args[0], conf,
buildTopology());
        }
    }
}
```

To run the application, begin by executing the `TwitterStreamConsumer` class, passing in a list of keywords you want to use to query the Twitter firehose. For example, if we want to build a graph of users discussing big data, we might use `bigdata` and `hadoop` as query parameters:

```
java TwitterStreamConsumer bigdata hadoop
```

The `TwitterStreamConsumer` class will connect to the Twitter Streaming API and begin queuing data to Kafka. With the `TwitterStreamConsumer` application running, we can then deploy `TwitterGraphTopology` to begin populating the Titan database.

Let `TwitterStreamConsumer` and `TwitterGraphTopology` run for a while. Depending on the popularity of the keywords used for the query, it may take some time for the dataset to grow to a meaningful level. We can then connect to Titan with the Gremlin shell to analyze the data with graph queries.

Querying the graph with Gremlin

To query the graph, we need to launch the Gremlin shell and create a `TitanGraph` instance connected to the local Cassandra backend:

```
$ cd titan
$ ./bin/gremlin.sh
         \,,,/
         (o o)
-----oOOo-(_)-oOOo-----
gremlin> conf = new BaseConfiguration()
gremlin> conf.setProperty('storage.backend', 'cassandra')
gremlin> conf.setProperty('storage.hostname', 'localhost')
gremlin> g = TitanFactory.open(conf)
```

The `g` variable now contains a `Graph` object we can use to issue graph traversal queries. The following are a few sample queries you can use to get started:

- To find all the users who have tweeted #hadoop hashtag and to show the number of times they have done this, use the following code:

  ```
  gremlin> g.V('type', 'hashtag').has('value', 'hadoop').in.userid.
  groupCount.cap
  ```

- To count the number of times the #hadoop hashtag has been tweeted, use the following code:

  ```
  gremlin> g.V.has('type', 'hashtag').has('value', 'java').inE.
  count()
  ```

The Gremlin DSL is very powerful; covering the complete API could fill an entire chapter (if not a whole book). To further explore the Gremlin language, we encourage you to explore the following online documentation:

- The official Gremlin Wiki at `https://github.com/tinkerpop/gremlin/wiki`

- GremlinDocs reference guide at `http://gremlindocs.com`

- SQL2Gremlin (sample SQL queries and their Gremlin equivalents) at `http://sql2gremlin.com`

Summary

In this chapter, we introduced you to graph databases by creating a topology that monitors a subset of the Twitter firehose and persists that information to the Titan graph database for further analysis. We've also demonstrated the reuse of generic components by using generic building blocks from earlier chapters such as the Logback Kafka appender.

While graph databases are not perfect for every use case, they represent a powerful weapon in your arsenal of polyglot persistence tools. Polyglot persistence is a term often used to describe a software architecture that involves multiple types of data stores such as relational, key-value, graph, document, and so on. Polyglot persistence is all about choosing the right database for the right job. In this chapter, we introduced you to graph data models, and have hopefully inspired you to explore situations where a graph may be the best data model to support a given use case. Later in the book, we will create a Storm application that persists data to multiple data stores, each for a specific purpose.

6
Artificial Intelligence

In earlier chapters, we saw a pattern that combined real-time analytics using Storm with batch processing using Hadoop. In this chapter, we will go in the other direction. We will incorporate Storm into an operational system that must respond in real time to end user queries.

Typical applications of Storm focus on a never-ending stream of data. The data is often queued and processed as fast as possible by persistent topologies. The system includes a queue to accommodate varying amounts of load. At times of light load, the queue is empty. During heavy load, the queue will persist the data for eventual processing.

Even the untrained eye will recognize that such a system does not provide true real-time data processing. Storm monitors tuple timeouts, but it is focused on the processing time of tuple(s) after the spout emits the data.

To support real-time scenarios more completely, timeouts and **Service Level Agreements (SLA)** must be monitored from the reception of the data to the delivery of the response. These days, requests are often received via an HTTP-based API and response time SLAs must be subsecond.

HTTP is a synchronous protocol. It often introduces an asynchronous mechanism like a queue, complicates the system, and introduces added latency. For this reason, when exposing features and functions via HTTP, we typically prefer synchronous integrations with components involved.

In this chapter, we will explore Storm's place in an architecture that exposes a web services API. Specifically, we will construct the world's best tic-tac-toe **Artificial Intelligence** (**AI**) system. Our system will include both synchronous and asynchronous subsystems. The asynchronous portion of the system will work continually, exploring the best options for game states. The synchronous component exposes a web services interface that, given a game state, returns the best move possible.

This chapter covers the following topics:

- Recursion in Storm
- Distributed Remote Procedure Call (DRPC)
- Distributed Read-before-write paradigm

Designing for our use case

The "hello world" of the artificial intelligence world is tic-tac-toe. Sticking to the tradition, we will also use this as our subject game, although the architecture and approach extend well beyond this simple example (for example, Global Thermonuclear War; for other use cases, refer to John Badham's *War Games*).

Tic-tac-toe is a two-player game of Xes and Os. The board is a 3 x 3 grid. One player has the symbol O and the other has the symbol X, and the play alternates. On a turn, a player places their symbol in any open cell in the grid. If by placing their symbol, it completes a horizontal, vertical, or diagonal line of three contiguous symbols, that player wins. If all cells are filled without forming a line of three, then the game is a tie.

A common approach to developing Artificial Intelligence programs for games with alternating turns is to explore the game tree recursively searching for the game state that evaluates best for the current player (or worse for the opposition). A game tree is a tree structure whose nodes are game states. A node's immediate children are game states that can be achieved by making a legal move from that node's game state.

A sample game tree for tic-tac-toe is shown in the following diagram:

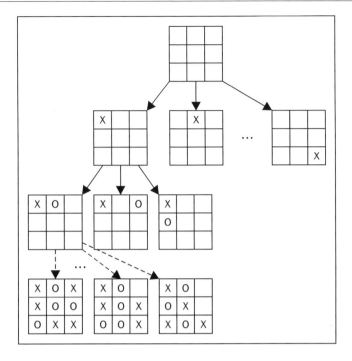

The simplest of algorithms that traverses a game tree searching for the best move is the **Minimax** algorithm. The algorithm scores each board recursively and returns the best score found. For this algorithm, we assume that a good score for the opposition is a bad score for the current player. Thus, the algorithm actually alternates between maximizing and minimizing the score of the current board. The Minimax algorithm can be summarized with the following pseudocode:

```
miniMax (board, depth, maximizing)
   if (depth <= 0)
      return score (board)
   else
      children = move(board)
      if (maximizing)
         bestValue = -∞
      for (child : children)
         value = miniMax (child, depth-1, false)
         if (value > bestValue)
            bestValue = value
         end
```

```
      end
   return bestValue
         else // minimizing
            bestValue = ∞
         for (child : children)
            value = miniMax (child, depth-1, false)
            if (value < bestValue)
               bestValue = value
            end
   end
   return bestValue
   end
   end
```

A client invokes the algorithm with a game state, a depth, and a Boolean variable that indicates whether or not the algorithm should seek to maximize or minimize the score. In our use case, the game state is fully encapsulated by the board, which is a 3 x 3 grid partially filled with Xes and Os.

The algorithm is recursive. The first few lines of the code are the base case. This ensures that the algorithm does not recurse endlessly. This conditions on the depth variable. In a game of alternating turns, the depth indicates how many turns the algorithm should explore.

In our use case, the Storm topology need not track the depth. We will let the Storm topology explore endlessly (or until there are no new boards returned from the move method).

Typically, each player is given a set amount of time and must make his or her move within the allotted time. Since we will more likely have antsy human players competing against the AI, let's assume the system needs to respond in fewer than 200 milliseconds.

After the algorithm checks for the base case, it calls the move() method, which returns boards for all possible moves. The algorithm then cycles through all possible child boards. If maximizing, the algorithm finds the child board that leads to the highest score. If minimizing, the algorithm finds the board that leads to the least score.

The **Negamax** algorithm accomplishes the same more succinctly by alternating the sign of the score. Additionally, in a real-world scenario, we might apply Alpha-Beta pruning, which attempts to trim the branches of the tree that are explored. The algorithm only considers branches that fall within a threshold. In our use case, this is not necessary because the search space is small enough to explore in its entirety.

In our simple use case, it is possible to enumerate the entire game tree. In more complicated games such as Chess, the game tree is impossible to enumerate. In an extreme case such as Go, experts have calculated the number of legal boards to be in excess of 2 x 10170.

The goal of the Minimax algorithm is to traverse the game tree and assign a score to each node. In our Storm topology, which is not beholden to any SLA, the score of any non-leaf node is simply the maximum (or minimum) of its descendants. For a leaf node, we must interpret the game state into a corresponding score. In our simple use case, there are three possible outcomes: we win, our opponent wins, or the game is a tie.

In our synchronous system, however, we might very well run out of time before we reach a leaf node. In this case, we need to calculate the score from the current state of the board. Scoring heuristics are often the most difficult aspect of developing an AI application.

For our simple use case, we will compute the score for any board by considering the lines in the grid. There are eight lines to consider: three horizontal, three vertical, and two diagonals. Each line contributes to the score according to the following table:

Status	Score
Three in a row for the current player	+1000
Two in a row for the current player	+10
One in a row for current player	+1
Three in a row for an opponent	-1000
Two in a row for an opponent	-10
One in a row for an opponent	-1

The preceding table applies only if the remaining cells in the line are empty. Although there are improvements to the preceding heuristic, it suffices for this example. And, since we expect Storm to work continually on our game tree, we hope not to rely on the heuristic all that much. Instead, we would rely directly on the minimum (or maximum) of the leaf scores, which will always be a win (+1000), loss (-1000), or draw (0).

Finally, armed with an approach, our algorithm and a scoring function, we are able to move on to the architecture and design.

Establishing the architecture

Examining the preceding algorithm, there are a number of interesting design and architectural considerations, especially given the current state of Storm. The algorithm requires recursion. We also need a means of synchronously processing requests. Recursion within Storm is an evolving topic, and while Storm provides a means of interacting with topologies synchronously, when combined with a demand for recursion, this presents some unique and interesting challenges.

Examining the design challenges

Originally, native Storm provided a mechanism to service asynchronous procedure calls. The feature is **Distributed Remote Procedure Call** (**DRPC**). DRPC allowed a client to make requests of a topology by submitting data directly to the topology. With DRPC, a simple RPC client acts as a spout.

With the advent of Trident, DRPC was deprecated in native Storm and is now officially supported only in Trident.

Although there has been some exploratory work into recursive/nonlinear DRPC, which is what we would require here, it is not a mainstream functionality (`https://groups.google.com/forum/#!topic/storm-user/hk3opTiv3Kc`).

Additionally, that work would rely on the deprecated classes within the native Storm. Thus, we need to find alternative means to create a recursive structure without relying on Storm.

Once we find a construct to implement the recursion, we need to be able to invoke the same functionality synchronously. Seeking to leverage what Storm provides means incorporating DRPC calls into our architecture.

Implementing the recursion

If we map our algorithm directly to Storm constructs, we would expect a means of allowing a stream to feed back data into itself. We can imagine a topology similar to the following logical data flow:

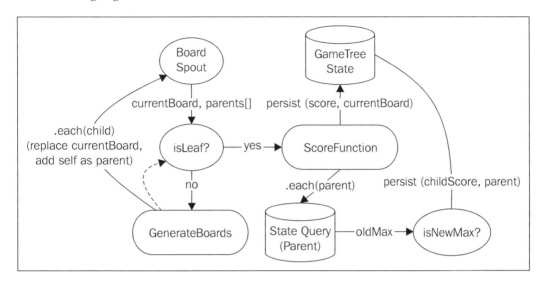

The BoardSpout function emits a board (for example, the 3 x 3 array) in the currentBoard field with a second field named parents that will be used to store all parent nodes. The parents field will be empty initially.

The isLeaf filter decides whether this is an end state (for example, win, loss, or draw). If the currentBoard field is not an end state, the GenerateBoards function emits all the new boards, replacing the value of the currentBoard field with the child board and adding the currentBoard field to the list of nodes in the parents field. The GenerateBoards function could emit the tuple back through the spout or directly into the isLeaf filter, bypassing the spout.

If the isLeaf filter determines that this is an end state, we need to score the currentBoard field and then update all the parents to reflect that new score. The ScoreFunction computes the score of the board and persists that to the GameTree State.

To update the parents, we iterate over each of the parents and query the current maximum (or minimum) for that node. If the child's score is a new maximum (or minimum), then we would persist the new values.

This is only a logical data flow. Constructing such a topology is not only impossible, but also not recommended for reasons described in the following sections.

You can already see that this data flow is not as straightforward as our pseudocode. There are a few constraints within Trident and Storm that force us to introduce additional complexities, and furthermore, not all the operations articulated in the data flow are available in Storm/Trident. Let's examine this data flow more closely.

Accessing the function's return values

Firstly, notice that we are forced to maintain our own call stack in the form of a list of parents because Storm and Trident do not have any mechanisms to access the results of functions downstream in the topology. In classic recursion, the results of the recursive method call are immediately available within the function and can be incorporated into the results of that method. Thus, the preceding data flow resembles a more iterative approach to the problem.

Immutable tuple field values

Secondly, in the preceding data flow, we invoke a magical ability to replace the value of a field. We do that in the recursive emit from the `GenerateBoards` function. Replacing the `currentBoard` field with the new board is not possible. Additionally, adding the `currentBoard` field to the parents list would require updating the value of the `parents` field. In Trident, tuples are immutable.

Upfront field declaration

To get around tuple immutability, we could always add additional fields to the tuple—one for each layer of the recursion—but Trident requires that all fields be declared prior to deployment.

Tuple acknowledgement in recursion

We have additional problems when we consider tuple acknowledgement in this data flow. At what point do we acknowledge the initial tuple that triggered the processing? From a logical data flow perspective, that initial tuple shouldn't be acknowledged until all the children for that node have been considered and the game tree state reflects those scores. Surely, however, the processing time to compute large subsections of the game tree for any non-trivial game would most likely exceed any tuple timeouts.

Output to multiple streams

Another issue with topology is the multiple paths that emit from the `isLeaf` filter. Presently, there is no way to output to multiple streams within Trident. The enhancement can be found at `https://issues.apache.org/jira/browse/STORM-68`.

As we will see, you can work around this by forking the stream and affecting the decision as filters on both streams.

Read-before-write

Lastly, because we do not have access to the return values, updating the parent scores requires a read-before-write paradigm. This is an anti-pattern in any distributed system. The following sequence diagram demonstrates the issues that arise in read-before-write constructs in the absence of locking mechanisms:

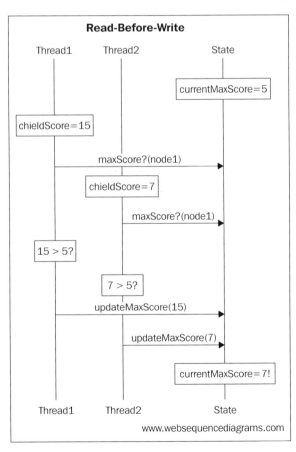

In the preceding diagram, there are two threads operating independently. In our use case, this occurs when multiple children complete simultaneously and attempt to resolve the maximum score of a parent node at the same time.

The first thread is resolving a child score of **7**. The second thread is resolving a child score of **15**. They are both resolving the same node. At the end of the process, the new maximum should be **15**, but because there was no coordination between the threads, the maximum score becomes **7**.

The first thread reads the current maximum score for the node, which returns **5**. Then, the second thread reads from the state and also receives **5**. Both threads compare the current maximum to their respective child scores and update the maximum with new values. Since the second thread's update takes place after the first, the result is an incorrect maximum value for the parent node.

In the next section, we will see how to properly address the preceding constraints to produce a functional system.

Solving the challenges

To accommodate the constraints outlined in the preceding section, we will break the topology into two parts. The first topology will perform the actual recursion. The second topology will resolve the scores. This is shown in the following diagram:

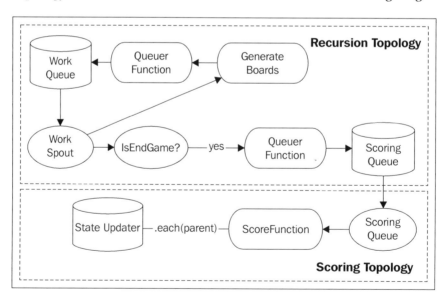

The system is broken down into two topologies: the **Recursion Topology** and the **Scoring Topology**. The **Recursion Topology** attempts to enumerate all the boards in the system. The Scoring Topology attempts to score all of the boards enumerated by the Recursion Topology.

To affect the recursion, we introduce two queues in the system. The first queue, **Work Queue**, contains a list of nodes that we need to visit. The Recursion Topology consumes from that queue via the **Work Spout**. If the node is not a leaf, the topology queues the child boards. The format of the messages on the Work Queue is as follows:

```
(board, parents[])
```

Each `board` is a 3 x 3 array. The `parents` array contains all of the parent boards.

If the node is a leaf node, the board is queued on the **Scoring Queue** using the same message format. The Scoring Topology reads from the Scoring Queue via the **Scoring Spout**. The **Scoring Function** scores the node. The board is necessarily a leaf node because that is the only type of node queued for scoring. Then, the Scoring Function emits a tuple for the current node and each parent.

We then need to update the state. The query-and-write paradigms are encapsulated in a single function because of the race condition we outlined previously. In the following design, we will demonstrate how we accommodate the race condition introduced by read-before-write.

However, before we move on to the design, notice that because we introduced queues, we clearly delineated lines along which we can acknowledge tuples. In the first topology, a tuple is acknowledged when either of the cases is true:

*   The topology has enumerated and queued the descendants of a node
*   The topology has queued the node for scoring

In the second topology, a tuple is acknowledged when the current board and all of its parents have been updated to reflect the value in the leaf node.

Also notice that we do not need to introduce new fields or mutate existing fields during processing. The only fields used in the first topology are `board` and `parents`. The second topology is the same but adds a single additional field to capture the score.

Notice also that we forked the stream coming out of the Work Spout. This was done to accommodate the fact that we cannot emit to multiple streams from a single function. Instead, both `GenerateBoards` and `IsEndGame` must determine whether the game has ended and react accordingly. In `GenerateBoards`, the tuple is filtered to avoid an infinite recursion. In `IsEndGame`, the tuple is passed along for scoring. When functions are able to emit to different streams, we will be able to collapse this function into a single "decision" filter that choses which stream a tuple should proceed with.

Implementing the architecture

Let's now delve into the details of the implementation. For example purposes, the following code assumes the topology is running locally. We use an in-memory queue instead of a persistent queue, and a hash map as our storage mechanism. In a real production implementation, we would most likely use a durable queuing system such as Kafka and a distributed storage mechanism such as Cassandra.

The data model

We will look at each of the topologies in depth, but first, let's have a look at the data model. To simplify things, we've encapsulated the game logic and the data model into two classes: Board and GameState.

The following is a listing of the Board class:

```
public class Board implements Serializable {
public static final String EMPTY = ' ';
    public String[][] board = { { EMPTY, EMPTY, EMPTY },
{ EMPTY, EMPTY, EMPTY }, { EMPTY, EMPTY, EMPTY } };

public List<Board> nextBoards(String player) {
        List<Board> boards = new ArrayList<Board>();
        for (int i = 0; i < 3; i++) {
            for (int j = 0; j < 3; j++) {
                if (board[i][j].equals(EMPTY)) {
                    Board newBoard = this.clone();
                    newBoard.board[i][j] = player;
                    boards.add(newBoard);
                }
            }
        }
        return boards;
    }

    public boolean isEndState() {
        return (nextBoards('X').size() == 0
|| Math.abs(score('X')) > 1000);
    }

    public int score(String player){
        return scoreLines(player) -
            scoreLines(Player.next(player));
    }
```

```java
    public int scoreLines(String player) {
        int score = 0;
        // Columns
        score += scoreLine(board[0][0], board[1][0], board[2][0],
player);
        score += scoreLine(board[0][1], board[1][1], board[2][1],
player);
        score += scoreLine(board[0][2], board[1][2], board[2][2],
player);

        // Rows
        score += scoreLine(board[0][0], board[0][1], board[0][2],
player);
        score += scoreLine(board[1][0], board[1][1], board[1][2],
player);
        score += scoreLine(board[2][0], board[2][1], board[2][2],
player);

        // Diagonals
        score += scoreLine(board[0][0], board[1][1], board[2][2],
player);
        score += scoreLine(board[2][0], board[1][1], board[0][2],
player);
        return score;
    }

    public int scoreLine(String pos1, String pos2, String pos3, String
player) {
        int score = 0;
        if (pos1.equals(player) && pos2.equals(player) && pos3.
equals(player)) {
            score = 10000;
        } else if ((pos1.equals(player) && pos2.equals(player) &&
pos3.equals(EMPTY)) ||
                (pos1.equals(EMPTY) && pos2.equals(player) && pos3.
equals(player)) ||
                (pos1.equals(player) && pos2.equals(EMPTY) && pos3.
equals(player))) {
            score = 100;
        } else {
            if (pos1.equals(player) && pos2.equals(EMPTY) && pos3.
equals(EMPTY) ||
                    pos1.equals(EMPTY) && pos2.equals(player) && pos3.
equals(EMPTY) ||
                    pos1.equals(EMPTY) && pos2.equals(EMPTY) && pos3.
equals(player)){
```

```
                    score = 10;
                }
            }
            return score;
        }
    ...

    public String toKey() {
        StringBuilder sb = new StringBuilder();
        for (int i = 0; i < 3; i++) {
            for (int j = 0; j < 3; j++) {
                sb.append(board[i][j]);
            }
        }
        return sb.toString();
    }
}
```

The `Board` class provides three main functions. The `Board` class encapsulates
the board itself in a multidimensional string array as a member variable. It then
provides functions that will generate the child boards (for example, `nextBoards()`),
determines whether the game has ended (for example, `isEndState()`), and finally,
provides a method to compute the score of the board when a player is provided
(for example, `nextBoards(player)`, and its supporting methods).

Notice also that the `Board` class provides a `toKey()` method. This key uniquely
represents the board and is what we will use as a unique identifier when accessing
our persistence mechanism. In this case, the unique identifier is just a concatenation
of the values from the board grid.

To completely represent the game state, we also need to know which player is
currently taking their turn. Thus, we have one higher-level object that encapsulates
the board and the current player. This is the `GameState` object whose listing is shown
in the following code snippet:

```
public class GameState implements Serializable {
private Board board;
    private List<Board> history;
    private String player;

    ...

    public String toString(){
        StringBuilder sb = new StringBuilder('GAME [');
```

```
        sb.append(board.toKey()).append(']');
        sb.append(': player(').append(player).append(')\n');
        sb.append('   history [');
        for (Board b : history){
            sb.append(b.toKey()).append(',');
        }
        sb.append(']');
        return sb.toString();
    }
}
```

There is nothing terribly surprising in this class except for the `history` variable. This member variable tracks all the previous board states for this path through the game tree. This is the breadcrumb trail required to update the game tree with the score from the leaf node.

Finally, we represent the player in the game with the `Player` class, which is shown in the following code snippet:

```
public class Player {
    public static String next(String current){
        if (current.equals('X')) return 'O';
        else return 'X';
    }
}
```

Examining the recursive topology

With the data model outlined previously, we can create a topology that recurses down the game tree. In our implementation, this is the `RecursiveTopology` class. The code for the topology is shown in the following code snippet:

```
public class RecursiveTopology {

    public static StormTopology buildTopology() {
        LOG.info('Building topology.');
        TridentTopology topology = new TridentTopology();

        // Work Queue / Spout
        LocalQueueEmitter<GameState> workSpoutEmitter =
new LocalQueueEmitter<GameState>('WorkQueue');
        LocalQueueSpout<GameState> workSpout =
```

```
new LocalQueueSpout<GameState>(workSpoutEmitter);
        GameState initialState =
new GameState(new Board(),
new ArrayList<Board>(), 'X');
        workSpoutEmitter.enqueue(initialState);

        // Scoring Queue / Spout
        LocalQueueEmitter<GameState> scoringSpoutEmitter =
new LocalQueueEmitter<GameState>('ScoringQueue');

        Stream inputStream =
topology.newStream('gamestate', workSpout);

        inputStream.each(new Fields('gamestate'),
new isEndGame())
                .each(new Fields('gamestate'),
                    new LocalQueuerFunction<GameState>(scoringSpoutEmi
tter),                new Fields(''));

        inputStream.each(new Fields('gamestate'),
new GenerateBoards(),
new Fields('children'))
                .each(new Fields('children'),
                    new LocalQueuerFunction<GameState>(workSpoutEmitt
er),
                    new Fields());

        return topology.build();
    }
...
}
```

The first section configures the in-memory queues for work and scoring. The input stream is configured from a single spout working off of the Work Queue. This queue is seeded with the initial game state.

The stream is then forked. The first prong of the fork is filtered for only endgame boards, which are then passed along to the Scoring Queue. The second prong of the fork generates new boards and queues the descendants.

The queue interaction

For this example implementation, we used an in-memory queue. In a real production system, we would rely on the Kafka spout. The listing for the `LocalQueueEmitter` class is shown in the following code snippet. Note that queues are instances of a `BlockingQueue` instance within a map, which links a queue name to the `BlockingQueue` instance. This is a handy class when testing topologies that use a single queue as the input and output (that is, recursive topologies):

```
public class LocalQueueEmitter<T> implements Emitter<Long>,
Serializable {
public static final int MAX_BATCH_SIZE=1000;
public static AtomicInteger successfulTransactions =
new AtomicInteger(0);
    private static Map<String, BlockingQueue<Object>> queues =
 new HashMap<String, BlockingQueue<Object>>();
private static final Logger LOG =
LoggerFactory.getLogger(LocalQueueEmitter.class);
    private String queueName;

    public LocalQueueEmitter(String queueName) {
        queues.put(queueName, new LinkedBlockingQueue<Object>());
        this.queueName = queueName;
    }

    @Override
    public void emitBatch(TransactionAttempt tx,
 Long coordinatorMeta, TridentCollector collector) {
        int size=0;
        LOG.debug('Getting batch for [' +
tx.getTransactionId() + ']');
        while (getQueue().peek() != null &&
size <= MAX_BATCH_SIZE) {
            List<Object> values = new ArrayList<Object>();
            try {
                LOG.debug('Waiting on work from [' +
 this.queueName + ']:[' +
getQueue().size() + ']');
                values.add(getQueue().take());
                LOG.debug('Got work from [' +
this.queueName + ']:[' +
getQueue().size() + ']');
            } catch (InterruptedException ex) {
                // do something smart
            }
```

```
            collector.emit(values);
            size++;
        }
        LOG.info('Emitted [' + size + '] elements in [' +
            tx.getTransactionId() + '], [' + getQueue().size()
+ '] remain in queue.');
    }
...
    public void enqueue(T work) {
        LOG.debug('Adding work to [' + this.queueName +
 ']:[' + getQueue().size() + ']');
        if (getQueue().size() % 1000 == 0)
            LOG.info('[' + this.queueName + '] size = [' +
                getQueue().size() + '].');
        this.getQueue().add(work);
    }

    public BlockingQueue<Object> getQueue() {
        return LocalQueueEmitter.queues.get(this.queueName);
    }
...
}
```

The main method in this class is the `emitBatch` implementation for the `Emitter` interface. This simply reads from the queue while it has data and while the maximum batch size has not been reached.

Also, note that the class provides an `enqueue()` method. The `enqueue()` method is used by our `LocalQueueFunction` class to complete the recursion. The listing for the `LocalQueueFunction` class is shown in the following code snippet:

```
public class LocalQueuerFunction<T> extends BaseFunction {
    private static final long serialVersionUID = 1L;
    LocalQueueEmitter<T> emitter;

    public LocalQueuerFunction(LocalQueueEmitter<T> emitter){
        this.emitter = emitter;
    }

    @SuppressWarnings('unchecked')
    @Override
    public void execute(TridentTuple tuple, TridentCollector
collector) {
```

```
            T object = (T) tuple.get(0);
            Log.debug('Queueing [' + object + ']');
            this.emitter.enqueue(object);
        }
    }
```

Note that the function is actually instantiated with the `emitter` function used by the spout. This allows the function to enqueue data directly into the spout. Again, this construct is useful when developing recursive topologies, but real production topologies would most likely use durable storage. Without durable storage, there is a chance for data loss since tuples are acknowledged before the processing (recursion) is complete.

Functions and filters

Now, we turn our attention to the functions and filters specific to this topology. The first is a simple filter used to filter out the endgame boards. The code for the `IsEndGame` filter is shown in the following code snippet:

```
public class IsEndGame extends BaseFilter {
...
    @Override
    public boolean isKeep(TridentTuple tuple) {
        GameState gameState = (GameState) tuple.get(0);
        boolean keep = (gameState.getBoard().isEndState());
        if (keep){
            LOG.debug('END GAME [' + gameState + ']');
        }
        return keep;
    }
}
```

Note that this class is not necessary if Trident had support for emitting tuples to different streams from a single function. In the following listing for the `IsEndGame` function, it performs the same check/filter function:

```
public class GenerateBoards extends BaseFunction {

    @Override
    public void execute(TridentTuple tuple,
TridentCollector collector) {
        GameState gameState = (GameState) tuple.get(0);
        Board currentBoard = gameState.getBoard();
        List<Board> history = new ArrayList<Board>();
```

```
        history.addAll(gameState.getHistory());
        history.add(currentBoard);

        if (!currentBoard.isEndState()) {
            String nextPlayer =
                Player.next(gameState.getPlayer());
            List<Board> boards =
                gameState.getBoard().nextBoards(nextPlayer);
            Log.debug('Generated [' + boards.size() +
'] children boards for [' + gameState.toString() +
']');
            for (Board b : boards) {
                GameState newGameState =
new GameState(b, history, nextPlayer);
                List<Object> values = new ArrayList<Object>();
                values.add(newGameState);
                collector.emit(values);
            }
        } else {
            Log.debug('End game found! [' + currentBoard + ']');
        }
    }
}
```

The function adds the current board to the history list, and then queues a new
`GameState` object, with the child board position.

 Alternatively, we could have implemented `IsEndGame` as a function, adding another field to capture the results; however, it was more constructive to use this as an example to motivate having multiple stream capabilities within functions.

The following is a sample output from the Recursive Topology:

```
2013-12-30 21:53:40,940-0500 | INFO [Thread-28] IsEndGame.isKeep(20) |
END GAME [GAME [XXO X OOO]: player(O)
    history [        ,       O ,     X O ,    X OO ,X   X OO ,X O X OO
,XXO X OO ,]]
2013-12-30 21:53:40,940-0500 | INFO [Thread-28] IsEndGame.isKeep(20) |
END GAME [GAME [X OXX OOO]: player(O)
    history [        ,       O ,     X O ,    X OO ,X   X OO ,X O X OO
,X OXX OO ,]]
2013-12-30 21:53:40,940-0500 | INFO [Thread-28] LocalQueueEmitter.
enqueue(61) | [ScoringQueue] size = [42000]
```

Examining the Scoring Topology

The Scoring Topology is more straightforward in that it is linear. The complicated aspect is the state's update to avoid the read-before-write race condition.

The code for the topology is as follows:

```
public static StormTopology buildTopology() {
TridentTopology topology = new TridentTopology();

GameState exampleRecursiveState =
 GameState.playAtRandom(new Board(), 'X');
LOG.info('SIMULATED STATE : [' + exampleRecursiveState + ']');

// Scoring Queue / Spout
LocalQueueEmitter<GameState> scoringSpoutEmitter =
new LocalQueueEmitter<GameState>('ScoringQueue');
scoringSpoutEmitter.enqueue(exampleRecursiveState);
LocalQueueSpout<GameState> scoringSpout =
new LocalQueueSpout<GameState>(scoringSpoutEmitter);

Stream inputStream =
topology.newStream('gamestate', scoringSpout);

inputStream.each(new Fields('gamestate'), new IsEndGame())
            .each(new Fields('gamestate'),
                  new ScoreFunction(),
                  new Fields('board', 'score', 'player'))
            .each(new Fields('board', 'score', 'player'),
new ScoreUpdater(), new Fields());
return topology.build();
}
```

There are only two functions: `ScoreFunction` and `ScoreUpdater`. The `ScoreFunction` scores the current board and emits that score for each board in the history.

The listing for `ScoreFunction` is shown in the following code snippet:

```
public class ScoreFunction extends BaseFunction {

@Override
public void execute(TridentTuple tuple,
TridentCollector collector) {
```

```
        GameState gameState = (GameState) tuple.get(0);
        String player = gameState.getPlayer();
        int score = gameState.score();

        List<Object> values = new ArrayList<Object>();
        values.add(gameState.getBoard());
        values.add(score);
        values.add(player);
        collector.emit(values);

        for (Board b : gameState.getHistory()) {
            player = Player.next(player);
            values = new ArrayList<Object>();
            values.add(b);
            values.add(score);
            values.add(player);
            collector.emit(values);
        }
    }
}
```

The function simply scores the current board and emits a tuple for the current board. Then, the function loops through the player emitting tuples for each board, swapping the player with each turn.

Lastly, we have the ScoreUpdater function. Again, we kept it simple for the example. The following is the code for this class:

```
public class ScoreUpdater extends BaseFunction {
...
private static final Map<String, Integer> scores =
  new HashMap<String, Integer>();
private static final String MUTEX = 'MUTEX';

@Override
public void execute(TridentTuple tuple,
TridentCollector collector) {
    Board board = (Board) tuple.get(0);
    int score = tuple.getInteger(1);
    String player = tuple.getString(2);
    String key = board.toKey();
    LOG.debug('Got (' + board.toKey() + ') => [' + score +
  '] for [' + player + ']');
```

```
    // Always compute things from X's perspective
    // We'll flip things when we interpret it if it is O's turn.
    synchronized(MUTEX){
            Integer currentScore = scores.get(key);
            if (currentScore == null ||
(player.equals('X') && score > currentScore)){
                    updateScore(board, score);
                } else if (player.equals('O') &&
score > currentScore){
                    updateScore(board, score);
                }
        }
    }

    public void updateScore(Board board, Integer score){
        scores.put(board.toKey(), score);
        LOG.debug('Updating [' + board.toString() +
']=>[' + score + ']');
    }
}
```

Addressing read-before-write

Notice in the preceding code that we used a mutex to sequence the updates to scores, thereby eliminating the race condition mentioned earlier. This only works because we are operating in a single/local JVM. When this topology is deployed to a real cluster, this will not work; however, we do have a few options to address the issue.

Distributed locking

As we see in other chapters, it is possible to leverage a distributed locking mechanism such as ZooKeeper. In this approach, ZooKeeper provides a mechanism for maintaining a mutex across multiple hosts. This is certainly a viable approach, but distributed locks come at a cost to performance. Every operation incurs overhead to accommodate what in reality might be an infrequent occurrence.

Retry when stale

Another pattern that might be useful is the *retry when stale* approach. In this scenario, along with the data, we also pull back a version number, timestamp, or checksum. Then, we perform a conditional update, including the version/timestamp/checksum information in a clause that will fail the update if that metadata has changed (for example, adding the WHERE clause to the UPDATE statement in the SQL/CQL paradigm). If the metadata has changed, it indicates that the value on which we based our decision is now stale and we should reselect the data.

Obviously, there are trade-offs between these approaches. With retries, in the extreme case where there is a tremendous amount of contention, a thread may have to be retried a number of times in order to commit an update. However, with distributed locking, you may run into timeout issues if a single thread gets stuck, loses communication with the server, or fails entirely.

Recently, there have been advances in this area. I suggest that you should look at Paxos and Cassandra's use of that algorithm to affect conditional updates at the following URLs:

- http://research.microsoft.com/en-us/um/people/lamport/pubs/paxos-simple.pdf
- http://www.datastax.com/dev/blog/lightweight-transactions-in-cassandra-2-0

In our simple case, we are extremely lucky, and we can actually incorporate the logic into the update directly. Consider the following SQL statement:

```
UPDATE gametree SET score=7 WHERE
boardkey = '000XX OXX' AND score <=7;
```

As we have resolved our read-before-write issues, the topology is suitable to score all of the boards queued by the Recursive Topology. The topology assigns a value to the endgame state and propagates that value up the game tree, persisting the proper score with the respective game state. In a real production system, we would access that state from our DRPC topology to be able to look ahead multiple turns.

Executing the topology

The following is sample output for the Scoring Topology:

```
2013-12-31 13:19:14,535-0500 | INFO [main] ScoringTopology.
buildTopology(29) | SIMULATED LEAF NODE : [
---------
|X||O||X|
---------
|O||O||X|
---------
|X||X||O|
---------
] w/ state [GAME [XOXOOXXXO]: player(O)
   history [          ,   X     ,  OX      ,  OX  X   ,  OX  X  O, OX  XX  O,
OXO XX  O, OXO XXXO, OXOOXXXO,]]
```

```
2013-12-31 13:19:14,536-0500 | INFO [main] LocalQueueEmitter.enqueue(61)
| [ScoringQueue] size = [0].
2013-12-31 13:19:14,806-0500 | INFO [main] ScoringTopology.main(52) |
Topology submitted.
2013-12-31 13:19:25,566-0500 | INFO [Thread-24] DefaultCoordinator.
initializeTransaction(25) | Initializing Transaction [1]
2013-12-31 13:19:25,570-0500 | DEBUG [Thread-30] LocalQueueEmitter.
emitBatch(37) | Getting batch for [1]
2013-12-31 13:19:25,570-0500 | DEBUG [Thread-30] LocalQueueEmitter.
emitBatch(41) | Waiting on work from [ScoringQueue]:[1]
2013-12-31 13:19:25,570-0500 | DEBUG [Thread-30] LocalQueueEmitter.
emitBatch(43) | Got work from [ScoringQueue]:[0]
2013-12-31 13:19:25,571-0500 | DEBUG [Thread-30] LocalQueueEmitter.
emitBatch(41) | Waiting on work from [ScoringQueue]:[0]
2013-12-31 13:19:25,571-0500 | INFO [Thread-28] IsEndGame.isKeep(20) |
END GAME [GAME [XOXOOXXXO]: player(O)
   history [          , X       , OX       , OX  X   , OX  X  O, OX  XX O,
OXO XX O, OXO XXXO, OXOOXXXO,]]
...
  ScoreUpdater.updateScore(43) | Updating [
---------
|  | |O| |X|
---------
|O| |  | |X|
---------
|X| |X| |O|
---------
]=>[0]
2013-12-31 13:19:25,574-0500 | DEBUG [Thread-28] ScoreUpdater.execute(27)
| Got ( OXOOXXXO) => [0] for [X]
2013-12-31 13:19:25,574-0500 | DEBUG [Thread-28] ScoreUpdater.
updateScore(43) | Updating [
---------
|  | |O| |X|
---------
|O| |O| |X|
---------
|X| |X| |O|
---------
]=>[0]
```

It is resolving a tie-game leaf node, shown at the beginning of the listing. You can see that the value propagates through the parents after that, updating the current score for those nodes.

Enumerating the game tree

The final result of combining the Recursive Topology with the Scoring Topology is a set of topologies working together continually to enumerate as much of the problem space as possible. Most likely, this process would be combined with heuristics that would only store key nodes. Also, we would prune the search space using heuristics to reduce the number of boards we need to evaluate. Regardless, however, we will need to interact with the system through an interface in order to determine the best move, given a current game state. This is what we will tackle in the next section.

Distributed Remote Procedure Call (DRPC)

Now that we have a functioning Recursive Topology that will continually seek to compute the entire game tree, let's take a look at a synchronous invocation. The DRPC capabilities that Storm provided were ported to Trident and deprecated in Storm. This was the major motivation for using Trident in this example.

With DRPC, you construct a topology much like you would in the asynchronous case. The following diagram show our DRPC topology:

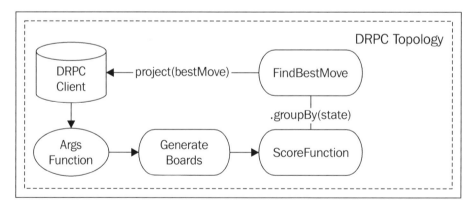

The DRPC client acts as a spout. The output of the client passes through the ArgsFunction, which normalizes the input so we can reuse the existing functions: GenerateBoards and ScoreFunction. Then, we use .groupBy(state) and aggregate the results using an Aggregator class's FindBestMove. We then perform a simple projection to return only the best move to the client.

You might also want to take a look at Spring Breeze, which allows you to wire POJOs together into a Storm topology. This is another approach to gain reuse, because those same POJOs could be exposed via web services without introducing DRPC.

```
https://github.com/internet-research-network/breeze
```

First, we will have a look at the code for the topology:

```java
public static void main(String[] args) throws Exception {
final LocalCluster cluster = new LocalCluster();
final Config conf = new Config();

LocalDRPC client = new LocalDRPC();
TridentTopology drpcTopology = new TridentTopology();

drpcTopology.newDRPCStream('drpc', client)
                .each(new Fields('args'),
new ArgsFunction(),
new Fields('gamestate'))
                .each(new Fields('gamestate'),
new GenerateBoards(),
new Fields('children'))
                .each(new Fields('children'),
new ScoreFunction(),
new Fields('board', 'score', 'player'))
                .groupBy(new Fields('gamestate'))
                .aggregate(new Fields('board', 'score'),
new FindBestMove(), new Fields('bestMove'))
                .project(new Fields('bestMove'));

cluster.submitTopology('drpcTopology', conf,
        drpcTopology.build());

Board board = new Board();
board.board[1][1] = 'O';
board.board[2][2] = 'X';
board.board[0][1] = 'O';
board.board[0][0] = 'X';
LOG.info('Determining best move for O on:' +
                board.toString());
LOG.info('RECEIVED RESPONSE [' +
client.execute('drpc', board.toKey()) + ']');
}
```

For this example, we use a `LocalDRPC` client. This is passed in as an argument to the `newDRPCStream` call, which is the crux of a DRPC topology. From there on, the topology functions as a normal topology.

You can see the actual remote procedure call takes place via the `client.execute()` method. Presently, the signature for that method takes and returns only strings. There is an outstanding enhancement request to change this signature. You can find that enhancement at `https://issues.apache.org/jira/browse/STORM-42`.

Since the current signature only accepts strings, we need to marshal the input. This takes place in the `ArgsFunction` as shown in the following code snippet:

```
@Override
public void execute(TridentTuple tuple,
TridentCollector collector) {
        String args = tuple.getString(0);
        Log.info('Executing DRPC w/ args = [' + args + ']');
        Board board = new Board(args);
        GameState gameState =
new GameState(board, new ArrayList<Board>(), 'X');
        Log.info('Emitting [' + gameState + ']');

        List<Object> values = new ArrayList<Object>();
        values.add(gameState);
        collector.emit(values);
    }
```

The second parameter to the call we made to `client.execute()` was a string that contained our input. In this case, you can see it in the topology code that we passed in the key for the board. This was the 3 x 3 grid, with the cells concatenated as a string. In order to marshal that string into a board, we added a constructor to the `Board` class that parses the string into a board as shown in the following code snippet:

```
public Board(String key) {
    for (int i = 0; i < 3; i++) {
        for (int j = 0; j < 3; j++) {
            this.board[i][j] = '' + key.charAt(i*3+j);
        }
    }
}
```

The next two functions applied in the DRPC topology demonstrate the reuse that you can achieve by leveraging DRPC as a synchronous interface. In this case, we are leveraging the functions in isolation, but you can imagine that you could reuse more complicated data flows as well.

Using the GenerateBoard function, we emit all the children for the current board. Then, the ScoreFunction scores each of those boards.

As it was in the Scoring Topology, the output of the ScoreFunction is a triple of board, score, and player. These are the scores for each of the children boards. To determine our next best move, we simply need to maximize (or minimize) the value. This can be done using a simple Aggregator. We created an aggregating function named FindBestMove as shown in the following code snippet:

```
public class FindBestMove extends BaseAggregator<BestMove> {
    private static final long serialVersionUID = 1L;

    @Override
    public BestMove init(Object batchId,
TridentCollector collector) {
        Log.info('Batch Id = [' + batchId + ']');
        return new BestMove();
    }

    @Override
    public void aggregate(BestMove currentBestMove,
TridentTuple tuple, TridentCollector collector) {
        Board board = (Board) tuple.get(0);
        Integer score = tuple.getInteger(1);
        if (score > currentBestMove.score){
            currentBestMove.score = score;
            currentBestMove.bestMove = board;
        }
    }

    @Override
    public void complete(BestMove bestMove,
TridentCollector collector) {
        collector.emit(new Values(bestMove));
    }

}
```

This aggregation extends `BaseAggregator`, which is a Java generic. In this case, we want to emit the best possible move, combined with its score. Thus, we parameterize the `BaseAggregator` class with a `BestMove` class, which is simply as follows:

```
public class BestMove {
    public Board bestMove;
    public Integer score = Integer.MIN_VALUE;

    public String toString(){
        return bestMove.toString() + '[' + score + ']';
    }
}
```

If you recall, for aggregation, Trident initially calls the `init()` method, which returns the initial aggregate value. In our case, we simply seed the `BestMove` class with the worst move. Note that the score variable of the `BestMove` class is seeded with the absolute minimum value. Then, Trident makes subsequent calls to the `aggregate()` method, which allows the function to incorporate the tuple into the aggregate value. An aggregation can also emit values here, but since we are only concerned with the final best move, we do not emit anything form the `aggregate()` method. Finally, Trident calls the `complete()` method when all values of tuples have been aggregated. It is in this method that we emit the final best move.

The following is the output from the topology:

```
2013-12-31 13:53:42,979-0500 | INFO [main] DrpcTopology.main(43) |
Determining best move for O on:

---------
|X||O|| |
---------
| ||O|| |
---------
| || ||X|
---------


00:00   INFO: Executing DRPC w/ args = [XO O   X]
00:00   INFO: Emitting [GAME [XO O   X]: player(X)
   history []]
00:00   INFO: Batch Id = [storm.trident.spout.RichSpoutBatchId@1e8466d2]
```

```
2013-12-31 13:53:44,092-0500 | INFO [main] DrpcTopology.main(44) |
RECEIVED RESPONSE [[[

---------

|X||O|| |

---------

| ||O|| |

---------

| ||O||X|

---------

[10000]]]]
```

In this example, it is O's turn, and he or she has a scoring opportunity. You can see that the topology correctly identifies the scoring opportunity and returns it as the best possible move (with the appropriate score value).

Remote deployment

What we showed is local invocation of a DRPC topology. To invoke a remote topology, you need to launch the DRPC server. You do this, just like any other Storm service, by executing the Storm script with `drpc` as the parameter as shown in the following code snippet:

```
bin/storm drpc
```

The Storm cluster will connect to the DRPC server to receive invocations. In order for it to do that, it needs to know the location(s) of the DRPC servers. These are specified in the `storm.yaml` file as follows:

```
drpc.servers:
- 'drpchost1 '
- 'drpchost2'
```

With the servers configured and the DRPC server started, the topology is submitted like any other topology, and the DRPC client can be used from any Java application that requires large-scale synchronous distributed processing. To switch from a local DRPC client to a remote, the only line that needs to change is the instantiation of the DRPC client. Instead of instantiating a local DRPC client, you need to use the following line:

```
DRPCClient client = new DRPCClient('drpchost1', 3772);
```

The parameters specify the host and port of the DRPC server and should match the configuration in the YAML file.

Summary

In this chapter, we took on an AI use case. There are many problems within that domain that leverage tree and graph data structures, and the algorithms most appropriate for those data structures are often recursive. To demonstrate how those algorithms translate to Storm, we took the Minimax algorithm and implemented it using Storm's constructs.

Along the way, we noted a few constraints within Storm that make it more complicated than expected, and we saw patterns and approaches that work around those constraints to produce a working/scalable system.

Additionally, we introduced DRPC. DRPC can be used to expose a synchronous interface to clients. DRPC also allows the design to reuse code and data flows between synchronous and asynchronous interfaces.

Combining synchronous and asynchronous topologies, with shared state, is a powerful pattern not only for AI applications, but also for analytics. Often, new data arrives in the background continuously, but users interrogate that data through synchronous interfaces. When you combine DRPC with the Trident state capabilities covered in other chapters, you should be able to build a system that can accommodate the real-time analytics' use cases.

In the next chapter, we integrate Storm with a non-transactional real-time analytics system, Druid. We will also look deeper into distributed state management with Trident and ZooKeeper.

7
Integrating Druid for Financial Analytics

In this chapter, we will extend the use of Trident to create a real-time financial analytics dashboard. The system will process financial messages to provide stock pricing information over time at various levels of granularity. The system will demonstrate integration with a non-transactional system using custom state implementations.

In the previous example, we used Trident to tally running totals of events over time. It was sufficient for the simple use case that analyzed only a single dimension of the data, but the architectural design was not flexible. To introduce a new dimension would have required Java development and the deployment of new code.

Traditionally, data warehousing techniques and business intelligence platforms are used to compute and store dimensional analytics. The warehouses are deployed as part of an **On-line Analytics Processing** (**OLAP**) system, which is separated out from the **On-line Transaction Processing** (**OLTP**). Data propagates down to the OLAP system, but typically after some lag. This is a sufficient model for retrospective analytics, but does not suffice in situations that require real-time analytics.

Similarly, other approaches use batch-processing techniques to empower data scientists. Data scientists use languages such as PIG to express their queries. Then, these queries compile down into jobs that run over large sets of data. Fortunately, they run on platforms such as Hadoop that distribute the processing across many machines, but this still introduces a substantial delay.

Both of these approaches fall short for financial systems, which cannot afford such a lag in the availability of the analytics. The overhead alone of spinning up a batch-processing job might be too much of a delay for the real-time demands of a financial system.

In this chapter, we will extend our use of Storm to deliver a flexible system that requires only minimal effort to introduce new dimensions, while simultaneously providing real-time analytics. By that, we mean only a short delay between data ingestion and availability of the dimensional analytics.

In this chapter, we will cover the following topics:

- Custom state implementations
- Integration with non-transactional storage
- Use of ZooKeeper for distributed state
- Druid and real-time aggregate analytics

Use case

In our use case, we will tap into orders for shares of stock in a financial system. Using this information, we will deliver pricing information over time, which is available via a **REpresentational State Transfer (REST)** interface.

The canonical message format in the financial industry is the **Financial Information eXchange (FIX)** format. The specification for this format can be found at `http://www.fixprotocol.org/`.

An example FIX message is shown as follows:

```
23:25:1256=BANZAI6=011=135215791235714=017=520=031=032=037=538=1
000039=054=155=SPY150=2151=010=2528=FIX.4.19=10435=F34=649=BANZ
AI52=20121105-
```

FIX messages are essentially streams of key-value pairs. The ASCII character 01, which is **Start of Header (SOH)**, delimits the pairs. FIX refers to the keys as tags. As shown in the preceding message, tags are identified by integers. Each tag has an associated field name and data type. For a full reference of tag types go to `http://www.fixprotocol.org/FIXimate3.0/en/FIX.4.2/fields_sorted_by_tagnum.html`.

The important fields for our use case are shown in the following table:

Tag ID	Field name	Description	Data type
11	CIOrdID	This is the unique identifier for message.	String
35	MsgType	This is the type of the FIX message.	String
44	Price	This is the stock price per share.	Price

Tag ID	Field name	Description	Data type
55	Symbol	This is the stock symbol.	String

FIX is a layer on top of the TCP/IP protocol. Thus, in a real system, these messages are received over TCP/IP. For ease of integration with Storm, the system could queue those messages in Kafka. However, for our example, we will simply ingest a file filled with the FIX messages. FIX supports multiple message types. Some are used for control messages (for example, Logon, Heartbeat, and so on). We will filter out those messages, passing only the types that include price information to the analytics engine.

Integrating a non-transactional system

To extend on our previous example, we could develop a framework for the configuration that would allow the user to specify the dimensions along which they would like to aggregate events. Then, we could use that configuration in our topology to maintain a set of in-memory data sets to accumulate the aggregations, but any in-memory store is susceptible to faults. To address fault-tolerance, we could then make those aggregations persist in a database.

We would need to anticipate and support all the different types of aggregations the user would like to perform (for example, sum, average, geospatial, and so on). This seems like a substantial endeavor.

Fortunately, there are options for real-time analytics engines. One popular open-source option is Druid. The following article is taken from their whitepaper found at http://static.druid.io/docs/druid.pdf:

> *Druid is an open source, real-time analytical data store that supports fast ad-hoc queries on large-scale data sets. The system combines a column-oriented data layout, a shared-nothing architecture, and an advanced indexing structure to allow for the arbitrary exploration of billion-row tables with sub-second latencies. Druid scales horizontally and is the core engine of the Metamarkets data analytics platform.*

From that excerpt, Druid exactly fits our requirements. Now, the challenge is integrating it with Storm.

Druid's technology stack fits naturally into a Storm-based ecosystem. Like Storm, it uses ZooKeeper to coordinate between its nodes. Druid also supports direct integration with Kafka. For some cases, this may be appropriate. In our example, to demonstrate integration of a non-transactional system, we will integrate Druid with Storm directly.

We will include a brief description of Druid here. However, for more detailed information on Druid, refer to the following website:

```
https://github.com/metamx/druid/wiki
```

Druid collects information via its **Real-time** nodes. Based on a configurable granularity, the **Real-time** nodes collect the event information into segments that are persisted permanently in a deep storage mechanism. Druid persistently stores the metadata for those segments in MySQL. The **Master** node recognizes the new segment, identifies **Compute** nodes for that segment based on rules, and notifies the **Compute** nodes to pull the new segment. A **Broker** node sits in front of the **Compute** nodes, receives REST queries from consumers, and distributes those queries to the appropriate **Compute** nodes.

Thus, an architecture that integrates Storm with Druid looks similar to what is shown in the following diagram:

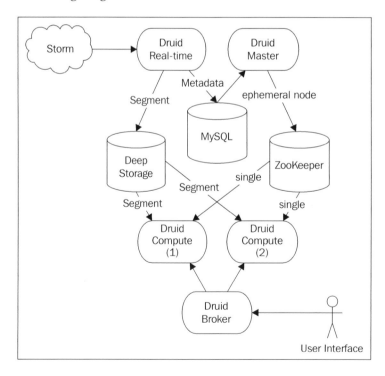

As depicted in the preceding diagram, there are three data storage mechanisms involved. The **MySQL** database is a simple metadata repository. It contains all the metadata information for all of the segments. The **Deep Storage** mechanism contains the actual segment information. Each segment contains a merged index of the events for a specific time period based on the dimensions and aggregations defined in a configuration file. As such, segments can be large (for example, 2 GB blobs). In our example, we will use Cassandra as our deep storage mechanism.

Finally, the third data storage mechanism is **ZooKeeper**. The storage in **ZooKeeper** is transient and is used for control information only. When a new segment is available, the **Master** node writes an ephemeral node in **ZooKeeper**. The **Compute** Node is subscribed to the same path, and the ephemeral node triggers the **Compute** node to pull the new segment. After the segment is successfully retrieved, the **Compute** node removes the ephemeral node from **ZooKeeper**.

For our example, the entire sequence of events is as follows:

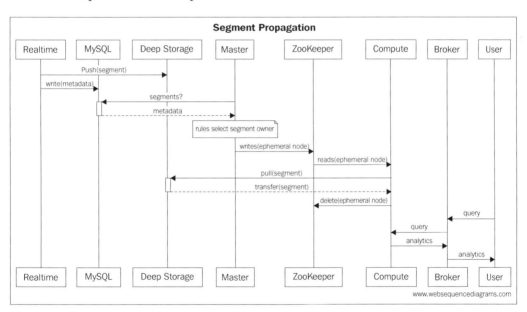

The preceding diagram lays out the event processing downstream from Storm. What is important to recognize in many real-time analytics engines is the inability to revert a transaction. The analytics systems are highly optimized to process speed and aggregation. The sacrifice is transactional integrity.

If we re-examine Trident's state classifications, there are three different flavors of state: Transactional, Opaque, and Non-Transactional. A Transactional state requires the contents of each batch to be constant over time. An Opaque Transactional state can tolerate batch composition changing over time. Finally, a Non-Transactional state cannot guarantee exactly one semantic at all.

Summarizing the Javadoc for the `storm.trident.state.State` object, there are three different kinds of state:

Non-Transactional state	In this state, commits are ignored.
	No rollback can be done.
	Updates are permanent.
Repeat Transactional state	The system is idempotent as long as all batches are identical.
Opaque Transactional state	State transitions are incremental. The previous state is stored along with the batch identifier to tolerate changing batch composition in the event of replay.

It is important to realize that introducing state into a topology effectively sequences any writes to storage. This can impact performance dramatically. When possible, the best approach is to ensure the entire system is idempotent. If all writes are idempotent, then you need not introduce transactional storage (or state) at all, because the architecture naturally tolerates tuple replay.

Often, if state persistence is backed by a database over which you control the schema, you can adjust the schema to add the additional information to participate in transactions: last committed batch identifier for repeat transactional and previous state for opaque transactional. Then, in the state implementation, you can leverage this information to ensure that your state object aligns with the type of spout you are using.

However, this is not always the case, especially in systems that perform aggregations such as counting, summing, averaging, and so on. Counter mechanisms in Cassandra have exactly this constraint. It is impossible to undo an addition to a counter, and it is impossible to make the addition idempotent. If a tuple is replayed, the counter is again incremented, and you have most likely overcounted elements in the system. For this reason, any state implementation backed by Cassandra counters is considered non-transactional.

Likewise, Druid is non-transactional. Once Druid consumes an event, the event cannot be undone. Thus, if a batch within Storm is partially consumed by Druid and then the batch is replayed, or the composition changes, there is no way for the aggregate dimensional analytics to recover. For this reason, it is interesting to consider integration between Druid and Storm, the steps we can take to address replays, and the power of such a coupling.

In short, to connect Storm to Druid, we will leverage the characteristics of a transactional spout to minimize the risk of overcounting when connecting to a non-transactional state mechanism like Druid.

The topology

With the architectural concepts in place, let's return to the use case. To keep things focused on the integration, we will keep the topology simple. The following diagram depicts the topology:

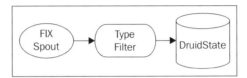

The **FIX Spout** emits tuples containing simple FIX messages. Then the filter checks the type of the message, filtering for stock orders that contain pricing information. Then, those filtered tuples flow to the DruidState object, which is the bridge to Druid.

The code for this simple topology is as follows:

```
public class FinancialAnalyticsTopology {

    public static StormTopology buildTopology() {
    TridentTopology topology = new TridentTopology();
    FixEventSpout spout = new FixEventSpout();
    Stream inputStream =
topology.newStream("message", spout);
        inputStream.each(new Fields("message"),
new MessageTypeFilter())
            .partitionPersist(new DruidStateFactory(),
new Fields("message"), new DruidStateUpdater());
        return topology.build();
    }

}
```

The spout

There are many parsers for the FIX message format. In the spout, we will use the FIX Parser, which is a Google project. For more information on this project, you can refer to https://code.google.com/p/fixparser/.

Just like the previous chapter, the spout itself is straightforward. It simply returns references to a coordinator and an emitter, as shown in the following code:

```
package com.packtpub.storm.trident.spout;

@SuppressWarnings("rawtypes")
public class FixEventSpout implements ITridentSpout<Long> {
    private static final long serialVersionUID = 1L;
    SpoutOutputCollector collector;
    BatchCoordinator<Long> coordinator = new DefaultCoordinator();
    Emitter<Long> emitter = new FixEventEmitter();
    ...
    @Override
    public Fields getOutputFields() {
        return new Fields("message");
    }
}
```

As shown in the preceding code, the Spout declares a single output field: message. This will contain the FixMessageDto object that is generated by the Emitter, as shown in the following code:

```
package com.packtpub.storm.trident.spout;

public class FixEventEmitter implements Emitter<Long>,
Serializable {
    private static final long serialVersionUID = 1L;
    public static AtomicInteger successfulTransactions =
new AtomicInteger(0);
    public static AtomicInteger uids = new AtomicInteger(0);

    @SuppressWarnings("rawtypes")
    @Override
    public void emitBatch(TransactionAttempt tx,
    Long coordinatorMeta, TridentCollector collector) {
    InputStream inputStream = null;
    File file = new File("fix_data.txt");
    try {
        inputStream =
new BufferedInputStream(new FileInputStream(file));
```

```
            SimpleFixParser parser = new SimpleFixParser(inputStream);
            SimpleFixMessage msg = null;
            do {
            msg = parser.readFixMessage();
            if (null != msg) {
                FixMessageDto dto = new FixMessageDto();
                for (TagValue tagValue : msg.fields()) {
                    if (tagValue.tag().equals("6")) { // AvgPx
                        // dto.price =
//Double.valueOf((String) tagValue.value());
                        dto.price =
                        new Double((int) (Math.random() * 100));
                    } else if (tagValue.tag().equals("35")) {
                        dto.msgType = (String)tagValue.value();
                    } else if (tagValue.tag().equals("55")) {
                      dto.symbol = (String) tagValue.value();
                    } else if (tagValue.tag().equals("11")){
                        // dto.uid = (String) tagValue.value();
                        dto.uid =
                        Integer.toString(uids.incrementAndGet());
                    }
                }
                new ObjectOutputStream(
                new ByteArrayOutputStream()).writeObject(dto);
                    List<Object> message = new ArrayList<Object>();
                    message.add(dto);
                    collector.emit(message);
            }
        } while (msg != null);
    } catch (Exception e) {
        throw new RuntimeException(e);
    } finally {
        IoUtils.closeSilently(inputStream);
    }
    }

    @Override
    public void success(TransactionAttempt tx) {
        successfulTransactions.incrementAndGet();
    }

    @Override
    public void close() {
    }
}
```

From the preceding code, you can see that we reparse the file for each batch. As we stated previously, in a real-time system we will probably receive the messages via TCP/IP and queue them in Kafka. Then, we would use the Kafka spout to emit the messages. It is a matter of preference; but, to fully encapsulate the data processing in Storm, the system would most likely queue the raw message text. In that design, we would parse the text in a function rather than the spout.

Although this Spout is only sufficient for this example, note that the composition of each batch is the same. Specifically, each batch contains all messages from the file. Since our state design relies on this characteristic, in a real system, we would need to use TransactionalKafkaSpout.

The filter

Like the spout, the filter is straightforward. It examines the msgType object and filters messages that are not fill orders. Fill orders are effectively stock purchase receipts. They contain the average price executed for that trade and the symbol for the stock purchased. The following code is the filter for this message type:

```
package com.packtpub.storm.trident.operator;

public class MessageTypeFilter extends BaseFilter {
    private static final long serialVersionUID = 1L;

    @Override
    public boolean isKeep(TridentTuple tuple) {
        FixMessageDto message = (FixMessageDto) tuple.getValue(0);
    if (message.msgType.equals("8")) {
        return true;
    }
    return false;
    }
}
```

This provides a good opportunity to point out the importance of serializability in Storm. Note that in the preceding code the filter is operating on a FixMessageDto object. It would have been easier to simply use the SimpleFixMessage object, but SimpleFixMessage is not serializable. This will not cause any problems when running on a local cluster. However, since tuples are exchanged between hosts during data processing in Storm, all the elements within a tuple must be serializable.

Developers often commit changes to data objects within tuples that are not serializable. This causes downstream deployment issues. To ensure that all objects in a tuple remain serializable, add unit tests that verify that objects are serializable. The test is a simple one; use the following code:

```
new ObjectOutputStream(
new ByteArrayOutputStream()).
writeObject(YOUR_OBJECT);
```

The state design

Now, let us proceed to the most interesting aspects of this example. In order to integrate Druid with Storm, we will embed a real-time Druid server into our topology and implement the necessary interfaces to connect the tuple stream to it. To mitigate the inherent risks of connecting to a non-transactional system, we leverage ZooKeeper to persist state information. That persistence will not prevent anomalies due to failures, but it will help identify what data is at risk when a failure occurs.

The high-level design is shown as follows:

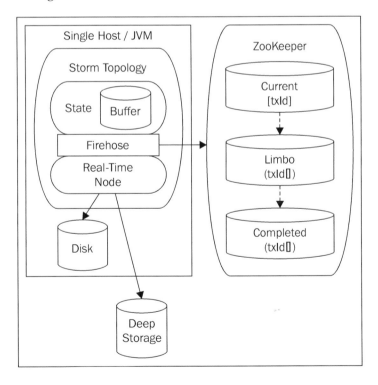

At a high level, Storm creates state objects within worker JVM processes by using a factory. A state object is created for every partition in the batch. The state factory object ensures that the real-time server is running before it returns any state objects and starts the server if it is not running. The state object then buffers those messages until Storm calls commit. When Storm calls commit, the state object unblocks the Druid **Firehose**. This sends the signals to Druid that the data is ready for aggregation. Then, we block Storm in the commit method, while the real-time server begins pulling the data via the **Firehose**.

To ensure that every partition is processed at most once, we associate a partition identifier with each partition. The partition identifier is a combination of the batch identifier and the partition index, which uniquely identifies a set of data since we are using a transactional spout.

The **Firehose** persists the identifier in **ZooKeeper** to maintain the state of the partition.

There are three states in **ZooKeeper**:

State	Description
inProgress	This Zookeeper path contains the partition identifiers that Druid is processing.
Limbo	This Zookeeper path contains the partition identifiers that Druid consumed in their entirety, but which may not be committed.
Completed	This Zookeeper path contains the partition identifiers that Druid successfully committed.

While a batch is in process, the **Firehose** writes the partition identifier to the inProgress path. When Druid has pulled the entirety of a Storm partition, the partition identifier is moved to **Limbo**, and we release Storm to continue processing while we wait for the commit message from Druid.

Upon receiving the commit message from Druid, the **Firehose** moves the partition identifier to the **Completed** path. At this point, we assume the data has been written to disk. We are still susceptible to losing data in the event of a disk failure. However, if we assume that we can reconstruct the aggregations using batch processing, then this is most likely an acceptable risk.

The following state machine captures the different phases of processing:

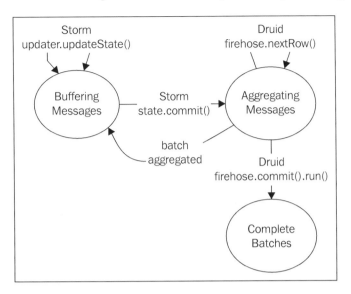

As depicted in the diagram, there is a loop between **Buffering Messages** and **Aggregating Messages**. The main control loop switches rapidly between these two states, splitting its time between the Storm processing loop and the Druid aggregation loop. The states are mutually exclusive: either the system is aggregating a batch, or it is buffering the next batch.

The third state is triggered when Druid has written the information to disk. When that happens (as we will see later), the **Firehose** is notified and we can update our persistence mechanism to indicate that the batch was safely processed. Until that commit is called, the batches consumed by Druid must remain in **Limbo**.

While in **Limbo**, no assumptions can be made about the data. Druid may or may not have aggregated the records.

In the event of a failure, Storm may leverage other `TridentState` instances to complete the processing. Thus, for every partition, the **Firehose** must execute the following steps:

1. The **Firehose** must check to see if the partition was already completed. If so, the partition is a replay, probably due to a downstream failure. Since the batch is guaranteed to have the same contents as before, it can safely be ignored since Druid has already aggregated its contents. The system may log a warning message.

2. The **Firehose** must check to see if the partition is in limbo. If this is the case, then Druid fully consumed the partition, but never called commit or the system failed after commit was called but before the **Firehose** updated **ZooKeeper**. The system should raise an alert. It should not attempt to complete the batch since it was fully consumed by Druid and we do not know the status of the aggregation. It simply returns, enabling Storm to continue to the next batch.

3. The **Firehose** must check to see if the partition is in progress. If this is the case, then for some reason, somewhere on the network, the partition is being processed by another instance. This should not happen during ordinary processing. In this case, the system should raise an alert for this partition. In our simple system, we will simply proceed, leaving it to our offline batch processing to correct the aggregation.

In many large scale real-time systems, the users are willing to tolerate slight discrepancies in the real-time analytics as long as the skews are infrequent and can be remedied fairly quickly.

It is important to note that this approach succeeds because we are using a transactional spout. The transactional spout guarantees that each batch has the same composition. Furthermore, for this approach to work, each partition within the batch must have the same composition. This is true if and only if the partitioning in the topology is deterministic. With deterministic partitioning and a transactional spout, each partition will contain the same data, even in the event of a replay. Had we used shuffle grouping, this approach would not work. Our example topology is deterministic. This guarantees that a batch identifier, when combined with a partition index, represents a consistent set of data over time.

Implementing the architecture

With the design in place, we can turn our attention to the implementation.
The sequence diagram for the implementation is shown as follows:

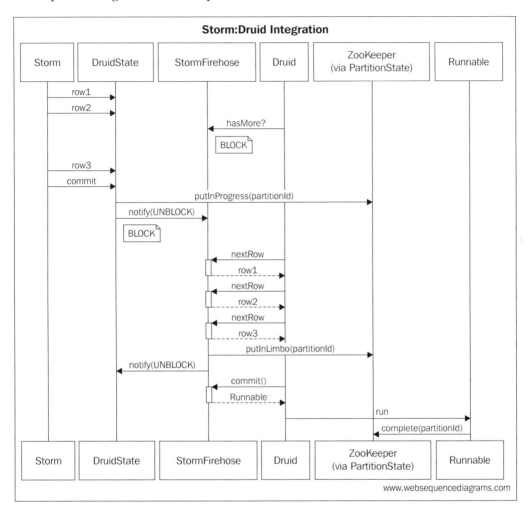

The preceding diagram implements the state machine shown in the design. Once the real-time server is started, Druid polls the StormFirehose object using the hasMore() method. The contract with Druid specifies that the Firehose object's implementation should block until data is available. While Druid is polling and the Firehose object is blocking, Storm delivers tuples into the DruidState object's message buffer. When the batch is complete, Storm calls the commit() method on the DruidState object. At that point, the PartitionStatus is updated. The partition is put in progress and the implementation unblocks the StormFirehose object.

Druid begins pulling data from the StormFirehose object via the nextRow() method. When the StormFirehose object exhausts the contents of the partition, it places the partition in limbo, and releases control back to Storm.

Finally, when the commit method is called on the StormFirehose, the implementation returns a Runnable, which is what Druid uses to notify a Firehose that the partition is persisted. When Druid calls run(), the implementation moves the partition to completion.

DruidState

First, we will look at the Storm side of the equation. In the previous chapter, we extended the NonTransactionalMap class to persist a state. That abstraction shielded us from the details of sequential batch processing. We simply implemented the IBackingMap interface to support the multiGet and multiPut calls, and the superclass took care of the rest.

In this scenario, we need more control over the persistence process than what the default implementations provide. Instead, we need to implement the base State interfaces ourselves. The following class diagram depicts the class hierarchy:

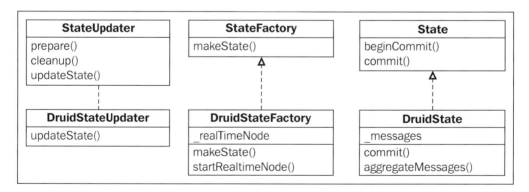

As evident in the diagram, the DruidStateFactory class manages the embedded real-time node. An argument could be made for the updater managing the embedded server. However, since there should be only a single instance of the real-time server per JVM and that instance needs to exist before any state objects, the lifecycle management of the embedded server seemed to fit more naturally in the factory.

The following code snippet contains the relevant sections of the DruidStateFactory class:

```
public class DruidStateFactory implements StateFactory {
    private static final long serialVersionUID = 1L;
    private static final Logger LOG =
LoggerFactory.getLogger(DruidStateFactory.class);
    private static RealtimeNode rn = null;

    private static synchronized void startRealtime() {
    if (rn == null) {
        final Lifecycle lifecycle = new Lifecycle();
        rn = RealtimeNode.builder().build();
        lifecycle.addManagedInstance(rn);
        rn.registerJacksonSubtype(
        new NamedType(StormFirehoseFactory.class, "storm"));

        try {
            lifecycle.start();
        } catch (Throwable t) {

        }
    }
    }

    @Override
    public State makeState(Map conf, IMetricsContext metrics,
        int partitionIndex, int numPartitions) {
            DruidStateFactory.startRealtime();
            return new DruidState(partitionIndex);
    }
}
```

Without going into too much detail, the preceding code starts a real-time node if one had not been started already. Also, it registers the StormFirehoseFactory class with that real-time node.

The factory also implements the `StateFactory` interface from Storm, which allows Storm to use this factory to create new `State` objects. The `State` object itself is fairly simple:

```
public class DruidState implements State {
private static final Logger LOG =
LoggerFactory.getLogger(DruidState.class);
private Vector<FixMessageDto> messages =
new Vector<FixMessageDto>();
    private int partitionIndex;

public DruidState(int partitionIndex){
    this.partitionIndex = partitionIndex;
}

@Override
    public void beginCommit(Long batchId) {
}

@Override
public void commit(Long batchId) {
    String partitionId = batchId.toString() + "-" +
                      partitionIndex;
    LOG.info("Committing partition [" +
        partitionIndex + "] of batch [" + batchId + "]");
    try {
        if (StormFirehose.STATUS.isCompleted(partitionId)) {
        LOG.warn("Encountered completed partition ["
            + partitionIndex + "] of batch [" + batchId
            + "]");
        return;
    } else if (StormFirehose.STATUS.isInLimbo(partitionId)) {
        LOG.warn("Encountered limbo partition [" + partitionIndex
                + "] of batch [" + batchId +
                "] : NOTIFY THE AUTHORITIES!");
        return;
    } else if (StormFirehose.STATUS.isInProgress(partitionId)) {
            LOG.warn("Encountered in-progress partition [\" +
            partitionIndex + \"] of batch [" + batchId +
            "] : NOTIFY THE AUTHORITIES!");
        return;
    }
```

```
        StormFirehose.STATUS.putInProgress(partitionId);
        StormFirehoseFactory.getFirehose()
            .sendMessages(partitionId, messages);
      } catch (Exception e) {
            LOG.error("Could not start firehose for [" +
                    partitionIndex + "] of batch [" +
                    batchId + "]", e);
      }
      }


  public void aggregateMessage(FixMessageDto message) {
      messages.add(message);
  }
  }
```

As you can see in the preceding code, the State object is a message buffer.
It delegates the actual commit logic to the Firehose object, which we will
examine shortly. However, there are a few critical lines in this class that
implement the failure detection we outlined earlier.

The conditional logic in the commit() method on the State object checks
the ZooKeeper status to determine if this partition was already successfully
processed (inCompleted), failed to commit (inLimbo), or failed during processing
(inProgress). We will dive deeper into the state storage when we examine the
DruidPartitionStatus object.

It is also important to note that the commit() method is called by Storm directly, but
the aggregateMessage() method is called by the updater. Even though Storm should
never call those methods concurrently, we chose to use a thread-safe vector anyway.

The DruidStateUpdater code is as follows:

```
public class DruidStateUpdater implements StateUpdater<DruidState> {
...
@Override
public void updateState(DruidState state,
List<TridentTuple> tuples, TridentCollector collector) {
for (TridentTuple tuple : tuples) {
    FixMessageDto message = (FixMessageDto) tuple.getValue(0);
    state.aggregateMessage(message);
  }
}
}
```

As shown in the preceding code, the updater simply loops through the tuples and
passes them to the state object to buffer.

Implementing the StormFirehose object

Before we turn our attention to the Druid side of the implementation, we should probably take a step back and discuss Druid in more detail. Druid feeds are configured via a spec file. In our example, this is `realtime.spec`, as shown in the following code:

```
[{
    "schema": {
        "dataSource": "stockinfo",
        "aggregators": [
            { "type": "count", "name": "orders"},
            { "type": "doubleSum", "fieldName": "price", "name":
              "totalPrice" }
        ],
        "indexGranularity": "minute",
        "shardSpec": {"type": "none"}
    },

    "config": {
        "maxRowsInMemory": 50000,
        "intermediatePersistPeriod": "PT30s"
    },

    "firehose": {
        "type": "storm",
        "sleepUsec": 100000,
        "maxGeneratedRows": 5000000,
        "seed": 0,
        "nTokens": 255,
        "nPerSleep": 3
    },

    "plumber": {
        "type": "realtime",
        "windowPeriod": "PT30s",
        "segmentGranularity": "minute",
        "basePersistDirectory":
        "/tmp/example/rand_realtime/basePersist"
    }
}]
```

For our example, the important elements in the preceding spec file are `schema` and `firehose`. The `schema` element defines the data and the aggregations that Druid should perform on that data. In our example, Druid will count the number of times we see a stock symbol in the `orders` field and track the total price paid in the `totalPrice` field. The `totalPrice` field will be used to calculate the running stock price average over time. Additionally, you need to specify an `indexGranularity` object that specifies the temporal granularity of the index.

The `firehose` element contains the configuration for the `Firehose` object. As we saw in the `StateFactory` interface, an implementation registers a `FirehoseFactory` class with Druid when the real-time server is started. That factory is registered as a `Jackson` subtype. When the real-time spec file is parsed, the type in the `firehose` element of the JSON is used to link back to the appropriate `FirehoseFactory` for a stream of data.

For more information on the JSON polymorphism, refer to the following website:

`http://wiki.fasterxml.com/JacksonPolymorphicDeserialization`

For more information on the spec file, refer to the following website:

`https://github.com/metamx/druid/wiki/Realtime`

Now, we can turn our attention to the Druid side of the implementation. `Firehose` is the main interface one must implement to contribute data into a Druid real-time server.

The code for our `StormFirehoseFactory` class is as follows:

```
@JsonTypeName("storm")
public class StormFirehoseFactory implements FirehoseFactory {
    private static final StormFirehose FIREHOSE =
    new StormFirehose();
    @JsonCreator
    public StormFirehoseFactory() {
    }

    @Override
    public Firehose connect() throws IOException {
        return FIREHOSE;
    }

    public static StormFirehose getFirehose(){
        return FIREHOSE;
    }
}
```

The factory implementation is straightforward. In this case, we simply return a static singleton object. Note that the object is annotated with `@JsonTypeName` and `@JsonCreator`. As stated in the preceding code, `Jackson` is the means through which `FirehoseFactory` objects are registered. Thus, the name specified as the `@JsonTypeName` must align with the type specified in the spec file.

The meat of the implementation is in the `StormFirehose` class. Within this class, there are four critical methods that we will examine one by one: `hasMore()`, `nextRow()`, `commit()`, and `sendMessages()`.

The `sendMessages()` method is the entry point into the `StormFirehose` class. It is effectively the handoff point between Storm and Druid. The code for this method is as follows:

```
public synchronized void sendMessages(String partitionId,
                    List<FixMessageDto> messages) {
    BLOCKING_QUEUE =
    new ArrayBlockingQueue<FixMessageDto>(messages.size(),
    false, messages);
    TRANSACTION_ID = partitionId;
    LOG.info("Beginning commit to Druid. [" + messages.size() +
    "] messages, unlocking [START]");
    synchronized (START) {
        START.notify();
    }
    try {
        synchronized (FINISHED) {
        FINISHED.wait();
        }
    } catch (InterruptedException e) {
        LOG.error("Commit to Druid interrupted.");
    }
    LOG.info("Returning control to Storm.");
}
```

This method is synchronized to prevent concurrency issues. Note that it does not do anything more than copy the message buffer into a queue and notify the `hasMore()` method to release the batch. Then, it blocks waiting for Druid to fully consume the batch.

Then, the flow proceeds to the `nextRow()` method, which is shown as follows:

```
@Override
public InputRow nextRow() {
    final Map<String, Object> theMap =
    Maps.newTreeMap(String.CASE_INSENSITIVE_ORDER);
    try {
    FixMessageDto message = null;
    message = BLOCKING_QUEUE.poll();

    if (message != null) {
    LOG.info("[" + message.symbol + "] @ [" +
     message.price + "]");
    theMap.put("symbol", message.symbol);
    theMap.put("price", message.price);
    }

    if (BLOCKING_QUEUE.isEmpty()) {
    STATUS.putInLimbo(TRANSACTION_ID);
    LIMBO_TRANSACTIONS.add(TRANSACTION_ID);
    LOG.info("Batch is fully consumed by Druid. "
    + "Unlocking [FINISH]");
    synchronized (FINISHED) {
        FINISHED.notify();

    }
    }
} catch (Exception e) {
    LOG.error("Error occurred in nextRow.", e);
    System.exit(-1);
}
final LinkedList<String> dimensions =
new LinkedList<String>();
dimensions.add("symbol");
dimensions.add("price");
return new MapBasedInputRow(System.currentTimeMillis(),
                            dimensions, theMap);
}
```

This method pulls a message off of the queue. If it is not null, the data is added to a map that is passed along to Druid as a `MapBasedInputRow` method. If there are no remaining messages in the queue, the `sendMessages()` method that we examined in the preceding code is released. From Storm's perspective, the batch is complete. Druid now owns the data. However, from a system perspective, the data is in limbo because Druid may not have persisted the data to disk. We are at a risk of losing the data entirely in the event of a hardware failure.

Druid will then poll the `hasMore()` method, which is shown in the following code:

```
@Override
public boolean hasMore() {
    if (BLOCKING_QUEUE != null && !BLOCKING_QUEUE.isEmpty())
        return true;
    try {
        synchronized (START) {
        START.wait();
        }
    } catch (InterruptedException e) {
        LOG.error("hasMore() blocking interrupted!");
    }
    return true;
}
```

Since the queue is empty, the method will block until `sendMessage()` is called again.

This leaves only one remaining piece of the puzzle, the `commit()` method. It is shown in the following code:

```
@Override
public Runnable commit() {
List<String> limboTransactions = new ArrayList<String>();
LIMBO_TRANSACTIONS.drainTo(limboTransactions);
return new StormCommitRunnable(limboTransactions);
}
```

This method returns `Runnable`, which is called by Druid after it's finished persisting the messages. Although all the other methods in the `Firehose` object are called from a single thread, the `Runnable` is called from a different thread and, therefore, must be thread-safe. For that reason, we copy the transactions in limbo into a separate list and pass it into the `Runnable` object's constructor. As you can see in the following code, the `Runnable` does nothing but moves the transactions into the completed state in `Zookeeper`.

```
public class StormCommitRunnable implements Runnable {
    private List<String> partitionIds = null;

    public StormCommitRunnable(List<String> partitionIds){
        this.partitionIds = partitionIds;
    }

    @Override
    public void run() {
    try {
        StormFirehose.STATUS.complete(partitionIds);
    } catch (Exception e) {
        Log.error("Could not complete transactions.", e);
    }
    }
}
```

Implementing the partition status in ZooKeeper

Now that we have examined all of the code, we can take a look at how the state is persisted in ZooKeeper. This enables the system to coordinate the distributed processing, especially in the event of a failure.

The implementation leverages ZooKeeper to persist the partition-processing status. ZooKeeper is another open source project. For more information, you can refer to `http://zookeeper.apache.org/`.

ZooKeeper maintains a tree of nodes. Each node has an associated path, much like a file system. The implementation uses ZooKeeper through a framework called Curator. For more information, you can refer to `http://curator.incubator.apache.org/`.

When connecting to ZooKeeper through Curator, you supply a namespace. Effectively, this is the top-level node under which the application data is stored. In our implementation, the namespace is `stormdruid`. The application then maintains three paths underneath that, where it stores batch status information.

The paths correspond to the states described in the design and are as follows:

- `/stormdruid/current`: This corresponds to the current state
- `/stormdruid/limbo`: This corresponds to the limbo state
- `/stormdruid/completed`: This corresponds to the completed state

In our implementation, all ZooKeeper's interactions for partition status are run through the `DruidPartitionStatus` class.

The code for this class is as follows:

```
public class DruidBatchStatus {
    private static final Logger LOG =
LoggerFactory.getLogger(DruidBatchStatus.class);
    final String COMPLETED_PATH = "completed";
    final String LIMBO_PATH = "limbo";
    final String CURRENT_PATH = "current";
    private CuratorFramework curatorFramework;

    public DruidBatchStatus() {
    try {
curatorFramework =
    CuratorFrameworkFactory.builder()
    .namespace("stormdruid")
    .connectString("localhost:2181")
    .retryPolicy(new RetryNTimes(1, 1000))
    .connectionTimeoutMs(5000)
            .build();
        curatorFramework.start();

        if (curatorFramework.checkExists()
    .forPath(COMPLETED_PATH) == null) {
        curatorFramework.create().forPath(COMPLETED_PATH);
        }

    }catch (Exception e) {
        LOG.error("Could not establish connection to Zookeeper",
                e);
    }
    }

    public boolean isInLimbo(String paritionId) throws Exception {
        return (curatorFramework.checkExists().forPath(LIMBO_PATH
        + "/" + paritionId) != null);
    }
```

```
public void putInLimbo(Long paritionId) throws Exception {
curatorFramework.inTransaction().
    delete().forPath(CURRENT_PATH + "/" + paritionId)
    .and().create().forPath(LIMBO_PATH + "/" +
                             paritionId).and().commit();
    }
}
```

In the interest of space, we have only shown the constructor and the methods related to the limbo status. In the constructor, the client connects to ZooKeeper and creates the three base paths as described in the preceding code. Then, it provides query methods to test if a transaction is in progress, limbo, or completed. It also provides methods that move a transaction between those states.

Executing the implementation

Enough with the code, let's get on with the demo! We start the topology using the main method of the FinancialAnalyticsTopology class. For a better demo, we introduce random prices between zero and one hundred. (Refer back to the Emitter code.)

Once the topology is started, you will see the following output:

```
2014-02-16 09:47:15,479-0500 | INFO [Thread-18]
DefaultCoordinator.initializeTransaction(24) | Initializing
Transaction [1615]
2014-02-16 09:47:15,482-0500 | INFO [Thread-22]
DruidState.commit(28) | Committing partition [0] of batch [1615]
2014-02-16 09:47:15,484-0500 | INFO [Thread-22]
StormFirehose.sendMessages(82) | Beginning commit to Druid. [7996]
messages, unlocking [START]
2014-02-16 09:47:15,511-0500 | INFO [chief-stockinfo]
StormFirehose.nextRow(58) | Batch is fully consumed by Druid.
Unlocking [FINISH]
2014-02-16 09:47:15,511-0500 | INFO [Thread-22]
StormFirehose.sendMessages(93) | Returning control to Storm.
2014-02-16 09:47:15,513-0500 | INFO [Thread-18]
DefaultCoordinator.success(30) | Successful Transaction [1615]
```

You can interrogate the processing from multiple dimensions.

Using the ZooKeeper client, you can examine the status of transactions. Take a look at the following listing; it shows the transaction/batch identifiers and their statuses:

```
[zk: localhost:2181(CONNECTED) 50] ls /stormdruid/current
[501-0]
[zk: localhost:2181(CONNECTED) 51] ls /stormdruid/limbo
[486-0, 417-0, 421-0, 418-0, 487-0, 485-0, 484-0, 452-0, ...
[zk: localhost:2181(CONNECTED) 82] ls /stormdruid/completed
[zk: localhost:2181(CONNECTED) 52] ls /stormdruid/completed
[59-0, 321-0, 296-0, 357-0, 358-0, 220-0, 355-0,
```

For alerting and monitoring, please note the following:

- If ever there is more than one batch in the `current` path, then alerts should go out
- If ever there are batch identifiers in `limbo` that are not sequential, or substantially behind the current identifier, alerts should go out

To clean up the state in ZooKeeper, you can execute the following code:

```
zk: localhost:2181(CONNECTED) 83] rmr /stormdruid
```

To monitor the segment propagation, you can use the MySQL client. Using the default schema, you will find segments by selecting them out of the `prod_segments` table with the following code:

```
mysql> select * from prod_segments;
```

Examining the analytics

Now, the moment we have all been waiting for; we can see average stock prices over time by using the REST API that Druid provides. To use the REST API, it is not necessary to run a full-blown Druid cluster. You will only be able to query the data seen by the singular embedded real-time node, but each node is capable of servicing requests and this makes testing easier. Using curl, you can issue a query of a real-time node using the following command:

```
curl -sX POST "http://localhost:7070/druid/v2/?pretty=true" -H
'content-type: application/json'  -d @storm_query
```

The final parameter of the `curl` statement references a file, the contents of which will be included as the body of the `POST` request. The file contains the following details:

```
{
    "queryType": "groupBy",
    "dataSource": "stockinfo",
    "granularity": "minute",
    "dimensions": ["symbol"],
    "aggregations":[
        { "type": "longSum", "fieldName": "orders",
          "name": "cumulativeCount"},
        { "type": "doubleSum", "fieldName": "totalPrice",
          "name": "cumulativePrice" }
    ],
    "postAggregations":[
    {   "type":"arithmetic",
        "name":"avg_price",
        "fn":"/",
        "fields":[ {"type":"fieldAccess","name":"avgprice",
        "fieldName":"cumulativePrice"},
                    {"type":"fieldAccess","name":"numrows",
        "fieldName":"cumulativeCount"}] }
    ],
    "intervals":["2012-10-01T00:00/2020-01-01T00"]
}
```

There are two types of aggregations happening in Druid. There are aggregations that happen as part of the indexing and there are aggregations that happen at query time. The aggregations that happen during indexing are defined in the spec file. If you recall, we had two aggregations in the spec file:

```
"aggregators": [
{ "type": "count", "name": "orders"},
    { "type": "doubleSum", "fieldName": "price",
"name": "totalPrice" }
],
```

The events we are aggregating have two fields: `symbol` and `price`. The preceding aggregations are applied at indexing time, and introduce two additional fields: `totalPrice` and `orders`. Recall that `totalPrice` is the sum of the prices on each event for that slice of time. The `orders` field contains the total count of events in that slice of time.

Then, when we perform the query, Druid applies a second set of aggregations based on the groupBy statement. In our query, we group by symbol at a granularity of a minute. The aggregations then introduce two new fields: cumulativeCount and cumulativePrice. These fields contain the sums of the previous aggregations.

Finally, we introduce a postaggregation method to calculate the average for that slice of time. The postaggregation method divides (""fn":"/") the two cumulative fields to yield a new avg_price field.

Issuing the curl statement to a running server results in the following response:

```
[ {
    "version" : "v1",
    "timestamp" : "2013-05-15T22:31:00.000Z",
    "event" : {
      "cumulativePrice" : 3464069.0,
      "symbol" : "MSFT",
      "cumulativeCount" : 69114,
      "avg_price" : 50.12108979367422
    }
  }, {
    "version" : "v1",
    "timestamp" : "2013-05-15T22:31:00.000Z",
    "event" : {
      "cumulativePrice" : 3515855.0,
      "symbol" : "ORCL",
      "cumulativeCount" : 68961,
      "avg_price" : 50.98323690201708
    }
  ...
  {
    "version" : "v1",
    "timestamp" : "2013-05-15T22:32:00.000Z",
    "event" : {
      "cumulativePrice" : 1347494.0,
      "symbol" : "ORCL",
      "cumulativeCount" : 26696,
      "avg_price" : 50.47550194785736
    }
  }, {
```

```
  "version" : "v1",
  "timestamp" : "2013-05-15T22:32:00.000Z",
  "event" : {
    "cumulativePrice" : 707317.0,
    "symbol" : "SPY",
    "cumulativeCount" : 13453,
    "avg_price" : 52.576897346316805
  }
} ]
```

Since we updated the code to generate random prices between zero and one hundred, it is no surprise that the averages are approximately fifty. (Woo hoo!)

Summary

In this chapter, we gained a deeper appreciation for the Trident State API. We created a direct implementation of the `State` and `StateUpdater` interfaces instead of relying on default implementations. Specifically, we implemented these interfaces to bridge the gap between a transactional spout and a non-transactional system, namely Druid. Although it is impossible to establish exactly-once semantics into a non-transactional store, we put mechanisms in place to alert when the system encounters issues. Ostensibly, upon failure we could then use a batch processing mechanism to reconstruct any suspect aggregation segments.

For future investigation, it would be beneficial to establish an idempotent interface between Storm and Druid. To do this, we could publish a single segment for each batch within Storm. Since segment propagation is atomic within Druid, this would give us a mechanism to commit each batch atomically to Druid. Additionally, batches could then be processed in parallel, improving throughput. Druid supports an ever-expanding set of query types and aggregation mechanisms. It is incredibly powerful, and the marriage of Storm and Druid is a powerful one.

8
Natural Language Processing

Some people believe Storm will eventually replace Hadoop as demand increases for real-time analytics and data processing. In this chapter, we will see how Storm and Hadoop actually complement each other.

Although Storm blurs the lines between traditional **On-Line Transactional Processing (OLTP)** and **On-Line Analytical Processing (OLAP)**, it can handle a high volume of transactions while performing aggregations and dimensional analysis typically associated with data warehouses. It is often the case that you still need additional infrastructure to perform historical analysis and to support ad hoc queries across the entire dataset. Additionally, batch processing is often used to correct anomalies where the OLTP system cannot ensure consistency in the event of failures. This is exactly what we encountered in the Storm-Druid integration.

For these reasons, batch processing infrastructure is often paired with real-time infrastructure. Hadoop provides us with such a batch processing framework. In this chapter, we will implement an architecture that supports historical and ad hoc analyses via batch processing.

This chapter covers the following topics:

- The CAP theorem
- Lambda architectures
- OLTP and OLAP integration
- An introduction to Hadoop

Motivating a Lambda architecture

First, from a logical perspective, let's take a look at the Storm-Druid integration. Storm, and more specifically Trident, is able to perform distributed analytics because it isolates state transitions. To do this, Storm makes certain assumptions about the underlying persistence mechanisms for state. Storm assumes that the persistence mechanism is both *consistent* and *available*. Specifically, Storm assumes that once a state transition is made, that new state is shared, consistent across all nodes, and immediately available.

From the CAP theorem, we know that it is difficult for any distributed system to provide all three of the following guarantees simultaneously:

- **Consistency**: The state is the same across all nodes
- **Availability**: The system can respond to a query with either success or failure
- **Partition Tolerance**: The system continues to respond despite loss of communication or partial system failure

More and more, web-scale architectures integrate persistence mechanisms that take a relaxed approach to Consistency in order to meet Availability and Partition Tolerance requirements. Often, these systems do so because the coordination required to provide transactional consistency across the entire system becomes untenable in large distributed systems. Performance and throughput are more important.

Druid made these same trade-offs. If we take a look at the persistence model for Druid, we see a few different stages:

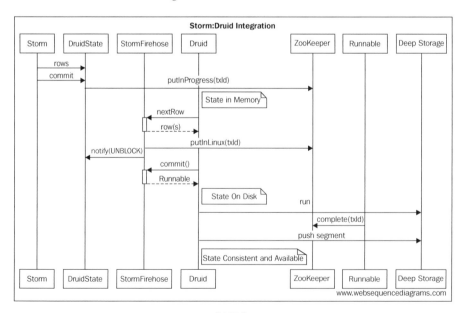

First, Druid consumes the data via the `Firehose` interface and places that data in the memory. Second, the data is persisted to the disk and the `Firehose` implementation is notified via the `Runnable` interface. Finally, this data is pushed to **Deep Storage**, which makes the data available to other parts of the system.

Now, if we consider the implications of inconsistent data to fault tolerance, we see that the data is at risk until it is persisted in Deep Storage. If we lose that node, we lose the analytics for all the data on that node we have consumed thus far via Storm, because we have already acknowledged the tuples.

One obvious solution to this problem is to push the segment to Deep Storage prior to acknowledging the tuples in Storm. This would be acceptable, but it would create a tenuous relationship between Storm and Druid. Specifically, batch sizes and timeouts would need to align with segment sizes and the timing of Druid's segment push to Deep Storage. If described in another way, the throughput of our transactional processing system would be limited and intimately tied to the system we are using for analytical processing. In the end, that is a dependency we most likely do not want.

However, we still want real-time analytics and are willing to tolerate those analytics missing some portion of the data in the unlikely event of a partial system failure. From this perspective, this integration is satisfactory. Ideally though, we would have a mechanism to correct and recover from any fault. To do this, we will introduce an offline batch processing mechanism to recover and correct data in the event of a failure.

For this to work, we will first persist the data prior to sending the data to Druid. Our batch processing system will read the data from that persistence mechanism offline. The batch processing system will be able to correct/update any data that the system may have lost during real-time processing. Combining these approaches, we can achieve the throughput we need during real-time processing with analytics that are accurate until there is a system failure and a mechanism that corrects those analytics if/when a failure occurs.

The de facto standard for distributed batch processing is Hadoop. Thus, we will incorporate the use of Hadoop for historical (that is, non-real-time) analytics. The following diagram depicts the pattern we will use here:

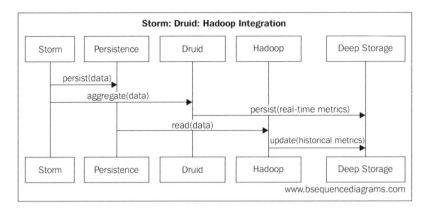

The preceding pattern shows how we can integrate OLTP and OLAP systems successfully while mostly providing consistent and complete analytics in real time with high throughput, availability, and partitioning. It also simultaneously provides mechanisms to account for partial system failures.

The other gap that this approach fills is the ability to introduce new analytics into the system. Since the Storm-Druid integration focuses on the real-time problem, there is no easy way to introduce new analyses into the system. Hadoop closes that gap since it can run over the historical data to populate new dimensions or perform additional aggregations.

Nathan Marz, the original author of Storm, refers to this approach as a **Lambda architecture**.

Examining our use case

Now, let's apply this pattern to the field of **Natural Language Processing** (**NLP**). In this use case, we will search Twitter for relevant tweets for a phrase (for example, "Apple Jobs"). The system will then process those tweets trying to find the most relevant words. Using Druid to aggregate the terms, we will be able to trend the most relevant words over time.

Let's define the problem a little more. Given a search phrase p, using the Twitter API, we will find the most relevant sets of Tweets, T. For each tweet, t in T, we will count the occurrences of each word, w. We will compare the frequency of that word in the tweets with the frequency of that word in a sample of English text, E. The system will then rank those words and display the top 20 results.

Mathematically, this equates to the following:

$$\forall t \in T, \forall w \in t : rank(w) = \frac{frequency(w) \in T}{frequency(w) \in E}$$

Here, the frequency of a word w in a corpus C is as follows:

$$frequency(w) \in C = \frac{count\ of\ occurrences\ of\ w\ in\ C}{total\ count\ of\ words\ in\ C}$$

Since we are only concerned with the relative frequency, and the total count of words in T and words in E are constant across all words, we can ignore them in the equations, reducing the complexity of the problem to the following:

$$\forall t \in T, \forall w \in t : rank(w) = \frac{count(w) \in T}{count(w) \in E}$$

For the denominator, we will use a freely available word frequency list from the following link:

`http://invokeit.wordpress.com/frequency-word-lists/`

We will use Storm to process the results of the Twitter search and enrich the tuple with the count information for the denominator. Druid will then count the occurrences for the numerator, and we will use a post-aggregation function to perform the actual relevance calculation.

Realizing a Lambda architecture

For this use case, we are focusing on a distributed computing pattern that integrates a real-time processing platform (that is, Storm) with an analytics engine (that is, Druid); we then pair it with an offline batch processing mechanism (that is, Hadoop) to ensure we have accurate historical metrics.

While that remains the focus, the other key goal we are trying to achieve is continuous availability and fault tolerance. More specifically, the system should tolerate the permanent loss of a node or even a data center. To achieve this kind of availability and fault tolerance, we need to focus a bit more on the persistence.

In a live system, we would use a distributed storage mechanism for persistence, ideally a storage mechanism that supported replication across data centers. Thus, even in a disastrous scenario, whereby a data center is entirely lost, the system can recover without losing data. When interacting with the persistent store, the client will demand a consistency level that replicates data across multiple data centers within the transaction.

For this discussion, assume we are using Cassandra as our persistence mechanism. With Cassandra, which has tunable consistency, writes will use a consistency level of EACH_QUORUM. This ensures that a copy of the data is written consistently to all data centers. Of course, this introduces the overhead of interdata center communication on each write. For less critical applications, LOCAL_QUORUM is most likely acceptable, which avoids the latency of interdata center communication.

Another benefit of using a distributed storage engine such as Cassandra is that a separate ring/cluster could be set up for offline / batch processing. Hadoop could then use that ring as the input, allowing the system to reingest the historical data without impacting transactional processing. Consider the following architecture diagram:

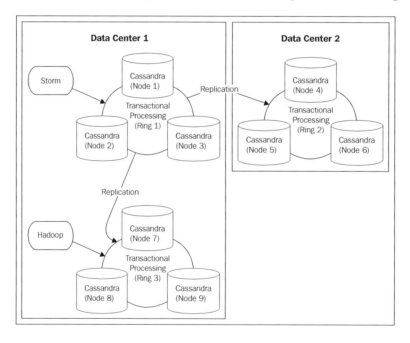

In the preceding diagram, we have two physical data centers, each with a Cassandra cluster servicing the transactional processing within Storm. This ensures that any write from the topology will replicate in real time to the data center, either before the tuple is acknowledged, if we use EACH_QUORUM consistency, or lazily, if we use LOCAL_QUORUM.

Additionally, we have a third *virtual* data center supporting the offline batch processing. **Ring 3** is a Cassandra cluster that is physically collocated with **Ring 1** but is configured as a second data center within Cassandra. When we run the Hadoop job to process the historical metrics, we can use a LOCAL_QUORUM. Since local quorum seeks to gain consensus within the local data center, read traffic from Hadoop will not cross over into our transactional processing cluster.

In general, this is a great pattern to deploy if your organization has data scientists/stewards that are running analyses on your data. Often, these jobs are data intensive. Isolating this workload from the transactional system is important.

Additionally, and arguably just as important as our ability to tolerate faults in the system, this architecture allows us to introduce new analytics into the system that we did not have at the time of data ingestion. Hadoop can run over all the relevant historical data using a new analytics configuration to populate new dimensions or perform additional aggregations.

Designing the topology for our use case

For this example, we will again use Trident and build on the topology that we constructed in the previous chapter. The Trident topology is depicted as follows:

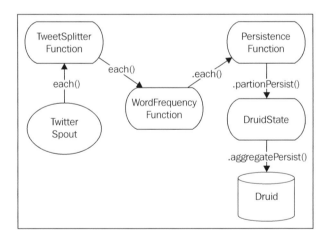

The TwitterSpout performs the search against the Twitter API periodically, emitting the tweets that it returns into a Trident stream. The TweetSplitterFunction then parses the tweets and emits a tuple for each word in the tweets. The WordFrequencyFunction enriches each tuple with the count for that word from a random sample of the English language. Finally, we let Druid consume that information to perform the aggregations over time. Druid partitions the data into temporal slices and persists that data as described previously.

In this case, because the persistence mechanism is our means of addressing fault tolerance/system failure, the persistence mechanism should distribute storage and provide both consistency and high-availability. Additionally, Hadoop should be capable of using the persistence mechanism as an input into a map/reduce job.

With its tunable consistency and support for Hadoop, Cassandra makes for an ideal persistence mechanism for this pattern. Since Cassandra and polyglot persistence are covered elsewhere, we will keep this example simple and use the local file storage.

Implementing the design

Let's first examine the real-time portion of the system beginning with the spout through to the Druid persistence. The topology is straightforward and mimics topologies we have written in previous chapters.

The following are the critical lines of the topology:

```
TwitterSpout spout = new TwitterSpout();
Stream inputStream = topology.newStream("nlp", spout);
try {
inputStream.each(new Fields("tweet"), new TweetSplitterFunction(), new
Fields("word"))
        .each(new Fields("searchphrase", "tweet", "word"), new
WordFrequencyFunction(), new Fields("baseline"))
        .each(new Fields("searchphrase", "tweet", "word",
"baseline"), new PersistenceFunction(), new Fields())
        .partitionPersist(new DruidStateFactory(), new
Fields("searchphrase", "tweet", "word", "baseline"), new
DruidStateUpdater());
} catch (IOException e) {
throw new RuntimeException(e);
}
return topology.build();
```

In the end, after parsing and enrichment, the tuples have four fields as shown in the following table:

Field name	Use
searchphrase	This field contains the search phrase being ingested. This is the phrase sent to the Twitter API. In reality, the system would most likely be monitoring multiple search phrases at a time. In this system, the value is hardcoded.

Field name	Use
tweet	This field contains tweets that are returned when searching the Twitter API for searchphrase. There is a 1:n relationship between searchphrase and tweet.
word	After parsing, this field contains the words found in the tweets. There is a 1:n relationship between tweet and word.
baseline	This field contains the count associated with the word in an ordinary sampled text. There is a 1:1 relationship between word and baseline.

TwitterSpout/TweetEmitter

Now, let's take a look at the spout/emitter. For this example, we will use the Twitter4J API, and the Emitter function is not much more than a thin glue layer between that API and the Storm API. As shown previously, it simply invokes the Twitter API using Twitter4J and emits all the results as a single batch within Storm.

In a more complex scenario, one might also tap into the Twitter Firehose and use a queue to buffer the live updates before emitting them into Storm. The following are the key lines in the Emitter portion of the spout:

```
query = new Query(SEARCH_PHRASE);
query.setLang("en");
result = twitter.search(query);
...
for (Status status : result.getTweets()) {
    List<Object> tweets = new ArrayList<Object>();
    tweets.add(SEARCH_PHRASE);
    tweets.add(status.getText());
    collector.emit(tweets);
}
```

Functions

This section covers the functions used in the topology. In this example, all the functions can either have side effects (for example, persistence) or they add fields and values to the tuple.

TweetSplitterFunction

The first function that the tweet passes through is the TweetSplitterFunction. This function simply parses the tweet and emits one tuple per word in the tweet. The code for this function is as follows:

```java
@Override
public void execute(TridentTuple tuple, TridentCollector collector) {
String tweet = (String) tuple.getValue(0);
LOG.debug("SPLITTING TWEET [" + tweet + "]");
Pattern p = Pattern.compile("[a-zA-Z]+");
Matcher m = p.matcher(tweet);
List<String> result = new ArrayList<String>();
    while (m.find()) {
        String word = m.group();
        if (word.length() > 0) {
          List<Object> newTuple = new ArrayList<Object>();
          newTuple.add(word);
          collector.emit(newTuple);
        }
    }
}
```

In a more sophisticated NLP system, this function will do more than simply split the tweet by whitespace. An NLP system would most likely try to parse the tweet, assigning parts of speech to the words and associating them with one another. Although, instant messages and tweets typically lack the traditional grammatical constructs that parsers are trained on, the system might still use elementary associations such as the distance between the words. In such systems, instead of word frequencies, systems use n-gram frequencies where each n-gram comprises multiple words.

To learn about the use of n-grams, visit http://books.google.com/ngrams.

WordFrequencyFunction

Now we move on to the WordFrequencyFunction. This function enriches the tuple with the baseline count. This is the number of times the word was encountered in a random sampled text.

The key code for this function is shown as follows:

```java
public static final long DEFAULT_BASELINE = 10000;
private Map<String, Long> wordLikelihoods =
new HashMap<String, Long>();

public WordFrequencyFunction() throws IOException {
File file = new File("src/main/resources/en.txt");
BufferedReader br = new BufferedReader(new FileReader(file));
String line;
while ((line = br.readLine()) != null) {
String[] pair = line.split(" ");
    long baseline = Long.parseLong(pair[1]);
    LOG.debug("[" + pair[0] + "]=>[" + baseline + "]");
    wordLikelihoods.put(pair[0].toLowerCase(), baseline);
    i++;
}
br.close();
}

@Override
public void execute(TridentTuple tuple,
TridentCollector collector) {
String word = (String) tuple.getValue(2);
Long baseline = this.getLikelihood(word);
List<Object> newTuple = new ArrayList<Object>();
newTuple.add(baseline);
collector.emit(newTuple);
}

public long getLikelihood(String word){
Long baseline = this.wordLikelihoods.get(word);
if (baseline == null)
return DEFAULT_BASELINE;
else
    return baseline;
}
```

The constructor in the code loads the word counts into the memory. The file format of `en.txt` is as follows:

```
you 4621939
the 3957465
i 3476773
to 2873389
...
of 1531878
that 1323823
in 1295198
is 1242191
me 1208959
what 1071825
```

Each line contains the word and the frequency count for that word. Again, since we are only worried about relative counts, we need not consider the total counts in the corpus. However, if we were calculating a true likelihood, we would need to consider the overall total word count as well.

The `execute` method of the function is straightforward and simply adds the baseline count to the tuple. However, if we examine the method that retrieves the count from the `HashMap` class, notice that it includes a `DEFAULT_BASELINE`. This is the value used when the system encounters a word that was not in the original corpus.

Since Twitter feeds contain many abbreviations, acronyms, and other terms that are not found typically in standard text, the `DEFAULT_BASELINE` becomes an important configuration parameter. In some cases, unique words are important and unique because they pertain to the `searchphrase` field. Others are anomalies because the sample corpus differs from the target corpus.

Ideally, the raw baseline counts would be drawn from the same source that the analytics are targeting. In this case, it would be ideal to have both word and n-gram counts calculated using the entire `Twitter Firehose`.

PersistenceFunction

We will not go into the details of a full multidata center Cassandra deployment here. Instead, for this example, we will keep it simple and use the local file storage. The code for the `PersistenceFunction` is as follows:

```
@Override
public void execute(TridentTuple tuple,
    TridentCollector collector) {
writeToLog(tuple);
```

```
collector.emit(tuple);
}

synchronized public void writeToLog(TridentTuple tuple) {
DateTime dt = new DateTime();
DateTimeFormatter fmt = ISODateTimeFormat.dateTime();
StringBuffer sb = new StringBuffer("{ ");
sb.append(String.format("\"utcdt\":\"%s\",", fmt.print(dt)));
sb.append(String.format("\"searchphrase\":\"%s\",", tuple.
getValue(0)));
sb.append(String.format("\"word\":\"%s\",", tuple.getValue(2)));
sb.append(String.format("\"baseline\":%s", tuple.getValue(3)));
sb.append("}");
BufferedWriter bw;
try {
bw = new BufferedWriter(new FileWriter("nlp.json", true));
bw.write(sb.toString());
    bw.newLine();
    bw.close();
} catch (IOException e) {
    throw new RuntimeException(e);
}
}
```

In the preceding code, the function simply persists the tuple in the native format that Druid expects to consume in the Hadoop indexing job. This code is inefficient in that we are opening up the file for writing each time. Alternatively, we could have implemented additional `StateFactory` and `State` objects that persisted the tuples; however, since this is just an example, we can tolerate the inefficient file access.

Additionally, notice that we generate a timestamp here that is not re-emitted with the tuple. Ideally, we would generate a timestamp and add it to the tuple, which would then be used downstream by Druid to align the temporal partitioning. For this example, we will accept the discrepancy.

Even though this function does not enrich the tuple at all, it must still re-emit the tuple. Since functions can also act as filters, it is the obligation of the function to declare which tuples are passed downstream.

The function writes the following lines to the `nlp.json` file:

```
{ "utcdt":"2013-08-25T14:47:38.883-04:00","searchphrase":"apple jobs",
"word":"his","baseline":279134}
{ "utcdt":"2013-08-25T14:47:38.884-04:00","searchphrase":"apple jobs",
"word":"annual","baseline":839}
{ "utcdt":"2013-08-25T14:47:38.885-04:00","searchphrase":"apple jobs",
"word":"salary","baseline":1603}
{ "utcdt":"2013-08-25T14:47:38.886-04:00","searchphrase":"apple jobs",
"word":"from","baseline":285711}
{ "utcdt":"2013-08-25T14:47:38.886-04:00","searchphrase":"apple jobs",
"word":"Apple","baseline":10000}
```

Examining the analytics

The Druid integration is the same that was used in the previous chapter. As a brief recap, this integration comprises the `StateFactory`, `StateUpdater`, and `State` implementations. The `State` implementation then communicates with a `StormFirehoseFactory` implementation and a `StormFirehose` implementation for Druid. At the heart of this implementation is the `StormFirehose` implementation, which maps the tuples into input rows for Druid. The listing for this method is shown as follows:

```
@Override
public InputRow nextRow() {
    final Map<String, Object> theMap =
Maps.newTreeMap(String.CASE_INSENSITIVE_ORDER);
try {
TridentTuple tuple = null;
    tuple = BLOCKING_QUEUE.poll();
    if (tuple != null) {
String phrase = (String) tuple.getValue(0);
        String word = (String) tuple.getValue(2);
        Long baseline = (Long) tuple.getValue(3);
        theMap.put("searchphrase", phrase);
        theMap.put("word", word);
        theMap.put("baseline", baseline);
}

    if (BLOCKING_QUEUE.isEmpty()) {
        STATUS.putInLimbo(TRANSACTION_ID);
        LIMBO_TRANSACTIONS.add(TRANSACTION_ID);
        LOG.info("Batch is fully consumed by Druid. Unlocking
[FINISH]");
```

```
        synchronized (FINISHED) {
            FINISHED.notify();
        }
    }
} catch (Exception e) {
LOG.error("Error occurred in nextRow.", e);
}
final LinkedList<String> dimensions = new LinkedList<String>();
dimensions.add("searchphrase");
dimensions.add("word");
return new MapBasedInputRow(System.currentTimeMillis(),
dimensions, theMap);
}
```

Looking at this method, there are two key data structures: `theMap` and `dimensions`. The first contains the data values for the row. The second contains the dimensions for that row, which is what Druid will use to perform the aggregations, and determines what queries you can run against the data. In this case, we will use the `searchphrase` and `word` fields as dimensions. This will allow us to perform counts and groupings in our queries, as we will see in a moment.

First, let's look at the Druid configuration for ingesting the data. We will largely use the same configuration for the embedded real-time server that we used in the previous chapter. Segments will be pushed to Cassandra for Deep Storage, while MySQL is used to write the segment metadata.

The following are the key configuration parameters from `runtime.properties`:

```
druid.pusher.cassandra=true
druid.pusher.cassandra.host=localhost:9160
druid.pusher.cassandra.keyspace=druid
druid.zk.service.host=localhost
druid.zk.paths.base=/druid
druid.host=127.0.0.1
druid.database.segmentTable=prod_segments
druid.database.user=druid
druid.database.password=druid
druid.database.connectURI=jdbc:mysql://localhost:3306/druid
druid.zk.paths.discoveryPath=/druid/discoveryPath
druid.realtime.specFile=./src/main/resources/realtime.spec
druid.port=7272
druid.request.logging.dir=/tmp/druid/realtime/log
```

This configuration points to the `realtime.spec` file, which is what specifies the details of the analytics performed by the real-time server. The following is the `realtime.spec` file for this use case:

```
[{
    "schema": {
        "dataSource": "nlp",
        "aggregators": [
            { "type": "count", "name": "wordcount" },
            { "type": "max", "fieldName": "baseline",
    name" : "maxbaseline" }
        ],
        "indexGranularity": "minute",
        "shardSpec": {"type": "none"}
    },

    "config": {
        "maxRowsInMemory": 50000,
        "intermediatePersistPeriod": "PT30s"
    },

    "firehose": {
        "type": "storm",
        "sleepUsec": 100000,
        "maxGeneratedRows": 5000000,
        "seed": 0,
        "nTokens": 255,
        "nPerSleep": 3
    },

    "plumber": {
        "type": "realtime",
        "windowPeriod": "PT10s",
        "segmentGranularity": "minute",
        "basePersistDirectory": "/tmp/nlp/basePersist"
    }
}]
```

In addition to the temporal granularities, we also specify the aggregators in this file. This tells Druid how to aggregate metrics between rows. Without aggregators, Druid cannot collapse the data. In this use case, there are two aggregators: `wordcount` and `maxbaseline`.

The `wordcount` field counts instances of rows that have the same values along the dimensions provided. Referring back to the `StormFirehose` implementation, the two dimensions are `searchphrase` and `word`. Thus, Druid can collapse the rows, adding a field named `wordcount`, which will contain the total count of the number of instances of that word found for that `searchphrase` and for that temporal slice.

The `maxbaseline` field contains the baseline for that word. In reality, the value for this is the same for each row. We simply use `max` as a convenient function to propagate the value into an aggregation that we can then use when we query the system.

Now, let's look at the query. The following is the query we use to retrieve the most relevant words:

```
{
    "queryType": "groupBy",
    "dataSource": "nlp",
    "granularity": "minute",
    "dimensions": ["searchphrase", "word"],
    "aggregations":[
        { "type": "longSum", "fieldName":"wordcount",
"name": "totalcount"},
        { "type": "max", "fieldName":"maxbaseline",
"name": "totalbaseline"}
    ],
    "postAggregations": [{
        "type": "arithmetic",
        "name": "relevance",
        "fn": "/",
        "fields": [
            { "type": "fieldAccess", "fieldName": "totalcount" },
            { "type": "fieldAccess", "fieldName": "totalbaseline" }
        ]
    }],
    "intervals":["2012-10-01T00:00/2020-01-01T00"]
}
```

The query needs to align with the `realtime.spec` file. At the bottom of the query, we specify the time interval in which we are interested. At the top of the file, we specify the dimensions in which we are interested, followed by the aggregations that allow Druid to collapse the rows to match the granularity requested. In this use case, the aggregations exactly match the aggregations that we are performing when indexing the data in real time.

Specifically, we introduce the `totalcount` field, which contains the sum of `wordcount`. This will therefore contain the total number of instances observed for that `word` and `searchphrase` combination. Additionally, we perform the same trick with `baseline` to pass that value through.

Finally, in this query, we include a post aggregation, which will combine the aggregations into a relevant score. The post aggregation divides the total count observed in the tweets by the baseline frequency.

The following is a simple Ruby file that processes the results of the query and returns the top 20 words:

```
. . .
url="http://localhost:7272/druid/v2/?pretty=true"
response = RestClient.post url, File.read("realtime_query"), :accept
=> :json, :content_type => 'appplication/json'
#puts(response)
result = JSON.parse(response.to_s)

word_relevance = {}
result.each do |slice|
   event = slice['event']
   word_relevance[event['word']]=event['relevance']
end

count = 0
word_relevance.sort_by {|k,v| v}.reverse.each do |word, relevance|
   puts("#{word}->#{relevance}")
   count=count+1
   if(count == 20) then
     break
   end
end
```

Notice that the URL we are using to access the server is the port of the embedded real-time server. In production, the queries go through a broker node.

Executing this script results in the following code snippet:

```
claiming->31.789579158316634
apple->27.325982081323225
purchase->20.985449735449734
Jobs->20.618
Steve->17.446
```

```
shares->14.802238805970148
random->13.480033984706882
creation->12.7524115755627
Apple->12.688
acts->8.82582081246522
prevent->8.702687877125618
farmer->8.640522875816993
developed->8.62642740619902
jobs->8.524986566362172
bottles->8.30523560209424
technology->7.535137701804368
current->7.21418826739427
empire->6.924050632911392
```

If you change the dimensions or metrics you are capturing, be sure to delete the local directory that the real-time server is using to cache the data. Otherwise, the real-time server may re-read old data that does not have the dimensions and/or metrics needed to fulfill the query; additionally, the query will fail because Druid is unable to find requisite metrics or dimensions.

Batch processing / historical analysis

Now, let's turn our attention to the batch processing mechanism. For this, we will use Hadoop. Although a complete description of Hadoop is well beyond the scope of this section, we will give a brief overview of Hadoop alongside the Druid-specific setup.

Hadoop provides two major components: a distributed file system and a distributed processing framework. The distributed file system is aptly named the **Hadoop Distributed Filesystem** (**HDFS**). The distributed processing framework is known as MapReduce. Since we chose to leverage Cassandra as our storage mechanism in the hypothetical system architecture, we will not need HDFS. We will, however, use the MapReduce portion of Hadoop to distribute the processing across all of the historical data.

In our simple example, we will run a local Hadoop job that will read the local file written in our `PersistenceFunction`. Druid comes with a Hadoop job that we will use in this example.

Hadoop

Before we jump to loading data, a quick overview of MapReduce is warranted. Although Druid comes prepackaged with a convenient MapReduce job to accommodate historical data, generally speaking, large distributed systems will need custom jobs to perform analyses over the entire data set.

An overview of MapReduce

MapReduce is a framework that breaks processing into two phases: a map phase and a reduce phase. In the map phase, a function is applied to the entire set of input data, one element at a time. Each application of the map function results in a set of tuples, each containing a key and a value. Tuples with similar keys are then combined via the reduce function. The reduce function emits another set of tuples, typically by combining the values associated with the key.

The canonical "Hello World" example for MapReduce is the word count. Given a set of documents that contain words, count the occurrences of each word. (Ironically, this is very similar to our NLP example.)

The following are Ruby functions that express the map and reduce functions for the word count example. The map function looks like the following code snippet:

```
def map(doc)
    result = []
doc.split(' ').each do |word|
result << [word, 1]
    end
    return result
end
```

The map function yields the following output, given the supplied input is as follows:

```
map("the quick fox jumped over the dog over and over again")
 => [["the", 1], ["quick", 1], ["fox", 1], ["jumped", 1], ["over",
1], ["the", 1], ["dog", 1], ["over", 1], ["and", 1], ["over", 1],
["again", 1]]
```

The corresponding reduce function looks like the following code snippet:

```
def reduce(key, values)
    sum = values.inject { |sum, x| sum + x }
    return [key, sum]
end
```

The MapReduce function would then group the values for each key and pass them to the preceding `reduce` function as follows, resulting in the total word count:

```
reduce("over", [1,1,1])
 => ["over", 3]
```

The Druid setup

With Hadoop as the background, let's take a look at our setup for Druid. In order for Druid to consume data from a Hadoop job, we need to start **Master** and **Compute** nodes (also known as **Historical** nodes). To do this, we will create a directory structure that has the Druid self-contained job at its root, with subdirectories that contain the configuration files for both the Master and Compute servers.

This directory structure looks like the following code snippet:

```
druid/druid-indexing-hadoop-0.5.39-SNAPSHOT.jar
druid/druid-services-0.5.39-SNAPSHOT-selfcontained.jar
druid/config/compute/runtime.properties
druid/config/master/runtime.properties
druid/batchConfig.json
```

The runtime properties for the Master and Compute nodes are largely the same as the real-time node with a few notable differences. They both include settings to cache segments as shown in the following code snippet:

```
# Path on local FS for storage of segments;
# dir will be created if needed
druid.paths.indexCache=/tmp/druid/indexCache
# Path on local FS for storage of segment metadata;
# dir will be created if needed
druid.paths.segmentInfoCache=/tmp/druid/segmentInfoCache
```

Also, note that if you are running the Master and Compute servers on the same machine, you will need to change the ports so that they do not conflict as follows:

```
druid.port=8082
```

Druid packages all the server components and their dependencies into a single self-contained JAR file. Using this JAR file, you can start the Master and Compute servers with the following commands.

For the Compute node, we use the following code snippet:

```
java -Xmx256m -Duser.timezone=UTC -Dfile.encoding=UTF-8 \
-classpath ./druid-services-0.5.39-SNAPSHOT-selfcontained.jar:config/
compute \
com.metamx.druid.http.ComputeMain
```

For the Master node, we use the following code snippet:

```
java -Xmx256m -Duser.timezone=UTC -Dfile.encoding=UTF-8 \
-classpath ./druid-services-0.5.39-SNAPSHOT-selfcontained.jar:config/
compute \
com.metamx.druid.http.ComputeMain
```

Once both nodes are running, we are ready to load data with the Hadoop job.

HadoopDruidIndexer

With our servers up and running, we can examine the internals of the Druid MapReduce job. The `HadoopDruidIndexer` function uses a JSON configuration file much like the `realtime.spec` file.

The file is specified on the command line when the Hadoop job is started, as shown in the following code snippet:

```
java -Xmx256m -Duser.timezone=UTC -Dfile.encoding=UTF-8 \
-Ddruid.realtime.specFile=realtime.spec -classpath druid-services-
0.5.39-SNAPSHOT-selfcontained.jar:druid-indexing-hadoop-0.5.39-
SNAPSHOT.jar \
com.metamx.druid.indexer.HadoopDruidIndexerMain batchConfig.json
```

The following is the `batchConfig.json` file we used in this example:

```
{
  "dataSource": "historical",
  "timestampColumn": "utcdt",
  "timestampFormat": "iso",
  "dataSpec": {
    "format": "json",
    "dimensions": ["searchphrase", "word"]
  },
  "granularitySpec": {
    "type":"uniform",
    "intervals":["2013-08-21T19/PT1H"],
    "gran":"hour"
  },
```

```
        "pathSpec": { "type": "static",
                      "paths": "/tmp/nlp.json" },
        "rollupSpec": {
                "aggs": [ { "type": "count", "name": "wordcount" },
                          { "type": "max", "fieldName": "baseline",
                                            "name" : "maxbaseline" } ],
           "rollupGranularity": "minute"},
           "workingPath": "/tmp/working_path",
        "segmentOutputPath": "/tmp/segments",
        "leaveIntermediate": "false",
        "partitionsSpec": {
          "targetPartitionSize": 5000000
        },
        "updaterJobSpec": {
          "type":"db",
          "connectURI":"jdbc:mysql://localhost:3306/druid",
          "user":"druid",
          "password":"druid",
          "segmentTable":"prod_segments"
        }
    }
}
```

Much of the configuration will look familiar. The two fields of particular interest are the `pathSpec` and `rollupSpec` fields. The `pathSpec` field contains the location of the file that was written by the `PersistenceFunction`. The `rollupSpec` field contains the same aggregation functions that we included in the `realtime.spec` file during transactional processing.

Additionally, notice that the timestamp column and format are specified, which aligns with the field that we are outputting in the persisted file:

```
{ "utcdt":"2013-08-25T14:47:38.883-04:00","searchphrase":"apple jobs",
"word":"his","baseline":279134}
{ "utcdt":"2013-08-25T14:47:38.884-04:00","searchphrase":"apple jobs",
"word":"annual","baseline":839}
{ "utcdt":"2013-08-25T14:47:38.885-04:00","searchphrase":"apple jobs",
"word":"salary","baseline":1603}
{ "utcdt":"2013-08-25T14:47:38.886-04:00","searchphrase":"apple jobs",
"word":"from","baseline":285711}
{ "utcdt":"2013-08-25T14:47:38.886-04:00","searchphrase":"apple jobs",
"word":"Apple","baseline":10000}
```

The `HadoopDruidIndexer` function loads the preceding configuration file and performs the `map`/`reduce` functions to construct the index. If we look more closely at that job, we can see the specific functions it is running.

Hadoop jobs are started using the Hadoop job class. Druid runs a couple of jobs to index the data, but we will focus on the `IndexGeneratorJob`. In the `IndexGeneratorJob`, Druid configures the job with the following lines:

```
job.setInputFormatClass(TextInputFormat.class);
job.setMapperClass(IndexGeneratorMapper.class);
job.setMapOutputValueClass(Text.class);
. . .
job.setReducerClass(IndexGeneratorReducer.class);
job.setOutputKeyClass(BytesWritable.class);
job.setOutputValueClass(Text.class);
job.setOutputFormatClass(IndexGeneratorOutputFormat.class);
FileOutputFormat.setOutputPath(job,config.makeIntermediatePath());
config.addInputPaths(job);
config.intoConfiguration(job);
. . .
job.setJarByClass(IndexGeneratorJob.class);
job.submit();
```

The preceding properties are set on nearly all Hadoop jobs. They set the input and output classes for each phase of the processing and the classes that implement the `Mapper` and `Reducer` interfaces.

For a complete description of Hadoop job configurations, visit the following URL: `http://hadoop.apache.org/docs/r0.18.3/mapred_tutorial.html#Job+Configuration`

The job configuration also specifies the input paths, which specify the files or other data sources for processing. Within the call to `config.addInputPaths`, Druid adds the files from the `pathSpec` field to the Hadoop configuration for processing, as shown in the following code snippet:

```
@Override
public Job addInputPaths(HadoopDruidIndexerConfig config,
Job job) throws IOException {
   log.info("Adding paths[%s]", paths);
   FileInputFormat.addInputPaths(job, paths);
   return job;
}
```

You can see that out-of-the-box, Druid only supports instances of `FileInputFormat`. As an exercise for the reader, it might be fun to enhance the `DruidHadoopIndexer` function to support direct reads from Cassandra, as envisioned in the hypothetical architecture.

Looking back at the job configuration, the `Mapper` class used by Druid is the `IndexGeneratorMapper` class, and the `Reducer` class is the `IndexGeneratorReducer` class.

Let's first have a look at the `map` function within the `IndexGeneratorMapper` class. The `IndexGeneratorMapper` class actually subclasses from `HadoopDruidIndexerMapper`, which contains the implementation of the `map` method, delegating it to the `IndexGeneratorMapper` class to emit the actual values, as we see in the following code.

Within `HadoopDruidIndexerMapper`, we see the `map` method implementation as follows:

```
@Override
protected void map(LongWritable key, Text value, Context context
  ) throws IOException, InterruptedException
  {
    try {
      final InputRow inputRow;
      try {
        inputRow = parser.parse(value.toString());
      }
      catch (IllegalArgumentException e) {
        if (config.isIgnoreInvalidRows()) {
          context.getCounter(HadoopDruidIndexerConfig.
IndexJobCounters.INVALID_ROW_COUNTER).increment(1);
          return; // we're ignoring this invalid row
        } else {
          throw e;
        }
      }
      if(config.getGranularitySpec().bucketInterval(new
DateTime(inputRow.getTimestampFromEpoch())).isPresent()) {
        innerMap(inputRow, value, context);
      }
    }
    catch (RuntimeException e) {
      throw new RE(e, "Failure on row[%s]", value);
    }
  }
```

We can see that the superclass map method handles rows that do not parse, marking them invalid, and checks to see if the row contains the necessary data to carry out the map. Specifically, the superclass ensures that the row contains a timestamp. The map requires the timestamp because it partitions the data into time slices (that is, buckets) as we see in the abstract method call to innerMap, which is shown as follows:

```
@Override
protected void innerMap(InputRow inputRow,
        Text text,
        Context context
    ) throws IOException, InterruptedException{

  // Group by bucket, sort by timestamp
  final Optional<Bucket> bucket = getConfig().getBucket(inputRow);

  if (!bucket.isPresent()) {
  throw new ISE("WTF?! No bucket found for row: %s", inputRow);
  }

  context.write(new SortableBytes(
            bucket.get().toGroupKey(),
            Longs.toByteArray(inputRow.getTimestampFromEpoch())
          ).toBytesWritable(),text);
  }
```

The key line in this method and in any Hadoop-based map function is the call to context.write that emits the tuple from the map function. In this case, the map function is emitting a key of the type SortableBytes, which represents the bucket for the metric and the actual text read from the input source as the value.

At this point, after the map phase completes, we have parsed the file, constructed our buckets, and partitioned the data into those buckets, sorted by timestamp. Each bucket is then processed via calls to the reduce method, which is shown as follows:

```
@Override
protected void reduce(BytesWritable key, Iterable<Text> values,
final Context context
    ) throws IOException, InterruptedException{
SortableBytes keyBytes = SortableBytes.fromBytesWritable(key);
Bucket bucket = Bucket.fromGroupKey(keyBytes.getGroupKey()).lhs;

final Interval interval =
config.getGranularitySpec().bucketInterval(bucket.time).get();
final DataRollupSpec rollupSpec = config.getRollupSpec();
```

```
final AggregatorFactory[] aggs = rollupSpec.getAggs().toArray(
        new AggregatorFactory[rollupSpec.getAggs().size()]);

IncrementalIndex index = makeIncrementalIndex(bucket, aggs);
...
for (final Text value : values) {
context.progress();
    final InputRow inputRow =
index.getSpatialDimensionRowFormatter()
.formatRow(parser.parse(value.toString()));
        allDimensionNames.addAll(inputRow.getDimensions());
    ...
IndexMerger.persist(index, interval, file,
index = makeIncrementalIndex(bucket, aggs);
    ...
    }
    ...
);
...
serializeOutIndex(context, bucket, mergedBase,
 Lists.newArrayList(allDimensionNames));
...
}
```

As you can see, the reduce method contains the meat of the analytics. It constructs the index based on the aggregations in the roll up specification and dimensions specified in the batch configuration file. The final lines of the method write the segment to a disk.

In the end, when you run the DruidHadoopIndexer class, you will see something similar to the following code snippet:

```
2013-08-28 04:07:46,405 INFO [main] org.apache.hadoop.mapred.JobClient
-   Map-Reduce Framework
2013-08-28 04:07:46,405 INFO [main] org.apache.hadoop.mapred.JobClient
-     Reduce input groups=1
2013-08-28 04:07:46,405 INFO [main] org.apache.hadoop.mapred.JobClient
-     Combine output records=0
2013-08-28 04:07:46,405 INFO [main] org.apache.hadoop.mapred.JobClient
-     Map input records=201363
2013-08-28 04:07:46,405 INFO [main] org.apache.hadoop.mapred.JobClient
-     Reduce shuffle bytes=0
2013-08-28 04:07:46,406 INFO [main] org.apache.hadoop.mapred.JobClient
-     Reduce output records=0
```

```
2013-08-28 04:07:46,406 INFO [main] org.apache.hadoop.mapred.JobClient
-     Spilled Records=402726
2013-08-28 04:07:46,406 INFO [main] org.apache.hadoop.mapred.JobClient
-     Map output bytes=27064165
2013-08-28 04:07:46,406 INFO [main] org.apache.hadoop.mapred.JobClient
-     Combine input records=0
2013-08-28 04:07:46,406 INFO [main] org.apache.hadoop.mapred.JobClient
-     Map output records=201363
2013-08-28 04:07:46,406 INFO [main] org.apache.hadoop.mapred.JobClient
-     Reduce input records=201363
2013-08-28 04:07:46,433 INFO [main] com.metamx.druid.indexer.
IndexGeneratorJob - Adding segment historical_2013-08-
28T04:00:00.000Z_2013-08-28T05:00:00.000Z_2013-08-28T04:07:32.243Z to
the list of published segments
2013-08-28 04:07:46,708 INFO [main] com.metamx.druid.indexer.
DbUpdaterJob - Published historical_2013-08-28T04:00:00.000Z_2013-08-
28T05:00:00.000Z_2013-08-28T04:07:32.243Z
2013-08-28 04:07:46,754 INFO [main] com.metamx.druid.indexer.
IndexGeneratorJob - Adding segment historical_2013-08-
28T04:00:00.000Z_2013-08-28T05:00:00.000Z_2013-08-28T04:07:32.243Z to
the list of published segments
2013-08-28 04:07:46,755 INFO [main] com.metamx.druid.indexer.
HadoopDruidIndexerJob - Deleting path[/tmp/working_path/
historical/2013-08-28T040732.243Z]
```

Notice that the segment added is named `historical`. To query the data loaded by the `historical` / batch processing mechanism, update the query to specify the historical data source and use the port of the Compute node. Provided everything is loaded properly, you will receive the aggregations we saw originally with the real-time server; an example of this is shown as follows:

```
{
  "version" : "v1",
  "timestamp" : "2013-08-28T04:06:00.000Z",
  "event" : {
    "totalcount" : 171,
    "totalbaseline" : 28719.0,
    "searchphrase" : "apple jobs",
    "relevance" : 0.005954246317768724,
    "word" : "working"
  }
}
```

Now, if we schedule the Hadoop job to run periodically, the historical index will lag the real-time index but will continually update the index, correcting errors and accounting for any system failures.

Summary

In this chapter, we saw that pairing a batch processing mechanism with a real-time processing engine such as Storm provides a more complete and robust overall solution.

We examined an approach to implementing a Lambda architecture. Such an approach delivers real-time analytics supported by a batch processing system retroactively correcting the analytics. Additionally, we saw how to configure a multidata center system architecture to isolate the offline processing from the transactional system while also providing continuous availability and fault tolerance via distributed storage.

The chapter also included an introduction to Hadoop, using Druid's implementation as an example.

In the next chapter, we will take an existing batch process that leverages Pig and Hadoop and demonstrate what it takes to convert that into a real-time system. At the same time, we will demonstrate how to deploy Storm onto the Hadoop infrastructure using Storm-YARN.

Deploying Storm on Hadoop for Advertising Analysis

In the previous two chapters, we saw how we might integrate Storm with a real-time analytics system. We then extended that implementation, supporting the real-time system with batch processing. In this chapter, we will explore the reverse.

We will examine a batch processing system that computes the effectiveness of an advertising campaign. We will take the system that was built on Hadoop and convert it into a real-time processing system.

To do this, we will leverage the Storm-YARN project out of Yahoo! The Storm-YARN project allows users to leverage YARN to deploy and run Storm clusters. The running of Storm on Hadoop allows enterprises to consolidate operations and utilize the same infrastructure for both real time and batch processing.

This chapter covers the following topics:

- An introduction to Pig
- YARN (resource management with Hadoop v2)
- Deploying Storm using Storm-YARN

Examining the use case

In our use case, we will process the logs of an advertising campaign to determine the most effective campaigns. The batch processing mechanism will process a single large flat file using a Pig script. Pig is a high-level language that allows users to perform data transformation and analysis. Pig is similar to SQL and compiles down into map/reduce jobs that typically deploy and run on Hadoop infrastructure.

In this chapter, we will convert the Pig script into a topology and deploy that topology using Storm-YARN. This allows us to transition from a batch processing approach to one that is capable of ingesting and reacting to real-time events (for example, clicks on a banner advertisement).

In advertising, an impression is an advertising event that represents an advertisement displayed in front of a user, regardless of whether or not it was clicked. For our analysis, we will track each impression and use a field to indicate whether the user clicked on the advertisement.

Each row in the flat file contains four fields that are described as follows:

Field	Description
cookie	This is a unique identifier from the browser. We will use this to represent users in the system.
campaign	This is a unique identifier that represents a specific set of advertising content.
product	This is the name of the product being advertised.
click-thru	This is the Boolean field that represents whether or not the user clicked on the advertisement: true if the user clicked on the ad; otherwise, false.

Typically, advertisers will run campaigns for products. A campaign may have a specific set of content associated with it. We want to calculate the most effective campaign per product.

In this context, we will calculate the effectiveness of a campaign by counting distinct click-thrus as a percentage of the overall impressions. We will deliver a report in the following format:

Product	Campaign	Distinct click-thrus	Impressions
X	Y	107	252

The number of impressions is simply the total count of impressions for the product and campaign. We do not distinct the impressions because we may have shown the same advertisement to the same user multiple times to attain a single click-thru. Since we are most likely paying per impression, we want to use the total number of impressions as a means of calculating the cost required to drive interest. Interest is represented as a click-thru.

Establishing the architecture

We touched on Hadoop in the previous chapter, but we focused mainly on the map/reduce mechanism within Hadoop. In this chapter, we will do the opposite and focus on the **Hadoop File System (HDFS)** and **Yet Another Resource Negotiator (YARN)**. We will leverage HDFS to stage the data, and leverage YARN to deploy the Storm framework that will host the topology.

The recent componentization within Hadoop allows any distributed system to use it for resource management. In Hadoop 1.0, resource management was embedded into the MapReduce framework as shown in the following diagram:

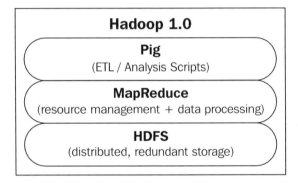

Hadoop 2.0 separates out resource management into YARN, allowing other distributed processing frameworks to run on the resources managed under the Hadoop umbrella. In our case, this allows us to run Storm on YARN as shown in the following diagram:

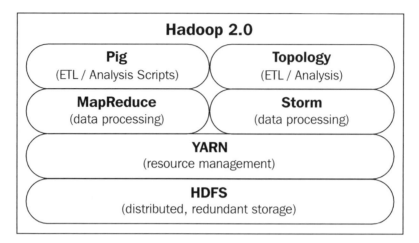

As shown in the preceding diagram, Storm fulfills the same function as MapReduce. It provides a framework for the distributed computation. In this specific use case, we use Pig scripts to articulate the ETL/analysis that we want to perform on the data. We will convert that script into a Storm topology that performs the same function, and then we will examine some of the intricacies involved in doing that transformation.

To understand this better, it is worth examining the nodes in a Hadoop cluster and the purpose of the processes running on those nodes. Assume that we have a cluster as depicted in the following diagram:

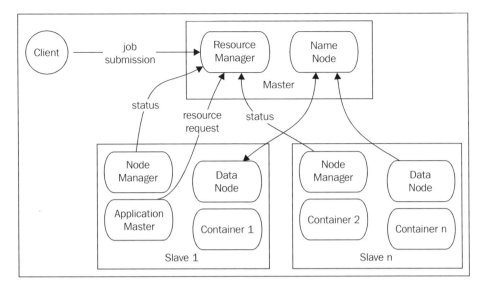

There are two different components/subsystems shown in the diagram. The first is YARN, which is the new resource management layer introduced in Hadoop 2.0. The second is HDFS. Let's first delve into HDFS since that has not changed much since Hadoop 1.0.

Examining HDFS

HDFS is a distributed filesystem. It distributes blocks of data across a set of slave nodes. The NameNode is the catalog. It maintains the directory structure and the metadata indicating which nodes have what information. The NameNode does not store any data itself, it only coordinates **create, read, update, and delete (CRUD)** operations across the distributed filesystem. Storage takes place on each of the slave nodes that run DataNode processes. The DataNode processes are the workhorses in the system. They communicate with each other to rebalance, replicate, move, and copy data. They react and respond to the CRUD operations of clients.

Examining YARN

YARN is the resource management system. It monitors the load on each of the nodes and coordinates the distribution of new jobs to the slaves in the cluster. The **ResourceManager** collects status information from the **NodeManagers**. The ResourceManager also services job submissions from clients.

One additional abstraction within YARN is the concept of an **ApplicationMaster**. An ApplicationMaster manages resource and container allocation for a specific application. The ApplicationMaster negotiates with the ResourceManager for the assignment of resources. Once the resources are assigned, the ApplicationMaster coordinates with the NodeManagers to instantiate **containers**. The containers are logical holders for the processes that actually perform the work.

The ApplicationMaster is a processing-framework-specific library. Storm-YARN provides the ApplicationMaster for running Storm processes on YARN. HDFS distributes the ApplicationMaster as well as the Storm framework itself. Presently, Storm-YARN expects an external ZooKeeper. Nimbus starts up and connects to the ZooKeeper when the application is deployed.

The following diagram depicts the Hadoop infrastructure running Storm via Storm-YARN:

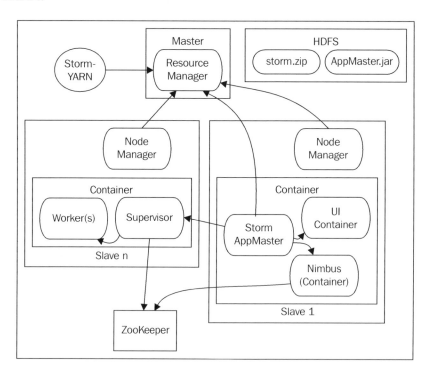

As shown in the preceding diagram, YARN is used to deploy the Storm application framework. At launch, Storm Application Master is started within a YARN container. That, in turn, creates an instance of Storm Nimbus and the Storm UI.

After that, Storm-YARN launches supervisors in separate YARN containers. Each of these supervisor processes can spawn workers within its container.

Both Application Master and the Storm framework are distributed via HDFS. Storm-YARN provides command-line utilities to start the Storm cluster, launch supervisors, and configure Storm for topology deployment. We will see these facilities later in this chapter.

To complete the architectural picture, we need to layer in the batch and real-time processing mechanisms: Pig and Storm topologies, respectively. We also need to depict the actual data.

Often a queuing mechanism such as Kafka is used to queue work for a Storm cluster. To simplify things, we will use data stored in HDFS. The following depicts our use of Pig, Storm, YARN, and HDFS for our use case, omitting elements of the infrastructure for clarity. To fully realize the value of converting from Pig to Storm, we would convert the topology to consume from Kafka instead of HDFS as shown in the following diagram:

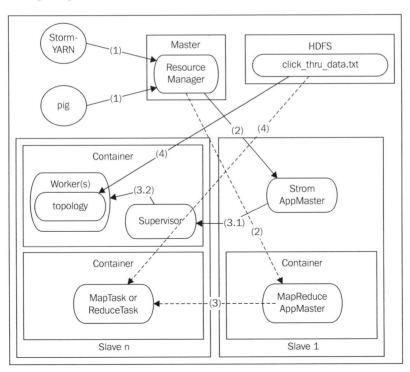

As the preceding diagram depicts, our data will be stored in HDFS. The dashed lines depict the batch process for analysis, while the solid lines depict the real-time system. In each of the systems, the following steps take place:

Step	Purpose	Pig Equivalent	Storm-Yarn Equivalent
1	The processing frameworks are deployed	The MapReduce Application Master is deployed and started	Storm-YARN launches Application Master and distributes Storm framework
2	The specific analytics are launched	The Pig script is compiled to MapReduce jobs and submitted as a job	Topologies are deployed to the cluster
3	The resources are reserved	Map and reduce tasks are created in YARN containers	Supervisors are instantiated with workers
4	The analyses reads the data from storage and performs the analyses	Pig reads the data out of HDFS	Storm reads the work, typically from Kafka; but in this case, the topology reads it from a flat file

Another analogy can be drawn between Pig and Trident. Pig scripts compile down into MapReduce jobs, while Trident topologies compile down into Storm topologies.

For more information on the Storm-YARN project, visit the following URL:

```
https://github.com/yahoo/storm-yarn
```

Configuring the infrastructure

First, we need to configure the infrastructure. Since Storm will run on the YARN infrastructure, we will first configure YARN and then show how to configure Storm-YARN for deployment on that cluster.

The Hadoop infrastructure

To configure a set of machines, you will need a copy of Hadoop residing on them or a copy that is accessible to each of them. First, download the latest copy of Hadoop and unpack the archive. For this example, we will use Version 2.1.0-beta.

Assuming that you have uncompressed the archive into `/home/user/hadoop`, add the following environment variables on each of the nodes in the cluster:

```
export HADOOP_PREFIX=/home/user/hadoop
export HADOOP_YARN_HOME=/home/user/hadoop
export HADOOP_CONF_DIR=/home/user/hadoop/etc/Hadoop
```

Add YARN to your execute path as follows:

```
export PATH=$PATH:$HADOOP_YARN_HOME/bin
```

All the Hadoop configuration files are located in `$HADOOP_CONF_DIR`. The three key configuration files for this example are: `core-site.xml`, `yarn-site.xml`, and `hdfs-site.xml`.

In this example, we will assume that we have a Master node named `master` and four slave-nodes named `slave01-04`.

Test the YARN configuration by executing the following command line:

```
$ yarn version
```

You should see output similar to the following:

```
Hadoop 2.1.0-beta
```

```
Subversion https://svn.apache.org/repos/asf/hadoop/common -r 1514472
```

```
Compiled by hortonmu on 2013-08-15T20:48Z
```

```
Compiled with protoc 2.5.0
```

```
From source with checksum 8d753df8229fd48437b976c5c77e80a
```

```
This command was run using /Users/bone/tools/hadoop-2.1.0-beta/share/
hadoop/common/hadoop-common-2.1.0-beta.jar
```

Configuring HDFS

As per the architecture diagram, to configure HDFS you need to start the NameNode and then connect one or more DataNode.

Configuring the NameNode

To start the NameNode, you need to specify a host and port. Configure the host and port in the `core-site.xml` file by using the following elements:

```
<configuration>
    <property>
        <name>fs.default.name</name>
        <value>hdfs://master:8020</value>
    </property>
</configuration>
```

Additionally, configure where the NameNode stores its metadata. This configuration is stored in the `hdfs-site.xml` file, in the `dfs.name.dir` variable.

To keep the example simple, we will also disable security on the distributed filesystem. To do this, we set `dfs.permissions` to `False`. After these edits, the HDFS configuration file looks like the following code snippet:

```
<configuration>
    <property>
        <name>dfs.name.dir</name>
        <value>/home/user/hadoop/name/data</value>
    </property>
    <property>
        <name>dfs.permissions</name>
        <value>false</value>
    </property>
</configuration>
```

The final step before starting the NameNode is the formatting of the distributed filesystem. Do this with the following command:

```
hdfs namenode -format <cluster_name>
```

Finally, we are ready to start the NameNode. Do so with the following command:

```
$HADOOP_PREFIX/sbin/hadoop-daemon.sh --config $HADOOP_CONF_DIR --script
hdfs start namenode
```

The last line of the startup will indicate where the logs are located:

```
starting namenode, logging to /home/user/hadoop/logs/hadoop-master.
hmsonline.com.out
```

Despite the message, the logs will actually be located in another file with the same name but with the suffix `log` instead of `out`.

Also, ensure that the name directory you declared in the configuration exists; otherwise, you will receive the following error in the logfile:

```
org.apache.hadoop.hdfs.server.common.
InconsistentFSStateException: Directory /home/user/
hadoop-2.1.0-beta/name/data is in an inconsistent
state: storage directory does not exist or is not
accessible.
```

Verify that the NameNode has started with the following code snippet:

```
boneill@master:~--> jps
30080 NameNode
```

Additionally, you should be able to navigate to the UI in a web browser. By default, the server starts on port 50070. Navigate to `http://master:50070` in a browser. You should see the following screenshot:

NameNode '   :8020' (active)

Started:	Mon Oct 07 21:25:06 EDT 2013
Version:	2.1.0-beta, 1514472
Compiled:	2013-08-15T20:48Z by hortonmu from branch-2.1.0-beta
Cluster ID:	CID-4784010b-4656-41f4-a58d-f55b5d5b4c6a
Block Pool ID:	BP-1724727417-10.13.10.76-1380028394770

Browse the filesystem
NameNode Logs

Cluster Summary

Security is OFF
651 files and directories, 608 blocks = 1259 total.
Heap Memory used 24.67 MB is 81% of Commited Heap Memory 30.44 MB. Max Heap Memory is 966.69 MB.
Non Heap Memory used 23.99 MB is 93% of Commited Non Heap Memory 25.69 MB. Max Non Heap Memory is 130 MB.

Configured Capacity	:	14.27 TB			
DFS Used	:	159.42 GB			
Non DFS Used	:	4.64 TB			
DFS Remaining	:	9.48 TB			
DFS Used%	:	1.09%			
DFS Remaining%	:	66.40%			
Block Pool Used	:	159.42 GB			
Block Pool Used%	:	1.09%			
DataNodes usages	:	Min %	Median %	Max %	stdev %
		0.25%	1.45%	1.45%	0.50%
Live Nodes	:	4 (Decommissioned: 0)			

Clicking on the **Live Nodes** link will show the nodes available and the space allocation per node, as shown in the following screenshot:

NameNode '   :8020'

Started:	Mon Oct 07 21:25:06 EDT 2013
Version:	2.1.0-beta, 1514472
Compiled:	2013-08-15T20:48Z by hortonmu from branch-2.1.0-beta
Cluster ID:	CID-4784010b-4656-41f4-a58d-f55b5d5b4c6a
Block Pool ID:	BP-1724727417-10.13.10.76-1380028394770

Browse the filesystem
NameNode Logs
Go back to DFS home

Live Datanodes : 4

Node	Last Contact	Admin State	Configured Capacity (TB)	Used (TB)	Non DFS Used (TB)	Remaining (TB)	Used (%)	Used (%)	Remaining (%)
	1	In Service	3.57	0.01	1.19	2.37	0.25		66.40
	1	In Service	3.57	0.04	1.16	2.37	1.21		66.40
	0	In Service	3.57	0.05	1.15	2.37	1.45		66.40
	2	In Service	3.57	0.05	1.15	2.37	1.45		66.40

Hadoop, 2013.

Finally, from the main page, you can also browse the filesystem by clicking on **Browse the filesystem**.

Configuring the DataNode

In general, it is easiest to share the core configuration file between nodes in the cluster. The data nodes will use the host and port defined in the `core-site.xml` file to locate the NameNode and connect to it.

Additionally, each DataNode needs to configure the location for local storage. This is defined in the following element within the `hdfs-site.xml` file:

```
<configuration>
    <property>
        <name>dfs.datanode.data.dir</name>
        <value>/vol/local/storage/</value>
    </property>
</configuration>
```

If this location is consistent across slave machines, then this configuration file can be shared as well. With this set, you can start the DataNode with the following command:

```
$HADOOP_PREFIX/sbin/hadoop-daemon.sh --config $HADOOP_CONF_DIR --script
hdfs start datanode
```

Once again, verify that the DataNode is running using `jps` and monitor the logs for any errors. In a few moments, the DataNode should appear in the **Live Nodes** screen of the NameNode as previously shown.

Configuring YARN

With HDFS up and running, it is now time to turn our attention to YARN. Similar to what we did with HDFS, we will first get the ResourceManager running and then we will attach slave nodes by running NodeManager.

Configuring the ResourceManager

The ResourceManager has various subcomponents, each of which acts as a server that requires a host and port on which to run. All of the servers are configured within the `yarn-site.xml` file.

For this example, we will use the following YARN configuration:

```
<configuration>
    <property>
        <name>yarn.resourcemanager.address</name>
        <value>master:8022</value>
    </property>
    <property>
        <name>yarn.resourcemanager.admin.address</name>
        <value>master:8033</value>
    </property>
    <property>
        <name>yarn.resourcemanager.resource-tracker.address</name>
         <value>master:8025</value>
    </property>
    <property>
        <name>yarn.resourcemanager.scheduler.address</name>
        <value>master:8030</value>
    </property>
    <property>
        <name>yarn.acl.enable</name>
        <value>false</value>
```

```
        </property>
        <property>
            <name>yarn.nodemanager.local-dirs</name>
            <value>/home/user/hadoop_work/mapred/nodemanager</value>
            <final>true</final>
        </property>
        <property>
            <name>yarn.nodemanager.aux-services</name>
            <value>mapreduce.shuffle</value>
        </property>
    </configuration>
```

The first four variables in the preceding configuration file assign host and ports for the subcomponents. Setting the `yarn.acl.enable` variable to `False` disables security on the YARN cluster. The `yarn.nodemanager.local-dirs` variable specifies the place on the local filesystem where YARN will place the data.

Finally, the `yarn.nodemanager.aux-services` variable starts an auxiliary service within the NodeManager's runtime to support MapReduce jobs. Since our Pig scripts compile down into MapReduce jobs, they depend on this variable.

Like the NameNode, start the ResourceManager with the following command line:

`$HADOOP_YARN_HOME/sbin/yarn-daemon.sh --config $HADOOP_CONF_DIR start resourcemanager`

Again, check for the existence of the process with `jps`, monitor the logs for exceptions, and then you should be able to navigate to the UI which by default runs on port 8088.

The UI is shown in the following screenshot:

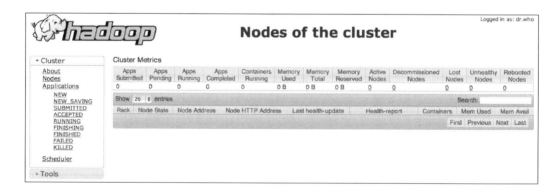

Configuring the NodeManager

The NodeManager uses the same configuration file (`yarn-site.xml`) to locate the respective servers. Thus, it is safe to copy or share that file between the nodes in the cluster.

Start the NodeManager with the following command:

```
$HADOOP_YARN_HOME/sbin/yarn-daemon.sh --config $HADOOP_CONF_DIR start
nodemanager
```

After all NodeManagers register with the ResourceManager, you will be able to see them in the ResourceManager UI after clicking on **Nodes**, as shown in the following screenshot:

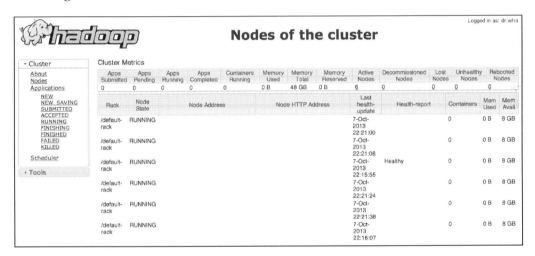

Deploying the analytics

With Hadoop in place, we can now focus on the distributed processing frameworks that we will use for analysis.

Performing a batch analysis with the Pig infrastructure

The first of the distributed processing frameworks that we will examine is Pig. Pig is a framework for data analysis. It allows the user to articulate analysis in a simple high-level language. These scripts then compile down to MapReduce jobs.

Although Pig can read data from a few different systems (for example, S3), we will use HDFS as our data storage mechanism in this example. Thus, the first step in our analysis is to copy the data into HDFS.

To do this, we issue the following Hadoop commands:

```
hadoop fs -mkdir /user/bone/temp
hadoop fs -copyFromLocal click_thru_data.txt /user/bone/temp/
```

The preceding commands create a directory for the data file and copy the click-thru data file into that directory.

To execute a Pig script against that data, we will need to install Pig. For this, we simply download Pig and expand the archive on that machine configured with Hadoop. For this example, we will use Version 0.11.1.

Just like we did with Hadoop, we will add the following environment variables to our environment:

```
export PIG_CLASSPATH=/home/user/hadoop/etc/hadoop
export PIG_HOME=/home/user/pig
export PATH=PATH:$HOME/bin:$PIG_HOME/bin:$HADOOP_YARN_HOME/bin
```

The `PIG_CLASSPATH` variable tells Pig where to find Hadoop.

Once you have those variables in your environment, you should be able to test your Pig installation with the following commands:

```
boneill@master:~-> pig
2013-10-07 23:35:41,179 [main] INFO  org.apache.pig.Main - Apache Pig
version 0.11.1 (r1459641) compiled Mar 22 2013, 02:13:53

...

2013-10-07 23:35:42,639 [main] INFO  org.apache.pig.backend.hadoop.
executionengine.HExecutionEngine - Connecting to hadoop file system at:
hdfs://master:8020

grunt>
```

By default, Pig will read the Hadoop configuration and connect to the distributed filesystem. You can see that in the previous output. It is connected to our distributed filesystem at `hdfs://master:8020`.

Via Pig, you can interact with HDFS in the same way as you would with a regular filesystem. For example, `ls` and `cat` both work as shown in the following code snippet:

```
grunt> ls /user/bone/temp/
hdfs://master:8020/user/bone/temp/click_thru_data.txt<r 3>        157

grunt> cat /user/bone/temp/click_thru_data.txt
boneill campaign7 productX true
lisalis campaign10 productX false
boneill campaign6 productX true
owen campaign6 productX false
collin campaign7 productY true
maya campaign8 productY true
boneill campaign7 productX true
owen campaign6 productX true
olive campaign6 productX false
maryanne campaign7 productY true
dennis campaign7 productY true
patrick campaign7 productX false
charity campaign10 productY false
drago campaign7 productY false
```

Performing a real-time analysis with the Storm-YARN infrastructure

Now that we have infrastructure working for batch processing, let's leverage the exact same infrastructure for real-time processing. Storm-YARN makes it easy to reuse the Hadoop infrastructure for Storm.

Since Storm-YARN is a new project, it is best to build from source and create the distribution using the instructions in the README file found at the following URL:

`https://github.com/yahoo/storm-yarn`

After building the distribution, you need to copy the Storm framework into HDFS. This allows Storm-YARN to deploy the framework to each of the nodes in the cluster. By default, Storm-YARN will look for the Storm library as a ZIP file in the launching user's directory on HDFS. Storm-YARN provides a copy of a compatible Storm in the `lib` directory of its distribution.

Assuming that you are in the Storm-YARN directory, you can copy the ZIP file into the correct HDFS directory with the following commands:

```
hadoop fs -mkdir /user/bone/lib/
hadoop fs -copyFromLocal ./lib/storm-0.9.0-wip21.zip /user/bone/lib/
```

You can then verify that the Storm framework is HDFS by browsing the filesystem through the Hadoop administration interface. You should see the following screenshot:

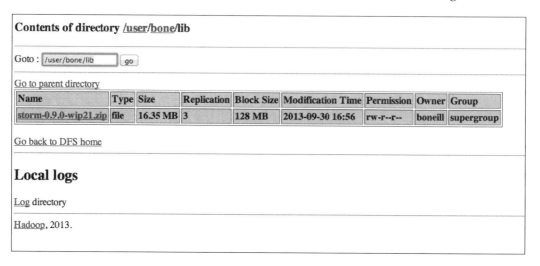

With the Storm framework staged on HDFS, the next step is to configure the local YAML file for Storm-YARN. The YAML file used with Storm-YAML is the configuration for both Storm-YAML and Storm. The Storm-specific parameters in the YAML file get passed along to Storm.

An example of the YAML file is shown in the following code snippet:

```
master.host: "master"
master.thrift.port: 9000
master.initial-num-supervisors: 2
master.container.priority: 0
master.container.size-mb: 5120
master.heartbeat.interval.millis: 1000
master.timeout.secs: 1000
yarn.report.wait.millis: 10000
nimbusui.startup.ms: 10000
```

```
ui.port: 7070

storm.messaging.transport: "backtype.storm.messaging.netty.Context"
storm.messaging.netty.buffer_size: 1048576
storm.messaging.netty.max_retries: 100
storm.messaging.netty.min_wait_ms: 1000
storm.messaging.netty.max_wait_ms: 5000

storm.zookeeper.servers:
    - "zkhost"
```

Many of the parameters are self-descriptive. However, take note of the last variable in particular. This is the location of the ZooKeeper host. Although it might not be the case always, for now Storm-YARN assumes you have a pre-existing ZooKeeper.

To monitor whether Storm-YARN will continue to require a pre-existing ZooKeeper instance, go through the information available at the following link:

https://github.com/yahoo/storm-yarn/issues/22

With the the Storm framework in HDFS and the YAML file configured, the command line to launch Storm on YARN is the following:

```
storm-yarn launch ../your.yaml --queue default -appname storm-yarn-2.1.0-
deta-demo --stormZip lib/storm-0.9.0-wip21.zip
```

You specify the location of the YAML file, the queue for YARN, a name for the application, and the location of the ZIP file, which is relative to the user directory unless a full path is specified.

Queues in YARN are beyond the scope of this discussion, but by default YARN is configured with a default queue that is used in the preceding command line. If you are running Storm on a pre-existing cluster, examine capacity-scheduler.xml in the YARN configuration to locate potential queue names.

After executing the preceding command line, you should see the application deployed in the YARN administration screen, as shown in the following screenshot:

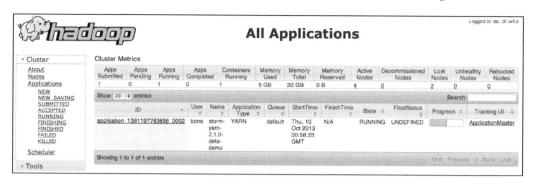

Clicking on the application shows where the application master is deployed. Examine the node value for the Application Master. This is where you will find the Storm UI as shown in the following screenshot:

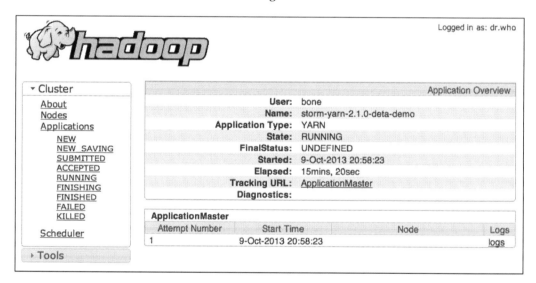

Drilling down one more level, you will be able to see the logfiles for Storm, as shown in the following screenshot:

Logs for
container_1381197763696_0003_01_000001

- ▾ ResourceManager
  - RM Home
- ▸ NodeManager
- ▸ Tools

nimbus.log : Total file length is 16156 bytes.
stderr : Total file length is 9196 bytes.
stdout : Total file length is 4640 bytes.
ui.log : Total file length is 296 bytes.

With any luck, the logs will show a successful startup of Nimbus and the UI. Examining the standard output stream, you will see Storm-YARN launching the supervisors:

```
13/10/09 21:40:10 INFO yarn.StormAMRMClient: Use NMClient to launch
supervisors in container.
13/10/09 21:40:10 INFO impl.ContainerManagementProtocolProxy: Opening
proxy : slave05:35847
13/10/09 21:40:12 INFO yarn.StormAMRMClient: Supervisor
log: http://slave05:8042/node/containerlogs/
container_1381197763696_0004_01_000002/boneill/supervisor.log
13/10/09 21:40:14 INFO yarn.MasterServer: HB: Received allocated
containers (1) 13/10/09 21:40:14 INFO yarn.MasterServer: HB:
Supervisors are to run, so queueing (1) containers...
13/10/09 21:40:14 INFO yarn.MasterServer: LAUNCHER: Taking container
with id (container_1381197763696_0004_01_000004) from the queue.
13/10/09 21:40:14 INFO yarn.MasterServer: LAUNCHER:
Supervisors are to run, so launching container id
(container_1381197763696_0004_01_000004)
13/10/09 21:40:16 INFO yarn.StormAMRMClient: Use NMClient to
launch supervisors in container.  13/10/09 21:40:16 INFO impl.
ContainerManagementProtocolProxy: Opening proxy : dlwolfpack02.
hmsonline.com:35125
13/10/09 21:40:16 INFO yarn.StormAMRMClient: Supervisor
log: http://slave02:8042/node/containerlogs/
container_1381197763696_0004_01_000004/boneill/supervisor.log
```

The key lines in the preceding output are highlighted. If you navigate to those URLs, you will see the supervisor logs for the respective instances. Looking back at the YAML file we used to launch Storm-YARN, notice that we specified the following:

```
master.initial-num-supervisors: 2
```

Navigate to the UI using the node that hosts the ApplicationMaster, and then navigate to the UI port specified in the YAML file used for launch (ui.port: 7070).

In a browser, open `http://node:7070/`, where node is the host for the Application Master. You should see the familiar Storm UI as shown in the following screenshot:

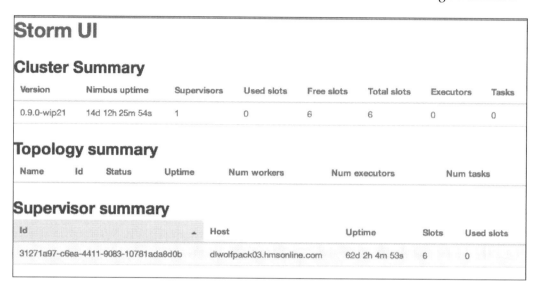

Storm UI

Cluster Summary

Version	Nimbus uptime	Supervisors	Used slots	Free slots	Total slots	Executors	Tasks
0.9.0-wip21	14d 12h 25m 54s	1	0	6	6	0	0

Topology summary

Name	Id	Status	Uptime	Num workers	Num executors	Num tasks

Supervisor summary

Id	Host	Uptime	Slots	Used slots
31271a97-c6ea-4411-9083-10781ada8d0b	dlwolfpack03.hmsonline.com	62d 2h 4m 53s	6	0

The infrastructure is now ready for use. To kill the Storm deployment on YARN, you can use the following command:

```
./storm-yarn shutdown -appId application_1381197763696_0002
```

In the preceding statement, the `appId` parameter corresponds to the `appId` parameter assigned to Storm-YARN, and it is visible in the Hadoop administration screen.

> Storm-YARN will use the local Hadoop configuration to locate the master Hadoop node. If you are launching from a machine that is not a part of the Hadoop cluster, you will need to configure that machine with the Hadoop environment variables and configuration files. Specifically, it launches through the ResourceManager. Thus, you will need the following variables configured in `yarn-site.xml`:
>
> `yarn.resourcemanager.address`

Performing the analytics

With both the batch and real-time infrastructure in place, we can focus on the analytics. First, we will take a look at the processing in Pig, and then we will translate the Pig script into a Storm topology.

Executing the batch analysis

For the batch analysis, we use Pig. The Pig script calculates the effectiveness of a campaign by computing the ratio between the distinct numbers of customers that have clicked-thru and the total number of impressions.

The Pig script is shown in the following code snippet:

```
click_thru_data = LOAD '../click_thru_data.txt' using PigStorage(' ')
  AS (cookie_id:chararray,
      campaign_id:chararray,
      product_id:chararray,
      click:chararray);

click_thrus = FILTER click_thru_data BY click == 'true';
distinct_click_thrus = DISTINCT click_thrus;
distinct_click_thrus_by_campaign = GROUP distinct_click_thrus BY
campaign_id;
count_of_click_thrus_by_campaign = FOREACH distinct_click_thrus_by_
campaign GENERATE group, COUNT($1);
-- dump count_of_click_thrus_by_campaign;

impressions_by_campaign = GROUP click_thru_data BY campaign_id;
count_of_impressions_by_campaign = FOREACH impressions_by_campaign
GENERATE group, COUNT($1);
-- dump count_of_impressions_by_campaign;

joined_data = JOIN count_of_impressions_by_campaign BY $0 LEFT OUTER,
count_of_click_thrus_by_campaign BY $0 USING 'replicated';
-- dump joined_data;

result = FOREACH joined_data GENERATE $0 as campaign, ($3 is null
? 0 : $3) as clicks, $1 as impressions, (double)$3/(double)$1 as
effectiveness:double;
dump result;
```

Let's take a closer look at the preceding code.

The first LOAD statement specifies the location of the data and a schema with which to load the data. Typically, Pig loads denormalized data. The location for the data is a URL. When operating in local mode, as previously shown, this is a relative path. When running in MapReduce mode, the URL will most likely be a location in HDFS. When running a Pig script against **Amazon Web Services (AWS)**, this will most likely be an S3 URL.

In the subsequent lines after the Load statement, the script calculates all the distinct click-thru. In the first line, it filters the dataset for only the rows that have True in the column, which indicates that the impression resulted in a click-thru. After filtering, the rows are filtered for only distinct entries. The rows are then grouped by campaign and each distinct click-thru is counted by campaign. The results of this analysis are stored in the alias count_of_click_thrus_by_campaign.

The second dimension of the problem is then computed in the subsequent lines. No filter is necessary since we simply want a count of the impressions by campaign. The results of this are stored in the alias count_of_impressions_by_campaign.

Executing the Pig script yields the following output:

```
(campaign6,2,4,0.5)
(campaign7,4,7,0.5714285714285714)
(campaign8,1,1,1.0)
(campaign10,0,2,)
```

The first element in the output is the campaign identifier. The number of all the distinct click-thru and the total number of impressions follow that. The last element is the effectiveness, which is the ratio of all the distinct click-thru to total number of impressions.

Executing real-time analysis

Now, let's translate the batch analysis into real-time analysis. A strict interpretation of the Pig script might result in the following topology:

```
Stream inputStream = topology.newStream("clickthru", spout);
Stream click_thru_stream = inputStream.each(
new Fields("cookie", "campaign", "product", "click"),
new Filter("click", "true"))
.each(new Fields("cookie", "campaign", "product", "click"),
new Distinct())
                .groupBy(new Fields("campaign"))
                .persistentAggregate(
new MemoryMapState.Factory(), new Count(),
new Fields("click_thru_count"))
                .newValuesStream();
```

```
Stream impressions_stream = inputStream.groupBy(
new Fields("campaign"))
                .persistentAggregate(
new MemoryMapState.Factory(), new Count(),
new Fields("impression_count"))
                .newValuesStream();


topology.join(click_thru_stream, new Fields("campaign"),
impressions_stream, new Fields("campaign"),
  new Fields("campaign", "click_thru_count", "impression_count"))
                .each(new Fields("campaign",
"click_thru_count", "impression_count"),
new CampaignEffectiveness(), new Fields("")));
```

In the preceding topology, we fork the stream into two separate streams: click_thru_stream and impressions_stream. The click_thru_stream contains the count of distinct impressions. The impressions_stream contains the total count of impressions. Those two streams are then joined using the topology.join method.

The issue with the preceding topology is the join. In Pig, since the sets are static they can easily be joined. Joins within Storm are done on a per batch basis. This would not necessarily be a problem. However, the join is also an inner join, which means records are only emitted if there are corresponding tuples between the streams. In this case, we are filtering records from the click_thru_stream because we only want distinct records. Thus, the cardinality of that stream is smaller than that of the impressions_stream, which means that tuples are lost in the join process.

Operations such as join are well defined for discrete sets, but it is unclear how to translate their definitions into a real-time world of infinite event streams. For more on this, visit the following URLs:

- https://cwiki.apache.org/confluence/display/PIG/Pig+on+Storm+Proposal
- https://issues.apache.org/jira/browse/PIG-3453

Instead, we will use Trident's state construct to share the counts between the streams.

This is shown in the corrected topology in the following diagram:

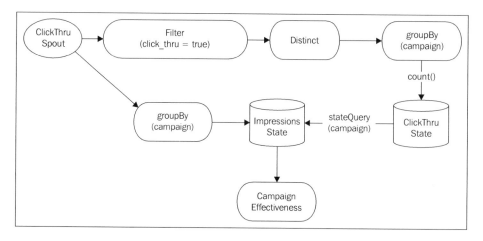

The code for this topology is as follows:

```
StateFactory clickThruMemory = new MemoryMapState.Factory();
ClickThruSpout spout = new ClickThruSpout();
Stream inputStream = topology.newStream("clithru", spout);
TridentState clickThruState = inputStream.each(
new Fields("cookie", "campaign", "product", "click"),
new Filter("click", "true"))
    .each(new Fields("cookie", "campaign", "product", "click"),
new Distinct())
    .groupBy(new Fields("campaign"))
    .persistentAggregate(clickThruMemory, new Count(),
new Fields("click_thru_count"));

inputStream.groupBy(new Fields("campaign"))
.persistentAggregate(new MemoryMapState.Factory(),
new Count(), new Fields("impression_count"))
.newValuesStream()
.stateQuery(clickThruState, new Fields("campaign"),
new MapGet(), new Fields("click_thru_count"))
.each(new Fields("campaign", "impression_count",
     "click_thru_count"),
new CampaignEffectiveness(), new Fields(""));
```

Let's first take a look at the spout. It simply reads the file, parses the rows, and emits the tuples, as shown in the following code snippet:

```
public class ClickThruEmitter
implements Emitter<Long>, Serializable {
...
@Override
public void emitBatch(TransactionAttempt tx,
Long coordinatorMeta, TridentCollector collector) {
    File file = new File("click_thru_data.txt");
    try {
        BufferedReader br =
new BufferedReader(new FileReader(file));
        String line = null;
        while ((line = br.readLine()) != null) {
         String[] data = line.split(" ");
         List<Object> tuple = new ArrayList<Object>();
         tuple.add(data[0]); // cookie
         tuple.add(data[1]); // campaign
         tuple.add(data[2]); // product
         tuple.add(data[3]); // click
         collector.emit(tuple);
        }
        br.close();
    } catch (Exception e) {
        throw new RuntimeException(e);
    }
}
    ...
}
```

In a real system, the preceding spout would most likely read from a Kafka queue. Alternatively, a spout could read directly from HDFS if we sought to recreate exactly what the batch processing mechanism was doing.

 There is some preliminary work on a spout that can read from HDFS; check out the following URL for more information:
`https://github.com/jerrylam/storm-hdfs`

To compute the distinct count of all the click-thru, the topology first filters the stream for only those impressions that resulted in a click-thru.

The code for this filter is as follows:

```
public class Filter extends BaseFilter {
    private static final long serialVersionUID = 1L;
    private String fieldName = null;
    private String value = null;

    public Filter(String fieldName, String value){
        this.fieldName = fieldName;
        this.value = value;
    }

    @Override
    public boolean isKeep(TridentTuple tuple) {
        String tupleValue = tuple.getStringByField(fieldName);
        if (tupleValue.equals(this.value)) {
          return true;
        }
        return false;
    }
}
```

Then, the stream filters for only distinct click-thrus. In this example, it uses an in-memory cache to filter for distinct tuples. In reality, this should use distributed state and/or a grouping operation to direct like tuples to the same host. Without persistent storage, the example would eventually run out of memory in the JVM.

 There is active work on algorithms to approximate distinct sets against data streams. For more information on **Streaming Quotient Filter (SQF)**, check out the following URL:

```
http://www.vldb.org/pvldb/vol6/p589-dutta.pdf
```

For our example, the Distinct function is shown in the following code snippet:

```
public class Distinct extends BaseFilter {
    private static final long serialVersionUID = 1L;
    private Set<String> distincter = Collections.synchronizedSet(new HashSet<String>());

    @Override
    public boolean isKeep(TridentTuple tuple) {
        String id = this.getId(tuple);
```

```
        return distincter.add(id);
      }

    public String getId(TridentTuple t){
        StringBuilder sb = new StringBuilder();
        for (int i = 0; i < t.size(); i++){
           sb.append(t.getString(i));
        }
        return sb.toString();
    }
  }
}
```

Once it has all the distinct click-thru, Storm persists that information into Trident
state using a call to persistAggregate. This collapses the stream by using the
Count operator. In the example, we use a MemoryMap. However, in a real system
we would most likely apply a distributed storage mechanism such as Memcache
or Cassandra.

The result of processing the initial stream is a TridentState object that contains the
count of all the distinct click-thru grouped by the campaign identifier. The critical
line that *joins* the two streams is shown as follows:

```
.stateQuery(clickThruState, new Fields("campaign"),
new MapGet(), new Fields("click_thru_count"))
```

This incorporates the state developed in the initial stream into the analysis developed
by the second stream. Effectively, the second stream queries the state mechanism for
the distinct count of all the click-thru for that campaign and adds it as a field to the
tuples processed in this stream. That field can then be leveraged in the effectiveness
computation, which is encapsulated in the following class:

```
public class CampaignEffectiveness extends BaseFunction {
    private static final long serialVersionUID = 1L;

    @Override
    public void execute(TridentTuple tuple, TridentCollector
collector) {
    String campaign = (String) tuple.getValue(0);
        Long impressions_count = (Long) tuple.getValue(1);
        Long click_thru_count = (Long) tuple.getValue(2);
        if (click_thru_count == null)
            click_thru_count = new Long(0);
        double effectiveness = (double) click_thru_count / (double)
impressions_count;
```

```
      Log.error("[" + campaign + "," + String.valueOf(click_thru_count) +
 "," + impressions_count + ", " + effectiveness + "]");
      List<Object> values = new ArrayList<Object>();
      values.add(campaign);
      collector.emit(values);
        }
  }
```

As shown in the preceding code, this class computes effectiveness by computing the ratio between the field that contains the total count and the field introduced by the state query.

Deploying the topology

To deploy the preceding topology, we must first retrieve the Storm-YAML configuration using the following command:

```
storm-yarn getStormConfig ../your.yaml --appId
application_1381197763696_0004 --output output.yaml
```

The preceding command interacts with the specified instance of the Storm-YARN application to retrieve a `storm.yaml` file that can be used to deploy topologies by using the standard mechanisms. Simply copy the `output.yaml` file into the appropriate location (typically, `~/.storm/storm.yaml`) and deploy using the standard `storm jar` command as follows:

```
storm jar <appJar>
```

Executing the topology

Executing the preceding topology results in the following output:

```
00:00 ERROR: [campaign10,0,2, 0.0]
00:00 ERROR: [campaign6,2,4, 0.5]
00:00 ERROR: [campaign7,4,7, 0.5714285714285714]
00:00 ERROR: [campaign8,1,1, 1.0]
```

Notice that the values are the same as those emitted by Pig. If we let the topology run, we eventually see decreasing effectiveness scores as shown in the following output:

```
00:03 ERROR: [campaign10,0,112, 0.0]
00:03 ERROR: [campaign6,2,224, 0.008928571428571428]
00:03 ERROR: [campaign7,4,392, 0.01020408163265306]
00:03 ERROR: [campaign8,1,56, 0.017857142857142856]
```

This stands to reason because we now have a real-time system, which is continually consuming the same impression events. Since we are only counting all the distinct click-thru and the entire set of click-thru has already been accounted for in the calculation, the effectiveness will continue to drop.

Summary

In this chapter, we saw a few different things. First, we saw the blueprint for converting a batch processing mechanism that leverages Pig into a real-time system that is implemented in Storm. We saw how a direct translation of that script would not work due to the limitations of joins in a real-time system, because traditional join operations require finite set of data. To overcome this problem, we used a shared state pattern with the forked streams.

Secondly, and perhaps most importantly, we examined Storm-YARN; it allows a user to reuse the Hadoop infrastructure to deploy Storm. Not only does this provide a means for existing Hadoop users to quickly transition to Storm, it also allows a user to capitalize on cloud mechanisms for Hadoop such as Amazon's **Elastic Map Reduce (EMR)**. Using EMR, Storm can be deployed quickly to cloud infrastructure and scaled to meet demand.

Finally, as future work, the community is exploring methods to run Pig scripts directly on Storm. This would allow users to directly port their existing analytics over to Storm.

To monitor this work, visit `https://cwiki.apache.org/confluence/display/PIG/Pig+on+Storm+Proposal`.

In the next chapter, we will explore automated Storm deployment to the cloud using Apache Whirr. Although not specifically addressed, the techniques in the next chapter can be used in cloud deployments.

10
Storm in the Cloud

In this chapter, we will introduce you to deploying and running Storm in a hosted environment of a cloud provider.

In *Chapter 2*, *Configuring Storm Clusters*, you were introduced to the steps necessary to set up Storm in a clustered environment, and the subsequent chapters covered the installation and configuration of complementary technologies such as Kafka, Hadoop, and Cassandra. While most installations are relatively straightforward, the cost to maintain even a modestly sized cluster—in terms of the physical asset requirements as well as the time necessary to configure and maintain the environment—can easily become a burden, if not an outright blocker to the adoption of distributed computing technologies.

Fortunately, today there are a number of cloud hosting providers that offer services for on-demand dynamic provisioning of multimachine computing environments. Most cloud hosting providers offer a wide range of services and options to fit most users' needs, ranging from a single small footprint server to a large-scale infrastructure consisting of hundreds or even thousands of machines. In fact, a common trend among high-profile Internet content providers is to choose a cloud hosting provider over an in-house data center.

One of the key benefits of using a cloud provider is the ability to deploy and undeploy computing resources as necessary, and on demand. An online retailer, for example, might provision additional servers and resources during the lead up to the holiday season in order to meet demand, scaling back later when the rush subsides. Also, as we'll see, cloud providers offer a cost-effective method for testing and prototyping distributed applications.

We'll start by provisioning a Storm cluster with a cloud provider. Later in the chapter, we'll show you how to provision and manage local, virtualized Storm instances for testing Storm applications in a fully clustered environment on your workstation.

In this chapter, we will cover the following topics:

- Provisioning virtual machines using the **Amazon Web Services** (**AWS**) **Elastic Compute Cloud** (**EC2**)

- Using Apache Whirr to automate the provisioning and deployment of Storm clusters to EC2

- Using Vagrant to launch and provision virtualized Storm clusters in a local environment for development and testing

Introducing Amazon Elastic Compute Cloud (EC2)

Amazon EC2 is the central part of many remote compute services offered by Amazon. EC2 allows users to rent virtual compute resources hosted on Amazon's network infrastructure on demand.

We'll begin by setting up an EC2 account and manually launching a virtual machine on Amazon's EC2 infrastructure.

Setting up an AWS account

Establishing an AWS account is easy but requires an Amazon account. If you don't already have an Amazon account, sign up for one at `http://www.amazon.com/`.

With your Amazon account established, you can set up an AWS account at `http://aws.amazon.com/`.

The AWS Management Console

The **AWS Management Console** acts as the main administrative interface to all the cloud services that Amazon offers. We're primarily interested in the EC2 service, so let's begin by logging in to the EC2 Management Console as shown in the following screenshot:

Creating an SSH key pair

Before you can launch any EC2 instances, you will need a key pair. To create a new key pair, click on the **Key Pairs** link to open the key pair manager, as shown in the following screenshot:

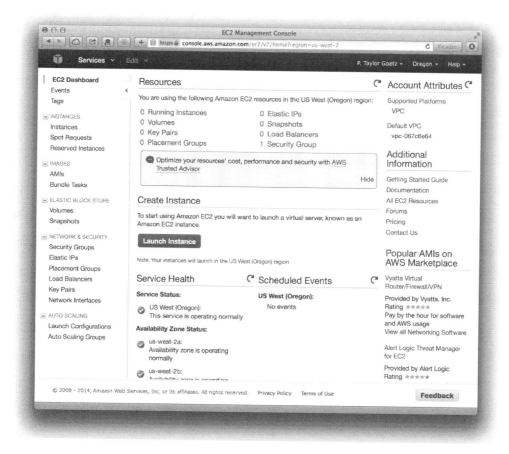

You will be prompted to give the key pair a name. Enter a name and click on the **Yes** button. At this point, depending on which browser you are using, you will be prompted to download your private certificate file or the file will be downloaded automatically.

It's very important that you keep this file safe since the key will give you full administrator access to any EC2 images launched with that key. Immediately after downloading your private key, you should change its file permissions so it is not publicly readable; for example, with UNIX, use the following command:

```
chmod 400 my-keyfile.pem
```

Many SSH clients will look at the permissions of the key file and issue a warning or refuse to use a key file that is publicly readable.

Launching an EC2 instance manually

Once you have created a key pair, you are ready to launch an EC2 instance.

The first step in launching an EC2 machine is to select an **Amazon Machine Image (AMI)**. An AMI is a virtual appliance template that can be run as a virtual machine on Amazon EC2.

Amazon provides a number of AMIs for popular operating system distributions such as Red Hat, Ubuntu, and SUSE. For our purposes, we will be using an Ubuntu Server instance as shown in the following screenshot:

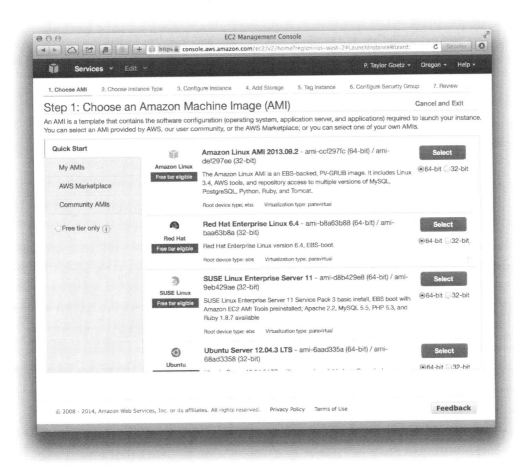

Once you've selected an AMI, you will be prompted to select an **instance type**. Instance types represent virtual hardware profiles with varying memory (RAM), CPU cores, storage, and I/O performance. Amazon charges by the hour for running instances, with prices ranging from a few cents per hour for its weakest instance type (**t1.micro**) to several dollars per hour for its most powerful instance type (**hs1.8xlarge**). The type you select will depend on your use case and budget. For example, a **t1.micro** instance (one CPU, 0.6 GB RAM, and low I/O performance) can be useful for testing purposes but is clearly not suited for heavy production loads.

After selecting an instance type, you are ready to launch the virtual machine by clicking on the **Review and Launch** button, reviewing the instance details, and then clicking on **Launch**. You will then be prompted to select a key pair for remote login and management of the instance. After a few minutes, your instance will be up and running as shown in the following screenshot:

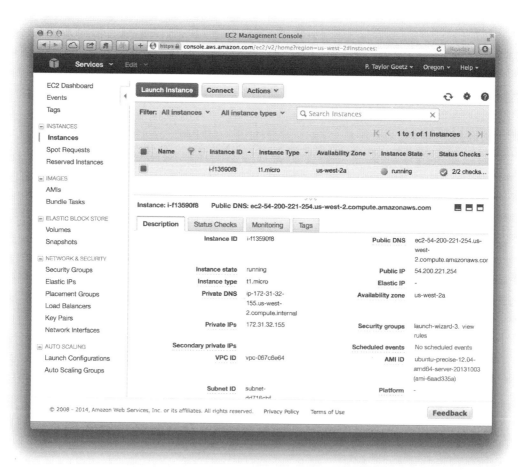

Logging in to the EC2 instance

When you launch an instance, EC2 will preconfigure SSH with the key pair you selected during the setup, allowing you to remotely log in to the machine. To log in to the instance remotely, you will need the private key file you downloaded earlier as well as the public DNS name (or public IP address) assigned to the instance. You can find this information in the EC2 Management Console by clicking on the instance and viewing the details.

You can now connect to the instance with the following command:

```
ssh -i [keypair] [username]@[public DNS or IP]
```

For example, to connect as the "ubuntu" user using the `my-keypair.pem` private key file:

```
ssh -i my-keypair.pem ubuntu@ec2-54-200-221-254.us-west-2.compute.
amazonaws.com
```

The Ubuntu user has administrator permissions on the remote host, giving you the ability to configure the machine the way you like.

At this point, you could install Storm or any other services you like. However, manually configuring instances for anything larger than a trivially sized cluster will quickly become time-consuming and unmanageable. In the next section, we'll introduce a way to automate this process as part of a more scalable workflow.

Introducing Apache Whirr

The Apache Whirr project (`http://whirr.apache.org`) provides a Java API and set of shell scripts for installing and running various services on cloud providers such as Amazon EC2 and Rackspace. Whirr allows you to define the layout of a cluster in terms of the number of nodes as well as control which services run on each node. Whirr also comes with a set of scripts for performing management operations such as launching new clusters, starting and stopping clusters, and terminating clusters.

Whirr began as a set of shell scripts for running Hadoop on Amazon EC2, and later matured to include a Java API based on the Apache jclouds (`http://jclouds.apache.org`) project, which allowed it to support multiple cloud providers. Whirr has also expanded beyond Hadoop to support many additional distributed computing services such as Cassandra, Elastic Search, HBase, Pig, and others.

Installing Whirr

Begin by downloading a recent release and unpacking it on the computer you will use to launch and manage your clusters:

```
wget http://www.apache.org/dist/whirr/whirr-0.8.2/whirr-0.8.2.tar.gz
tar -zxf whirr-0.8.2.tar.gz
```

For convenience, add Whirr's `bin` directory to your system's `PATH` environment variable so you can run the Whirr command from any directory as follows:

```
WHIRR_HOME=/Users/tgoetz/whirr-0.8.2
export PATH=$PATH:$WHIRR_HOME/bin
```

Whirr uses SSH to communicate with cloud instances, so we will create a dedicated key pair for using it with Whirr. Whirr requires that the key has an empty passphrase as shown in the following command:

```
ssh-keygen -t rsa -P '' -f ~/.ssh/id_rsa_whirr
```

In order for Whirr to interact with your cloud provider account, it needs to know your credentials. For EC2, this consists of your EC2 Access Key ID and your EC2 Secret Access Key. If your AWS account is new, you will need to generate new credentials; otherwise, you should already have downloaded your credentials to a safe location. To generate a new set of EC2 credentials, perform the following steps:

1. Log in to the **AWS Management Console**.
2. Click on the name in the top-right section of the navigation bar and select **Security Credentials**.
3. Expand the section titled **Access Keys (Access Key ID and Secret Access Key)** and click on the **Create New Access Key** button.
4. Click on the **Download Key File** to download your credentials to a safe location.

The key file you downloaded will contain your Access Key ID and Secret Access Key in the following format:

```
AWSAccessKeyId=QRIXIUUTWRXXXXTPW4UA
AWSSecretKey=/oA7m/XW+x1eGQiyxxxTsU+rxRSIxxxx3EbM1yg6
```

Whirr gives you three options for specifying your cloud credentials: command-line parameters, cluster configuration file, or a local credentials file (`~/.whirr/credentials`). We'll use the last option as it is the most convenient as follows:

```
mkdir ~/.whirr
echo "PROVIDER=aws-ec2" > ~/.whirr/credentials
echo "IDENTITY=[your EC2 Access Key ID]" >> ~/.whirr/credentials
echo "CREDENTIAL=[your EC2 Secret Access Key]" >> ~/.whirr/credentials
```

Configuring a Storm cluster with Whirr

Now that we have Whirr installed, let's turn our attention toward cluster configuration. Whirr's configuration files, or recipes, are just Java property files that contain Whirr properties which define the layout of nodes and services within a cluster.

Let's start by looking at the minimum configuration necessary to launch a 3-node ZooKeeper cluster:

```
whirr.cluster-name=zookeeper
whirr.instance-templates=3 zookeeper
```

The `whirr.cluster-name` property simply assigns a unique identifier to the cluster and is used when running management commands such as listing the hosts in a cluster or destroying a cluster.

The `whirr.instance-template` property defines the number of nodes in a cluster and the services that run on each node. In the preceding example, we've defined a cluster of three nodes, with each node assigned with the ZooKeeper role.

With just these two properties defined, we have enough to tell Whirr how to launch and manage a ZooKeeper cluster. Whirr will use default values for everything else. However, there are a few options that you will typically want to override. For example, we'll want Whirr to use the dedicated key pair we created earlier as shown in the following code snippet:

```
whirr.private-key-file=${sys:user.home}/.ssh/id_rsa_whirr
whirr.public-key-file=${whirr.private-key-file}.pub
```

Next, we'll configure Whirr with the hardware specification we want and the region in which our cluster should be hosted, as shown in the following code snippet:

```
whirr.image-id=us-east-1/ami-55dc0b3c
whirr.hardware-id=t1.micro
whirr.location=us-east-1
```

The `whirr.image-id` property is provider specific and specifies which machine image to use. Here, we've specified an Ubuntu 10.04 64-bit AMI.

Since we're just testing Whirr, we've chosen the smallest (and least expensive) instance type: `t1.micro`. Finally, we've specified that we want our cluster deployed in the `us-east-1` region.

For a complete list of public AMIs, perform the following steps:

1. From the EC2 Management Console, select a region from the drop-down menu in the upper-right corner.
2. In the left navigation pane, click on **AMIs**.
3. From the **Filter** drop-down menu at the top of the page, select **Public images**.

Whirr is most thoroughly tested with Ubuntu Linux images. While other operating systems may work, if you run into problems, try again with an Ubuntu image.

Launching the cluster

Our configuration file for a ZooKeeper cluster now looks like the following code snippet:

```
whirr.cluster-name=zookeeper
whirr.instance-templates=3 zookeeper
whirr.private-key-file=${sys:user.home}/.ssh/id_rsa_whirr
whirr.public-key-file=${whirr.private-key-file}.pub
whirr.image-id=us-east-1/ami-55dc0b3c
whirr.hardware-id=t1.micro
whirr.location=us-east-1
```

If we save those properties to a file named `zookeeper.properties`, we can then launch the cluster with the following command:

```
whirr launch-cluster --config zookeeper.properties
```

When the command completes, Whirr will output the list of instances created as well as the SSH command that can be used to connect to each instance.

You can log in to instances using the following SSH commands:

```
[zookeeper]: ssh -i /Users/tgoetz/.ssh/id_rsa_whirr -o
"UserKnownHostsFile /dev/null" -o StrictHostKeyChecking=no
storm@54.208.197.231
```

```
[zookeeper]: ssh -i /Users/tgoetz/.ssh/id_rsa_whirr -o
"UserKnownHostsFile /dev/null" -o StrictHostKeyChecking=no
storm@54.209.143.46

[zookeeper]: ssh -i /Users/tgoetz/.ssh/id_rsa_whirr -o
"UserKnownHostsFile /dev/null" -o StrictHostKeyChecking=no
storm@54.209.22.63
```

To destroy a cluster, run `whirr destroy-cluster` with the same options used to launch it.

When you are finished with the cluster, you can terminate all instances with the following command:

```
whirr destroy-cluster --config zookeeper.properties
```

Introducing Whirr Storm

The Whirr Storm project (`https://github.com/ptgoetz/whirr-storm`) is a Whirr service implementation for configuring Storm clusters. Whirr Storm supports the configuration of all Storm daemons as well as full control over Storm's `storm.yaml` configuration file.

Setting up Whirr Storm

To install the Whirr Storm service, simply place the JAR file in the `$WHIRR_HOME/lib` directory as follows:

```
wget http://repo1.maven.org/maven2/com/github/ptgoetz/whirr-
storm/1.0.0/whirr-storm-1.0.0.jar -P $WHIRR_HOME/lib
```

Next, verify the installation by running the `whirr` command without arguments to print a list of instance roles available to Whirr. The list should now include the roles provided by Whirr Storm as shown in the following code snippet:

```
$ whirr
...
  storm-drpc
  storm-logviewer
  storm-nimbus
  storm-supervisor
  storm-ui
```

Cluster configuration

In our previous Whirr example, we created a cluster of three nodes where each node had only the ZooKeeper role. Whirr allows you to assign multiple roles to a node, which we'll need to do for a Storm cluster. Before we get into the details of configuring Whirr for Storm, let's take a look at the different roles Whirr Storm defines as shown in the following table:

Role	Description
storm-nimbus	This is the role for running the Nimbus daemon. Only one node per cluster should be assigned with this role.
storm-supervisor	This is the role for running the supervisor daemon.
storm-ui	This is the role for running the Storm UI web service.
storm-logviewer	This is the role for running the Storm logviewer service. This role should only be assigned to nodes that also have the storm-supervisor role.
storm-drpc	This is the role for running the Storm DRPC service.
zookeeper	This role is provided by Whirr. Nodes with this role will be part of a ZooKeeper cluster. You must have at least one ZooKeeper node in a Storm cluster, and for multi-node ZooKeeper clusters, the number of nodes should be odd.

To use these roles in a Whirr configuration, we specify them in the whirr.instance-template property in the following format:

```
whirr.instance-templates=[# of nodes] [role 1]+[role 2],[# of nodes]
[role 3]+[role n]
```

For example, to create a single-node pseudocluster, where all Storm's daemons are run on one machine, we would use the following value for whirr.instance-template:

```
whirr.instance-template=1 storm-nimbus+storm-ui+storm-logviewer+storm-
supervisor+zookeeper
```

If we wanted to create a multinode cluster with one node running Nimbus and Storm UI, three nodes running the supervisor and logviewer daemons, and a 3-node ZooKeeper cluster, we would use the following configuration:

```
whirr.instance-templates=1 storm-nimbus+storm-ui,3 storm-
supervisor+storm-logviewer, 3 zookeeper
```

Customizing Storm's configuration

Whirr Storm will generate a `storm.yaml` configuration file with values for `nimbus.host`, `storm.zookeeper.servers`, and `drpc.servers` that are automatically calculated based on the hostnames of nodes in the cluster and which roles they have been assigned with. All other Storm configuration parameters will inherit default values unless specifically overridden. Note that if you attempt to override values for `nimbus.host`, `storm.zookeeper.servers`, or `drpc.servers`, Whirr Storm will ignore it and log a warning message.

> Although Whirr Storm will automatically calculate and configure the `nimbus.host` value for the cluster, you will still need to tell the Storm executable the host name of the Nimbus host when running the command locally. The easiest way to do this, and the most convenient if you have multiple clusters, is to specify a hostname for nimbus with the `-c` flag as follows:
>
> ```
> Storm <command> [arguments] -c nimbus.host=<nimbus
> hostname>
> ```

Other Storm configuration parameters can be specified in the Whirr configuration file by adding a property with a key prefixed with `whirr-storm`. For example, to set a value for the `topology.message.timeout.secs` parameter, we would add it to the Whirr configuration file as follows:

```
whirr-storm.topology.message.timeout.secs=30
```

The preceding code would result in the following line in `storm.yaml`:

```
topology.message.timeout.secs: 30
```

Configuration parameters that accept a list of values can be expressed in the Whirr configuration file as a comma-separated list, such as the following configuration for `supervisor.slots.ports`:

```
whirr-storm.supervisor.slots.ports=6700,6701,6702,6703
```

The preceding code would produce the following YAML:

```
supervisor.slots.ports:
    - 6700
    - 6701
    - 6702
    - 6703
```

Customizing firewall rules

When a new machine instance is launched on EC2, most of its network ports are blocked by a firewall by default. To enable network communication between instances, you must explicitly configure firewall rules to allow ingress and egress on specific ports between hosts.

By default, Whirr Storm will automatically create the security groups and firewall rules necessary for Storm components to communicate, such as opening the Nimbus Thrift port for topology submission and opening port 2181 between **Nimbus** and **Supervisor** nodes, and ZooKeeper nodes as shown in the following diagram:

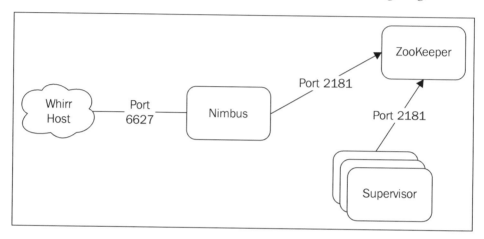

However, in many cases, Storm's worker processes will need to communicate with other services on arbitrary ports. For example, if you have a spout that consumes data from an external queue or a bolt that writes to a database, you will need additional firewall rules to enable that interaction.

Consider a scenario where we have a spout reading data from a Kafka queue and streaming data to a bolt that writes to a Cassandra database. In such scenarios, we would set up our cluster with the following `whirr.instance-template` value:

```
whirr.instance-templates=3 kafka,3 cassandra,1 storm-nimbus,3 storm-
supervisor, 3 zookeeper
```

With this setup, we need a firewall configuration that allows each of the Supervisor/ worker nodes to connect to each of the Kafka nodes on port 9092 and each of the Cassandra nodes on port 9126, as shown in the following diagram:

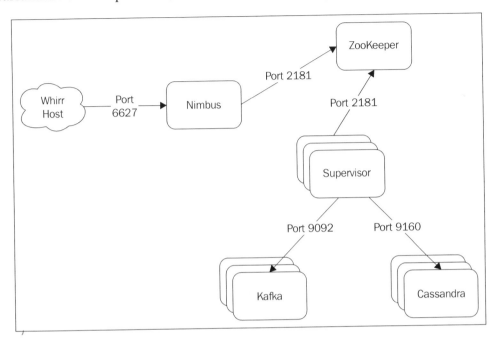

For this situation, Whirr Storm has the configuration property `whirr.storm.supervisor.firewall-rules` that allows you to open arbitrary ports on other nodes in the cluster. The property value is a comma-delimited list of role-port pairs as shown in the following code snippet:

```
whirr.storm.supervisor.firewall-rules=[role1]:[port1],[role2]:[port2]
```

For example, to set up the rules for our scenario, we would use the following setting:

```
whirr.storm.supervisor.firewall-rules=cassandra:9160,kafka:9092
```

This configuration will instruct Whirr Storm to create firewall rules that allow each Supervisor node to connect to each Cassandra node on port 9160 and each Supervisor node to connect to each Kafka node on port 9092.

Introducing Vagrant

Vagrant (http://www.vagrantup.com) is a tool similar to Apache Whirr in that it's designed to help provision virtual machine instances in an easy and repeatable manner. However, Whirr and Vagrant differ in a key way. While Whirr's primary purpose is to enable cloud-based provisioning, Vagrant focuses more on local virtualization with virtualization software such as VirtualBox and VMWare.

Vagrant supports several virtual machine providers, including VirtualBox (https://www.virtualbox.org) and VMWare (http://www.vmware.com). In this chapter, we'll cover the use of Vagrant with VirtualBox since it is free and well supported by Vagrant.

Prior to using Vagrant, you must install a 4.x Version of VirtualBox (Vagrant does not yet support Version 5.x). We covered the VirtualBox installation in *Chapter 2, Configuring Storm Clusters,* and will not repeat those instructions here. Installing VirtualBox is largely just a matter of running an installer, but if you run into issues, please refer to the instructions in *Chapter 2, Configuring Storm Clusters.*

Installing Vagrant

Linux packages and Vagrant installers for OS X and Windows are available on the Vagrant website (http://www.vagrantup.com/downloads.html). Be sure to install the latest version of Vagrant as it will include the most recent updates and bug fixes. The installation process will update your system's PATH variable to include the Vagrant executable. You can verify the installation by opening a terminal and typing vagrant --version as follows:

```
$ vagrant --version
Vagrant 1.3.5
```

If the command fails for any reason, consult the Vagrant website for solutions to common problems.

Launching your first virtual machine

Launching a virtual machine with Vagrant involves two steps. First, you initialize a new Vagrant project with the vagrant init command as follows:

```
$ vagrant init precise64 http://files.vagrantup.com/precise64.box
```

```
A `Vagrantfile` has been placed in this directory. You are now
ready to `vagrant up` your first virtual environment! Please read
the comments in the Vagrantfile as well as documentation on
`vagrantup.com` for more information on using Vagrant.
```

The two arguments to the `vagrant init` command are `name` and `URL` for a Vagrant *box*. A Vagrant box is a virtual machine image that is specially packaged for use with Vagrant. Since Vagrant boxes can be quite large (over 300 MB), Vagrant will store them locally on the disk rather than download them every time. The `name` parameter simply provides an identifier for the box, so it can be reused in other Vagrant configurations, while the `URL` parameter tells Vagrant about the download location for the box.

The next step is to launch the virtual machine as follows:

```
$ vagrant up
```

If the Vagrant box specified in the `vagrant init` command is not found on the local disk, Vagrant will download it. Vagrant will then clone the virtual machine, boot it, and configure networking so it is easily accessible from the host machine. When the command completes, a VirtualBox virtual machine running Ubuntu 12.04 LTS 64-bit will be running in the background.

You can then log in to the machine using SSH commands:

```
$ vagrant ssh
Welcome to Ubuntu 12.04 LTS (GNU/Linux 3.2.0-23-generic x86_64)


 * Documentation:  https://help.ubuntu.com/
Welcome to your Vagrant-built virtual machine.
Last login: Fri Sep 14 06:23:18 2012 from 10.0.2.2
vagrant@precise64:~$
```

The Vagrant user has administrative privileges so you are free to do anything you like with the virtual machine, such as install software packages and modify files. When you are finished with the virtual machine, you can shut it down and remove all traces of it with the `vagrant destroy` command:

```
$ vagrant destroy
Are you sure you want to destroy the 'default' VM? [y/N] y
[default] Forcing shutdown of VM...
[default] Destroying VM and associated drives...
```

Vagrant provides additional management commands for operations such as suspending, resuming, and halting the virtual machine. For an overview of the commands Vagrant provides, run the `vagrant --help` command.

The Vagrantfile and shared filesystem

When we ran the `vagrant init` command, Vagrant created a file named `Vagrantfile` in the directory where we ran the command. This file describes the type of machine(s) a project requires and how to provision and set up the machines. Vagrantfiles are written using a Ruby syntax that is easy to learn even if you are not a Ruby developer. The initial content of the `Vagrantfile` will be minimal and largely made up of documentation comments. With the comments removed, our Vagrant file looks like the following code snippet:

```
VAGRANTFILE_API_VERSION = "2"

Vagrant.configure(VAGRANTFILE_API_VERSION) do |config|
  config.vm.box = "precise64"
  config.vm.box_url = "http://files.vagrantup.com/precise64.box"
end
```

As you can see, the file simply contains the box name and URL that we passed to the `vagrant init` command. We will expand on this later as we build out a Vagrant project to provision a virtualized Storm cluster.

When you launch a machine with `vagrant up`, by default Vagrant will create a shared folder on the virtual machine (`/vagrant`) that will be synchronized with the contents of the project directory (the directory containing the `Vagrantfile`). You can verify this functionality by logging in to the virtual machine and listing the contents of that directory

```
$ vagrant ssh
vagrant@precise64:~$ ls /vagrant/
Vagrantfile
```

This is where we will store all our provisioning scripts and data files. While the `vagrant destroy` command removes all traces of a virtual machine, it leaves the contents of the project directory untouched. This allows us to store persistent project data that will always be available to our virtual machines.

Vagrant provisioning

Vagrant supports provisioning with shell scripts as well Puppet and Chef. We'll use the shell provisioner since it is the easiest to start with as it does not require any additional knowledge aside from basic shell scripting.

To illustrate how Vagrant shell provisioning works, we'll modify our Vagrant project to install the Apache web server in the Vagrant virtual machine. We will begin by creating a simple shell script to install Apache2 using Ubuntu's APT package manager. Save the following script as `install_apache.sh` in the same directory as the `Vagrantfile`:

```
#!/bin/bash
apt-get update
apt-get install -y apache2
```

Next, we'll modify our `Vagrantfile` to execute our script when Vagrant provisions our virtual machine by adding the following line:

```
config.vm.provision "shell", path: "install_apache.sh"
```

Finally, configure port forwarding so requests to port 8080 on the host machine are forwarded to port 8080 on the guest (virtual) machine:

```
config.vm.network "forwarded_port", guest: 80, host: 8080
```

Our complete Vagrantfile should now look like the following:

```
VAGRANTFILE_API_VERSION = "2"

Vagrant.configure(VAGRANTFILE_API_VERSION) do |config|
  config.vm.box = "precise64"
  config.vm.box_url = "http://files.vagrantup.com/precise64.box"
  config.vm.provision "shell", path: "install_apache.sh"
  config.vm.network "forwarded_port", guest: 80, host: 8080
end
```

If your virtual machine is still running, kill it now by running `vagrant destroy`, then execute `vagrant up` to bring up a new virtual machine. When Vagrant completes, you should be able to view the default Apache page by pointing your browser to `http://localhost:8080` on the host machine.

Configuring multimachine clusters with Vagrant

In order to model a virtualized Storm cluster with Vagrant, we need a way to configure multiple machines within a single Vagrant project. Fortunately, Vagrant supports multiple machines with a syntax that makes it easy to convert our existing single-machine project into a multimachine configuration.

For our multimachine setup, we'll define two virtual machines named www1 and www2. To avoid port conflicts on the host machine, we'll forward the host port 8080 to port 80 on www1 and the host port 7070 to port 80 on www2, as shown in the following code snippet:

```
VAGRANTFILE_API_VERSION = "2"

Vagrant.configure(VAGRANTFILE_API_VERSION) do |config|

  config.vm.define "www1" do |www1|
    www1.vm.box = "precise64"
    www1.vm.box_url = "http://files.vagrantup.com/precise64.box"
    www1.vm.provision "shell", path: "apache.sh"
    www1.vm.network "forwarded_port", guest: 80, host: 8080
  end

  config.vm.define "www2" do |www2|
    www2.vm.box = "precise64"
    www2.vm.box_url = "http://files.vagrantup.com/precise64.box"
    www2.vm.provision "shell", path: "apache.sh"
    www2.vm.network "forwarded_port", guest: 80, host: 7070
  end

end
```

With a multimachine setup, running `vagrant up` without arguments will bring up every machine defined in the `Vagrantfile`. This behavior applies to Vagrant's other management commands as well. To control an individual machine, add that machine's name to the command. For example, if we want to launch just the www1 machine, we would use the following command:

```
vagrant up www1
```

Likewise, to destroy virtual machine, we would use the following command:

```
vagrant destroy www1
```

Creating Storm-provisioning scripts

In *Chapter 2, Configuring Storm Clusters*, we covered the manual installation of Storm and its dependencies on Ubuntu Linux. We can leverage the commands we used in *Chapter 2, Configuring Storm Clusters*, by using them to create Vagrant provisioning scripts to automate what would otherwise be a manual process. If you don't understand some of the commands used in the provisioning scripts, refer to *Chapter 2, Configuring Storm Clusters*, for a more in-depth explanation.

ZooKeeper

ZooKeeper is available pre-packaged for most Linux platforms, which makes our installation script simple, letting the package manager do most of the work. The following is the command line to install ZooKeeper:

```
install-zookeeper.sh
```

And the commands to install ZooKeeper are as follows:

```
apt-get update
apt-get --yes install zookeeper=3.3.5* zookeeperd=3.3.5*
```

Storm

The Storm installation script is a little more complicated since it is not pre-packaged and must be installed manually. We'll take the commands we used in *Chapter 2, Configuring Storm Clusters*, assemble them into a script, and parameterize them to the script so it expects a Storm version string as an argument. This will allow us to easily switch between different Storm versions without having to modify the installation script as shown in the following code snippet:

```
install-storm.sh
```

```
apt-get update
apt-get install -y unzip supervisor openjdk-6-jdk

/etc/init.d/supervisor stop

groupadd storm
useradd --gid storm --home-dir /home/storm --create-home --shell /bin/
bash storm
```

```
unzip -o /vagrant/$1.zip -d /usr/share/
chown -R storm:storm /usr/share/$1
ln -s /usr/share/$1 /usr/share/storm
ln -s /usr/share/storm/bin/storm /usr/bin/storm

mkdir /etc/storm
chown storm:storm /etc/storm

rm /usr/share/storm/conf/storm.yaml
cp /vagrant/storm.yaml /usr/share/storm/conf/
cp /vagrant/cluster.xml /usr/share/storm/logback/
ln -s /usr/share/storm/conf/storm.yaml /etc/storm/storm.yaml

mkdir /var/log/storm
chown storm:storm /var/log/storm
```

The install-storm.sh script leverages the existence of the Vagrant shared directory (/vagrant). This allows us to keep the storm.yaml and logback.xml files in a convenient location right next to the Vagrantfile.

In the storm.yaml file, we will use hostnames instead of IP addresses and let Vagrant configure the name resolution as shown in the following code snippet:

storm.yaml

```
storm.zookeeper.servers:
    - "zookeeper"

nimbus.host: "nimbus"

# netty transport
storm.messaging.transport: "backtype.storm.messaging.netty.Context"
storm.messaging.netty.buffer_size: 16384
storm.messaging.netty.max_retries: 10
storm.messaging.netty.min_wait_ms: 1000
storm.messaging.netty.max_wait_ms: 5000

drpc.servers:
  - "nimbus"
```

Supervisord

The supervisord service is installed by the `install-storm.sh` script, but we still need to configure it to manage the Storm daemons. Instead of creating separate configuration files for each service, we'll write a script that generates the supervisord configuration with a service name as a parameter, as shown in the following code snippet:

`configure-supervisord.sh`

```
echo [program:storm-$1] | sudo tee -a /etc/supervisor/conf.d/storm-$1.
conf
echo command=storm $1 | sudo tee -a /etc/supervisor/conf.d/storm-$1.
conf
echo directory=/home/storm | sudo tee -a /etc/supervisor/conf.d/
storm-$1.conf
echo autorestart=true | sudo tee -a /etc/supervisor/conf.d/storm-$1.
conf
echo user=storm | sudo tee -a /etc/supervisor/conf.d/storm-$1.conf
```

The `configure-supervisord.sh` script expects a single argument representing the name of the Storm service to manage. For example, to generate a supervisord configuration for the Nimbus daemon, you would invoke the script using the following command:

`sh configure-supervisord.sh nimbus`

The Storm Vagrantfile

For our Storm cluster, we will create a cluster with one ZooKeeper node, one Nimbus node, and one or more Supervisor nodes. Because the `Vagrantfile` is written in Ruby, we have access to many of Ruby's language features, which will allow us to make the configuration file more robust. We will, for example, make the number of Supervisor nodes easily configurable.

In the `storm.yaml` file, we used hostnames rather than IP addresses, which means our machines must be able to resolve names to IP addresses. Vagrant does not come with a facility for managing entries in the `/etc/hosts` file, but fortunately, there is a Vagrant plugin that does. Before we delve into the `Vagrantfile` for the Storm cluster, install the `vagrant-hostmanager` plugin (https://github.com/smdahlen/vagrant-hostmanager) using the following command:

`vagrant plugin install vagrant-hostmanager`

The `vagrant-hostmanager` plugin will set up hostname resolution for all the machines in our cluster. It also has an option to add the name resolution between the host machine and virtual machines.

Next, let's look at the complete `Vagrantfile` and walk through it line by line:

```
require 'uri'
# Configuration
STORM_DIST_URL = "https://dl.dropboxusercontent.com/s/dj86w8ojecgsam7/
storm-0.9.0.1.zip"
STORM_SUPERVISOR_COUNT = 2
STORM_BOX_TYPE = "precise64"
# end Configuration


STORM_ARCHIVE = File.basename(URI.parse(STORM_DIST_URL).path)
STORM_VERSION = File.basename(STORM_ARCHIVE, '.*')


# Vagrantfile API/syntax version. Don't touch unless you know what
you're doing!
VAGRANTFILE_API_VERSION = "2"
Vagrant.configure(VAGRANTFILE_API_VERSION) do |config|

  config.hostmanager.manage_host = true
  config.hostmanager.enabled = true
  config.vm.box = STORM_BOX_TYPE

  if(!File.exist?(STORM_ARCHIVE))
    `wget -N #{STORM_DIST_URL}`
  end

  config.vm.define "zookeeper" do |zookeeper|
    zookeeper.vm.network "private_network", ip: "192.168.50.3"
    zookeeper.vm.hostname = "zookeeper"
    zookeeper.vm.provision "shell", path: "install-zookeeper.sh"
  end

  config.vm.define "nimbus" do |nimbus|
    nimbus.vm.network "private_network", ip: "192.168.50.4"
    nimbus.vm.hostname = "nimbus"
    nimbus.vm.provision "shell", path: "install-storm.sh", args:
STORM_VERSION
```

```
      nimbus.vm.provision "shell", path: "config-supervisord.sh", args:
  "nimbus"
      nimbus.vm.provision "shell", path: "config-supervisord.sh", args:
  "ui"
      nimbus.vm.provision "shell", path: "config-supervisord.sh", args:
  "drpc"
      nimbus.vm.provision "shell", path: "start-supervisord.sh"
    end

    (1..STORM_SUPERVISOR_COUNT).each do |n|
      config.vm.define "supervisor#{n}" do |supervisor|
        supervisor.vm.network "private_network", ip: "192.168.50.#{4 +
  n}"
        supervisor.vm.hostname = "supervisor#{n}"
        supervisor.vm.provision "shell", path: "install-storm.sh", args:
  STORM_VERSION
        supervisor.vm.provision "shell", path: "config-supervisord.sh",
  args: "supervisor"
        supervisor.vm.provision "shell", path: "config-supervisord.sh",
  args: "logviewer"
        supervisor.vm.provision "shell", path: "start-supervisord.sh"
      end
    end
  end
```

The first line of the file tells the Ruby interpreter to require the `uri` module, which we will use for URL parsing.

Next, we set up some variables representing the URL of the Storm distribution archive, the number of Supervisor nodes we want, and the name of the Vagrant box type for our virtual machines. These variables are intended to be changed by the user.

The `STORM_ARCHIVE` and `STORM_VERSION` values are set to the filename and version name of the Storm distribution by parsing the distribution URL using Ruby's `File` and `URI` classes. These values will be passed as arguments to the provisioning scripts.

Next, we enter the main Vagrant configuration section. We begin by configuring the `vagrant-hostmanager` plugin as follows:

```
      config.hostmanager.manage_host = true
      config.hostmanager.enabled = true
```

Here, we are telling the `vagrant-hostmanager` plugin to manage the hostname resolution between the host machine and virtual machines and that it should manage the `/etc/hosts` files on the virtual machines as well.

The next block checks to see whether the Storm distribution archive has already been downloaded; if not, it uses the `wget` command to download it as shown in the following code snippet:

```
if(!File.exist?(STORM_ARCHIVE))
  `wget -N #{STORM_DIST_URL}`
end
```

The preceding code will download the Storm archive to the same directory as the `Vagrantfile`, thus making it accessible to the provisioning scripts in the `/vagrant` shared directory.

The next two code blocks configure ZooKeeper and Nimbus and are relatively straightforward. They contain two new directives we have not seen before:

```
zookeeper.vm.network "private_network", ip: "192.168.50.3"
zookeeper.vm.hostname = "zookeeper"
```

The `zookeeper.vm.network` directive signals Vagrant to assign a specific IP address to the virtual machine using the VirtualBox host-only network adapter. The next line tells Vagrant to set the hostname on the virtual machine to a specific value. Finally, we invoke the provisioning scripts appropriate for each node.

The final block configures the Supervisor node(s). The Ruby code creates a loop iterating from `1` to the value of `STORM_SUPERVISOR_COUNT` and allows you to set the number of Supervisor nodes in the cluster. It will dynamically set the virtual machine name, hostname, and IP address based on the number of Supervisor nodes specified by the `STORM_SUPERVISOR_COUNT` variable.

Launching the Storm cluster

With our cluster defined in the `Vagrantfile` and our provisioning scripts in place, we're ready to launch the Vagrant cluster with `vagrant up`. With four machines and a considerable amount of software to install on each, this will take a while.

Once Vagrant has finished launching the cluster, you should be able to view the Storm UI from the host machine at `http://nimbus:8080`. To submit a topology to the cluster, you can do so with the following command:

```
storm jar myTopology.jar com.example.MyTopology my-topology -c nimbus.
host=nimbus
```

Summary

In this chapter, we've just scratched the surface of deploying Storm in a cloud environment but hopefully introduced you to the many possibilities available, from deploying it to a hosted cloud environment such as Amazon EC2 to deploying it to a local cloud provider on your workstation or even an in-house hypervisor server.

We encourage you to explore both cloud hosting providers such as AWS as well as virtualization options such as Vagrant in more depth to better equip your Storm deployment options. Between the manual installation procedures introduced in *Chapter 2*, *Configuring Storm Clusters*, and the technology introduced in this chapter, you should be well equipped to find the development, test, and deployment solution that best fits your needs.

Index

Gremlin Wiki
  URL 151
groupBy() method 84
guaranteed processing
  about 30
  reliability, in bolts 31, 32
  reliability, in spouts 30, 31
  reliability, in word count 32, 33

H

Hadoop
  about 10, 236
  Druid, setting up 237
  MapReduce overview 236
HadoopDruidIndexer function 238-240
Hadoop infrastructure
  configuring 255
HDFS (Hadoop Distributed Filesystem)
  about 235, 249
  configuring 255
  examining 251
Hiera 60-62
Historical nodes 237
HTTP 153

I

ICD-9-CM
  codes 73
  URL, for codes 66
immutable tuple field values 160
installation, Apache Whirr 286
installation, base operating system 41
installation, Cassandra 135
installation, Java 41
installation, Kafka 98, 99
installation, OpenFire 99
installation, Storm
  about 42
  on Linux 40
installation, Titan 133
installation, Vagrant 294
installation, ZooKeeper 42
install-storm.sh script 300
instance type 284
instant message (IM) 97

intrusion detection 96

J

jar command 50
Java
  about 40
  installing 41
JSON project function 108
JSONProjectFunction class 143

K

Kafka
  installing 98, 99
  log messages, sending to 100-105
  URL, for downloading 98
Kafka spout 97, 107, 127
kill command 51
Kryo
  URL 134

L

Lambda architecture
  motivating 218, 219
  realizing 221-223
Limbo 196
Linux
  Storm, installing on 40
localconfvalue command 53
local/shuffle grouping 27
log analysis topology
  about 106
  completing 120-122
  filtering, on thresholds 115-117
  JSON project function 108
  Kafka spout 107
  moving average, calculating 109, 110
  moving average function, implementing 114
  notifications, sending with XMPP protocol 117-119
  running 123
  sliding window, adding 110, 113
Logback Appender extension 127
logback framework 96

logback Kafka appender 97
log messages
  sending, to Kafka 100-105

M

management commands, Storm
  activate 51
  deactivate 51
  jar 50
  kill 51
  rebalance 52
  remoteconfvalue 52
mandatory settings, Storm cluster
  nimbus.host 47
  storm.local.dir 47
  storm.zookeeper.servers 46
  supervisor.slots.ports 47
manifests, Puppet 56, 57
map function 236
MapReduce 236
mark() method 113
Master node 188, 237
Metcalfe's law
  URL 126
Minimax algorithm
  about 155, 156
  goal 157
modules, Puppet 58
move() method 156
moving average
  calculating 109, 110
moving average function
  implementing 114
multimachine clusters
  configuring, with Vagrant 298
MySQL 189

N

NameNode
  configuring 256-258
Natural Language Processing (NLP)
  about 220
  analytics, examining 230-234
Negamax algorithm 157
nextTuple() method 15

n-grams
  URL, for info 226
nimbus.childopts setting 48
nimbus daemon 36
  overview 36
nimbus.host setting 47
nimbus node 292
NodeManager
  about 252
  configuring 261
none grouping 27
non-transactional spouts 69
non-transactional state 190
non-transactional system
  integrating 187-190
notifications
  sending, with XMPP 117-119

O

OAuth
  configuring 139
online advertising 96
On-Line Analytical Processing (OLAP) 185, 217
On-Line Transactional Processing (OLTP) 185, 217
opaque spouts 69
Opaque state 90, 92
Opaque Transactional state 190
OpenFire
  about 99
  installing 99
OpenFire XMPP server
  URL 98
operations, Trident
  about 75
  filters 76, 77
  functions 78-81
optional settings, Storm cluster 47
OutbreakDetectionTopology class 93
OutbreakTrendState object 91

P

parallelism
  in Storm 22

Thank you for buying
Storm Blueprints: Patterns for Distributed Real-time Computation

About Packt Publishing

Packt, pronounced 'packed', published its first book "*Mastering phpMyAdmin for Effective MySQL Management*" in April 2004 and subsequently continued to specialize in publishing highly focused books on specific technologies and solutions.

Our books and publications share the experiences of your fellow IT professionals in adapting and customizing today's systems, applications, and frameworks. Our solution based books give you the knowledge and power to customize the software and technologies you're using to get the job done. Packt books are more specific and less general than the IT books you have seen in the past. Our unique business model allows us to bring you more focused information, giving you more of what you need to know, and less of what you don't.

Packt is a modern, yet unique publishing company, which focuses on producing quality, cutting-edge books for communities of developers, administrators, and newbies alike. For more information, please visit our website: www.packtpub.com.

About Packt Open Source

In 2010, Packt launched two new brands, Packt Open Source and Packt Enterprise, in order to continue its focus on specialization. This book is part of the Packt Open Source brand, home to books published on software built around Open Source licenses, and offering information to anybody from advanced developers to budding web designers. The Open Source brand also runs Packt's Open Source Royalty Scheme, by which Packt gives a royalty to each Open Source project about whose software a book is sold.

Writing for Packt

We welcome all inquiries from people who are interested in authoring. Book proposals should be sent to author@packtpub.com. If your book idea is still at an early stage and you would like to discuss it first before writing a formal book proposal, contact us; one of our commissioning editors will get in touch with you.

We're not just looking for published authors; if you have strong technical skills but no writing experience, our experienced editors can help you develop a writing career, or simply get some additional reward for your expertise.

Storm Real-time Processing Cookbook

ISBN: 978-1-78216-442-5   Paperback: 254 pages

Efficiently process unbounded streams of data in real time

1. Learn the key concepts of processing data in real time with Storm.

2. Concepts ranging from Log stream processing to mastering data management with Storm.

3. Written in a Cookbook style, with plenty of practical recipes with well-explained code examples and relevant screenshots and diagrams.

Hadoop MapReduce Cookbook

ISBN: 978-1-84951-728-7   Paperback: 300 pages

Recipes for analyzing large and complex datasets with Hadoop MapReduce

1. Learn to process large and complex data sets, starting simply, then diving in deep

2. Solve complex big data problems such as classifications, finding relationships, online marketing, and recommendations

3. More than 50 Hadoop MapReduce recipes, presented in a simple and straightforward manner, with step-by-step instructions and real world examples

Please check **www.PacktPub.com** for information on our titles

Big Data Analytics with R and Hadoop

ISBN: 978-1-78216-328-2   Paperback: 238 pages

Set up an integrated infrastructure of R and Hadoop to turn your data analytics into big data analytics

1. Write Hadoop MapReduce within R

2. Learn data analytics with R and the Hadoop platform

3. Handle HDFS data within R

4. Understand Hadoop streaming with R

Scaling Big Data with Hadoop and Solr

ISBN: 978-1-78328-137-4   Paperback: 144 pages

Learn exciting new ways to build efficient, high performance enterprise search repositories for big data using Hadoop and Solr

1. Understand the different approaches of making Solr work on Big Data as well as the benefits and drawbacks

2. Learn from interesting, real-life use cases for big data search along with sample code

3. Work with the Distributed Enterprise Search without prior knowledge of Hadoop and Solr

Made in the USA
San Bernardino, CA
06 January 2015